Competency

Competency 1: Demonstrate Ethical and Professional Behavior

Behaviors:

Make ethical decisions by applying the standards of the NASW Code of Ethics, relevant laws and regulations, models for ethical decision-making, ethical conduct of research, and additional codes of ethics as appropriate to context	1,11,12,13,14, 15,16,17
Use reflection and self-regulation to manage personal values and maintain professionalism in practice situations	11,12,15,16
Demonstrate professional demeanor in behavior; appearance; and oral, written, and electronic communication	2,5,11,12,15
Use technology ethically and appropriately to facilitate practice outcomes	4,12,13
Use supervision and consultation to guide professional judgment and behavior	2,3,7,13

Competency 2: Engage Diversity and Difference in Practice

Behaviors:

Apply and communicate understanding of the importance of diversity and difference in shaping life experiences in practice at the micro, mezzo, and macro levels	5,7,8,9,1013,17
Present themselves as learners and engage clients and constituencies as experts of their own experiences	2,5,10,11,14, 15,16,17
Apply self-awareness and self-regulation to manage the influence of personal biases and values in working with diverse clients and constituencies	5,8,10,11,16

Competency 3: Advance Human Rights and Social, Economic, and Environmental Justice

Behaviors:

Apply their understanding of social, economic, and environmental justice to advocate for human rights at the individual and system levels	2,6,7,8,9,10,12, 13,14,17
Engage in practices that advance social, economic, and environmental justice	6,8,9,10,11,12, 13,15,16

Competency 4: Engage in Practice-informed Research and Research-informed Practice

Behaviors:

Use practice experience and theory to inform scientific inquiry and research	2,9,11,14,15,16
Apply critical thinking to engage in analysis of quantitative and qualitative research methods and research findings	4,9,10,14,15
Use and translate research evidence to inform and improve practice, policy, and service delivery	3,6,7,8,9,16

Competency 5: Engage in Policy Practice

Behaviors:

Assess how social welfare and economic policies impact the delivery of and access to social services	6,7,8,9,10,13, 14,15,17
Apply critical thinking to analyze, formulate, and advocate for policies that advance human rights and social, economic, and environmental justice	6,7,8,9,10,13, 14,15,17

Competency	Chapter
Competency 6: Engage with Individuals, Families, Groups, Organizations, and Communities	
Behaviors:	
Apply knowledge of human behavior and the social environment, person-in-environment, and other multidisciplinary theoretical frameworks to engage with clients and constituencies	4,5,6,7,8,9,13,14
Use empathy, reflection, and interpersonal skills to effectively engage diverse clients and constituencies	4,5,8,10,14,16
Competency 7: Assess Individuals, Families, Groups, Organizations, and Communities	
Behaviors:	
Collect and organize data, and apply critical thinking to interpret information from clients and constituencies	5,8,10,14
Apply knowledge of human behavior and the social environment, person-in-environment, and other multidisciplinary theoretical frameworks in the analysis of assessment data from clients and constituencies	8,9,10,14
Develop mutually agreed-on intervention goals and objectives based on the critical assessment of strengths, needs, and challenges within clients and constituencies	5,7,10,14
Select appropriate intervention strategies based on the assessment, research knowledge, and values and preferences of clients and constituencies	2,10,14
Competency 8: Intervene with Individuals, Families, Groups, Organizations, and Communities	
Behaviors:	
Critically choose and implement interventions to achieve practice goals and enhance capacities of clients and constituencies	10,11,14
Apply knowledge of human behavior and the social environment, person-in-environment, and other multidisciplinary theoretical frameworks in interventions with clients and constituencies	6,7,8,10,14
Use inter-professional collaboration as appropriate to achieve beneficial practice outcomes	5,6,8,14
Negotiate, mediate, and advocate with and on behalf of diverse clients and constituencies	5,6,7,8,10,14
Facilitate effective transitions and endings that advance mutually agreed-on goals	10,14,15
Competency 9: Evaluate Practice with Individuals, Families, Groups, Organizations, and Communities	
Behaviors:	
Select and use appropriate methods for evaluation of outcomes	10,14,15
Critically analyze, monitor, and evaluate intervention and program processes and outcomes	6,10,11,14,15
Apply evaluation findings to improve practice effectiveness at the micro, mezzo, and macro levels	3,7,14,15,17

Adapted with permission of Council on Social Work Education.

SEVENTH EDITION

The Social Work Practicum

A Guide and Workbook for Students

Cynthia L. Garthwait
The University of Montana

PEARSON

Boston Columbus Hoboken Indianapolis New York San Francisco
Amsterdam Cape Town Dubai London Madrid Milan Munich Paris Montréal Toronto
Delhi Mexico City São Paulo Sydney Hong Kong Seoul Singapore Taipei Tokyo

VP and Editorial Director: Jeffery W. Johnston
Executive Editor: Julie Peters
Program Manager: Megan Moffo
Editorial Assistant: Pamela DiBerardino
Executive Product Marketing Manager:
  Christopher Barry
Executive Field Marketing Manager: Krista Clark
Team Lead Project Management: Bryan Pirrmann
Team Lead Program Management: Laura Weaver
Procurement Specialist: Deidra Skahill
Art Director: Diane Lorenzo

Art Director Cover: Diane Ernsberger
Cover Design: Studio Montage
Cover Art: Rawpixel/Shutterstock
Media Producer: Allison Longley
Editorial Production and Composition Services:
  Lumina Datamatics, Inc.
Full-Service Project Manager: Raja Natesan
Printer/Binder: RR Donnelley
Cover Printer: RR Donnelley
Text Font: Dante MT Pro 10.5/13pt

Library of Congress Cataloging-in-Publication Data
Garthwait, Cynthia L., author.
  Social work practicum : a guide and workbook for students / Cynthia L. Garthwait. — 7th edition.
    pages cm
  Includes bibliographical references and index.
  ISBN 978-0-13-394841-7 — ISBN 0-13-394841-2 1. Social work education—United States—Outlines, syllabi, etc.
  2. Social work education—United States—Examinations, questions, etc. I. Title.
  HV11.7.H67 2015
  361.3076—dc23
                                                                  2015028455

3   16

Student Edition
ISBN 10: 0-13-394841-2
ISBN 13: 978-0-13-394841-7

Package
ISBN 10: 0-13-440332-0
ISBN 13: 978-0-13-440332-8

eText
ISBN 10: 0-13-394848-X
ISBN 13: 978-0-13-394848-6

PEARSON

Brief Contents

Contents

Foreword

Having served as the BSW and MSW Practicum Director at the University of Montana School of Social Work for the past 13 years, I heartily agree with the Council on Social Work Education that practicum is the signature pedagogy of social work education. For students, the practicum is where the real needs of real people must be addressed. It is in the practicum that students begin to practice what they have learned in the classroom, but now in actual social work settings. This growth from student to professional is not achieved easily, and students are often very nervous about beginning this journey. They understandably have many questions about the process and how they will remember and integrate their classroom knowledge in order to be effective social workers.

Students need much more than supervision in the practicum in order to integrate theory and practice. They also need help in navigating this integration process. Schools of social work have the responsibility for addressing what could be a gap between the classroom and practice, and this book can help them fulfill this responsibility. This book provides a user-friendly but in-depth format and guide for students in both BSW and MSW programs seeking to maximize the practicum experience.

Cynthia Garthwait, the author of this book, is an experienced social worker, educator, practicum director, and administrator. She has a thorough understanding of what social work students need in order to be successful in the field. She has designed the book to correlate with and build upon coursework that students have already taken. She has developed stimulating content, critical thinking questions, links to relevant videos, and workbook activities that will help students translate the theories and knowledge they acquired in the classroom into real skills in actual practice.

The Social Work Practicum: A Guide and Workbook for Students is the ultimate tool for students to utilize during their practicum. This book makes it very clear how students can integrate their classroom learning with the practicum setting. It also provides informative learning activities that can be used within practicum seminars and advanced practice courses, allowing for faculty-to-student immersion in the content. Many students have told me that this book was extremely helpful to them in the transition from the classroom to the field.

The book provides students with the educational tools needed to have a successful practicum and social work career. It is based on CSWE EPAS 2015 competencies and practice behaviors, and helps instructors by tying content and activities into the practice behaviors required for both practice and CSWE EPAS 2015. It helps students understand, prepare, and develop their practicum learning agreement to assure that they secure the best social work practicum experience possible. Because of this, they develop a deeper understanding of the planned change process and how it is utilized within their practicum site. Students also learn how to utilize the supervision provided by their agency field instructor in a constructive manner. *The Social Work Practicum: A guide and Workbook for Students* is a wonderful tool to assure that students get the best experience possible.

The book helps schools of social work meet the requirements of the Council on Social Work Education for teaching and measuring competencies and practice behaviors. It offers hands-on learning experiences which can be tailored to the needs and mission of individuals programs. This book also offers short essay questions and multiple-choice questions that can be used for measuring student learning outcomes.

As a social work educator I unconditionally recommend this book for all social work students in BSW/MSW practicum placements. It is definitely a highly effective tool to enhance the linkage between theory and practice, making for a highly successful experience in practicum and beyond.

Tondy Baumgartner, MSW, LCSW
BSW/MSW Practicum Director
University of Montana
School of Social Work

Preface

Social work educators who are intent on engaging students in the integrative experience of blending theory and practice know how challenging and exciting the practicum can be for both students and faculty members. This book is meant to be a resource for that endeavor and a central feature of a learning laboratory where classroom knowledge and real-life practice are integrated and blended into social work practice. Students seeking ways to apply the perspectives, theories, and models learned in an academic setting will find a valuable resource in this book. This text can help students translate academic learning into actual practice skills and behaviors, and can also support them as they learn to provide services to very real clients in very real settings. It can enhance the competencies required for practice, and facilitate the transition from student to professional.

Each chapter provides a focused, succinct summary of a topic that must be understood and applied in the practicum setting. The chapters provide a foundation for each other, each one informing the others and building toward a multifaceted and complete set of competencies necessary for effective practice. The chapters also offer critical thinking questions, links to videos that illustrate ideas presented, workbook activities that build skills, and additional suggested learning activities.

Because professional practice requires an ongoing commitment to acquiring knowledge and enhancing skills, this text offers a methodology for beginning social workers that can be carried into practice and used throughout a career. Using this book as intended, combining it with a university social work program mission, and tailoring it to individual career goals will produce intentional, values-based, and competent practice. Because the process of professional development is not complete when the practicum concludes, but rather begins at another level, it is my hope that you will use this book to guide your own unique professional journey.

New to This Edition

The Enhanced Pearson eText provides a rich, interactive learning environment designed to improve student mastery of content with the following multimedia features:

- Video links to topical videos accompanied by a question to encourage reflection or critical thinking.
- Essay-format quizzes on major sections in each chapter give students the opportunity to check their understanding of the section as they read. Feedback is provided to students after submitting their response.
- End-of-Chapter multiple choice quizzes allow students to demonstrate their understanding of the major concepts in the chapter. Feedback for the correct answer is provided to help scaffold learning.

This edition includes new content on:

- Guidelines for electronic communication and the use of social media
- Organizational communication that influences clients and practice outcomes
- Social problem analysis models and perspectives
- Principles of work with involuntary clients
- Community practice, including community development and community organization
- Policy practice in response to social problems
- Professional development plans, including licensure

Significantly revised content on the following is included:

- Personal safety for social workers
- Social policy analysis models
- Evaluation of practice, including understanding and learning from ineffective interventions

Acknowledgments

Designing a textbook that will effectively prepare students to enter the social work profession requires a blending of knowledge and professional skills gained over many years of both practice and social work education. The knowledge shared in this edition is drawn from exchanges with clients in a wide variety of social work settings, and is enhanced by their life stories of strength, perseverance, and courage. Their struggles and achievements, at times made easier by the support of a social worker, inform my efforts as an educator. My BSW and MSW students, when using resources such as this text to integrate theory with practice have taught me about commitment, enthusiasm, and fulfilling one's professional calling. Thanks go to Gary, who has always supported my commitment to students and the clients they are learning to help. Thanks also to the reviewers of this text: Erika Gaylean, Indiana University Purdue University; Dawn Marie Green, Southwestern Michigan College; Linda S. Helm, The Ohio State University; and Carlene Quinn, Indiana University.

1

Purpose and Expectations for Practicum

©ARYBICKII / FOTOLIA

STRUCTURE OF CHAPTERS

Although the chapters in the book are numbered in the conventional manner, this is not to suggest that you must move through the book sequentially, one chapter after another. Rather, the book is structured so that chapters build upon each other and at times can also be reviewed in conjunction with each succeeding chapter. It is expected that you will move back and forth between sections and will also revisit the same section several times as you gain experience in the practicum and begin to look at various questions and issues from new perspectives. The chapters may also be read in a different order to accommodate the structure and outline of your school's program.

Each chapter begins with a list of *Learning Outcomes* designed to help you focus on competencies and your efficacy as a social worker in specific practice areas. Each chapter contains a section titled *Chapter Preview*, which presents a short capsule of the chapter content and reasons that the focus of the chapter is essential. It also describes the relationship between this chapter and previous ones, while also linking it to chapters that follow. The first major section of each chapter, *Background and Context*, presents selected concepts and principles related to the topic addressed by the chapter. The concepts and definitions presented in this section are not a

1

Ethical and Professional Behavior

Behavior: Use reflection and self-regulation to manage personal values and maintain professionalism in practice situations.

Critical Thinking Question: Although you are just beginning your practicum, you have some of the strengths a social worker will need. As you complete this self-assessment, identify the strengths you already have.

substitute for a text book, but rather should act as a review of key ideas that set the stage for what follows. The ideas in the *Guidance and Direction* section of each chapter will stimulate creative thinking and raise important questions that need to be considered as you work your way through the practicum. These sections offer general suggestions, guidance, advice, and sometimes even a few specific do's and don'ts intended to encourage and facilitate learning in relation to the chapter's objectives and particular focus.

Several pages of each chapter have been cast into a workbook format and titled *A Workbook Activity*. You will be asked to engage in critical thinking activities and answer questions that will help you integrate knowledge, skills, and values needed for the professional competencies of social work practice. A section titled *Suggested Learning Activities* lists several specific tasks and activities that provide additional opportunities and experiences for learning.

Each chapter allows for *review and an informal testing* of your understanding of chapter content. Links are provided to a number of multiple-choice and short essay questions designed to help you cement your knowledge.

The *References* section at the end of each chapter lists books, articles, and links related to the topics addressed in the book. These suggestions serve as resources for additional information and encourage a more in-depth examination of the topics presented. Using textbooks and readings from courses you have taken as reference guides will also help you understand how social workers continue to build on their previous knowledge and skills as more advanced practice is expected over time.

CHAPTER PREVIEW

Congratulations on your entry to the practicum phase of your social work education. In order to help you think about how to maximize this challenge, this introductory chapter presents the concept of practicum as a unique learning experience. Your practicum will offer you the opportunity to review classroom *knowledge*, integrate this knowledge with the *skills* required in the social work profession, and support all your interventions with the *values* of the social work profession. This book will help you bring those three components of practice together. Also covered in this chapter are the *expectations for practicum* of the school, the practicum agency, your clients, and you as a student. You will learn how these expectations converge and how to clarify, understand, and meet them all. Content on the *skill-building continuum* experienced by all social work students and social workers will assist you in placing yourself developmentally along this trajectory with plans for professional development throughout your career. Finally, this chapter provides a tool entitled *Student Self-Assessment of Practice Strengths*, which you can use now and at the conclusion of your practicum to identify and build upon the strengths you bring to the social work practicum.

You are to be commended for embarking on the exciting social work practicum experience and applauded for reaching this stage in your professional education. You have been approved for a practicum based on your academic achievements and your professional readiness for this experience. The practicum is a unique opportunity to apply what you have learned in the classroom, expand your knowledge, develop your skills, and hone your use of professional values. It is time for you to move from the role of a student to that of a professional social worker. This book is designed to provide you with guidance and structure during the social work practicum. If used in a thoughtful manner throughout the practicum, it will help you make the best of whatever your practicum setting has to offer. It requires a real commitment and a willingness to invest time in the learning process.

BACKGROUND AND CONTEXT

The practicum experience is almost universally described by BSW and MSW social work students as the single most important, challenging, significant, and powerful learning experience of their formal social work education. It is in the practicum where the concepts, principles, theories, and models discussed in the classroom come to life because they are being applied with real people in real-life situations. During the practicum, students have the opportunity and responsibility to use and enhance the skills and techniques they previously rehearsed in classroom role-playing and simulations. It is also during the practicum that students make considerable progress in developing self-awareness and come to a better understanding of their individual strengths and limitations as well as the influence of their personal values, attitudes, and life experiences on their practice. The practicum can and should be a time when classroom theory is integrated with social work practice and when students apply the values and fundamental principles of their chosen profession.

You will quickly learn that there are many *stakeholders who have expectations for you and your practicum*. Both clients and professionals with a variety of points of view, experiences, and roles to play will have a stake in your learning. This includes you as the *practicum student*, your university *social work program*, your *agency*, and your *clients*. This combination of people and groups who have a stake in your learning is similar to actual social work practice in which there are also many stakeholders with an investment in the performance of social workers. While you are still a student, it is helpful to understand what those expectations are.

The specific objectives associated with a practicum can be found in your school's practicum manual, in official descriptions of your social work curriculum, and in other documents issued by the social work program. In addition, your faculty supervisors will guide you through the process of meeting your program's expectations for the development of competency. Agencies will have expectations of students, and so will clients. All parties to the practicum are expected to adhere to the *National Association of Social Workers (NASW) Code of Ethics* as well as the expectations for social work programs accredited by the *Council on Social Work Education (CSWE)*.

Engagement

Behavior: Apply knowledge of human behavior and the social environment, person-in-environment, and other multidisciplinary theoretical frameworks to engage with clients and constituencies.

Critical Thinking Question: Now that you have begun your practicum, what is your plan for drawing on the various sources or knowledge gained through your classroom experience?

Ethical and Professional Behavior

Behavior: Make ethical decisions by applying the standards of the NASW Code of Ethics, relevant laws and regulations, models for ethical decision-making, ethical conduct of research, and additional codes of ethics as appropriate to context.

Critical Thinking Question: A professional social worker must learn to apply the NASW Code of Ethics to all practice decisions. What can you do to make certain that you understand how to apply the ethical standards of the profession to each practicum assignment given to you?

Given the fact that you are in the process of learning to become a social worker, you must consider how this lack of skill and experience might affect your clients and the quality of the services provided to them. Even though you are a student, you will have a great deal to offer your clients, and when the work expected of you is beyond your level of knowledge and skill, consult with your field instructor for guidance and suggestions. Review your classroom learning, drawing upon theory and any skill-building exercises in which you have participated. The clients served by a student social worker are to be made aware that they are being served or assisted by a student. However, most clients will see you as a developing professional and will be cooperative and trusting of you, your knowledge, and your skills.

Refer to Table 1.1, Practicum Stakeholder Expectations, to identify all the parties involved in your practicum experience. Compare their views of your role, how you should be prepared and trained, how your work is to be organized, what supervision will consist of, and how you are to be evaluated. This information can help you understand the

Table1.1   Practicum Stakeholder Expectations

Student Expectations for Practicum

As a student, you expect a high quality learning experience in your practicum. You have worked and studied a long time in preparation for this experience with real clients and no doubt have hopes that this experience will prepare you for professional social work practice. Below are commonly held expectations of all stakeholders involved in your practicum. Notice how the secondary and primary roles expected of you by the various stakeholders vary between the parties based on their role in the practicum.

Primary Role of Student	Secondary Role of Student	Preparation of Student	Organization of Student Work	Supervision of Student	Evaluation of Student Performance
Learn and integrate theory and practice	Provide services to clients and client systems	Classroom content and experience	Assignments given by field instructor	Daily tasks supervised in agency	Ongoing evaluation by field instructor
		Orientation by agency field instructor	Learning goals required by university	Integration of theory and practice supervised by university	Academic grade given by university

Agency Expectations for Practicum

Your agency and field instructor also have much at stake in your practicum. They serve real clients facing real-life challenges and expect you to engage in activities with those clients that are ethical, professional, and effective. Their expectations for you and the practicum experience include the following:

Primary Role of Student	Secondary Role of Student	Preparation of Student	Organization of Student Work	Supervision of Student	Evaluation of Student Performance
Provide services to clients and client systems	Learn and integrate theory and practice	Orientation by field instructor	Task assignments given by field instructor	Daily tasks supervised in agency	Ongoing and final evaluation by field instructor
				Supervision training provided by university	

Table 1.1 *continued*

University Expectations for Practicum

Your university social work program has invested itself in developing curriculum, designing learning experiences, and building a partnership with your agency, and expects that you will be able to use this experience to integrate classroom learning with practicum learning opportunities. The program has an obligation to ensure that its graduates are competent to practice social work and view the practicum as an opportunity to demonstrate this competency. The program's expectations are in line with its goals in education.

Primary Role of Student	Secondary Role of Student	Preparation of Student	Organization of Student Work	Supervision of Student	Evaluation of Student
Learn and integrate theory and practice	Provide services to clients and client systems	Classroom content and experience Orientation by field instructor	Learning goals required by university	Integration of theory and practice supervised by university	Academic grade given by university

Client or Client System Expectations for Practicum

Although your clients do not yet know that you will be working with them, they will expect to receive professional services from you and your agency, and that you will be prepared to help them address their needs and concerns ethically, under supervision, and with respect. In many ways, their expectations may be the most important of all, since it is their lives and concerns that are at the center of your practicum. If you are working with a client system on a larger level, this family, group, organization, or community will have the same expectations.

Primary Role of Student	Secondary Role of Student	Preparation of Student	Organization of Student Work	Supervision of Student	Evaluation of Student
Receipt of services by competent social workers and students	Allowing self to be served by student	Not aware of services to be provided by student	Tasks designed to meet client needs and goals	Ongoing supervision by social worker	Professional-level services expected Effectiveness defined by client

varied perspectives on your learning and the services you will provide as a practicum student. As can be expected, you and your university will see your *primary role* as that of a learner and your *secondary role* as a service provider. In contrast, the agency and its clients will tend to view your primary role as a service provider and your secondary role as a student. Although this makes sense to all parties involved, this may seem complex to you. Work hard to meet all the expectations for your practicum and work to understand how this same set of varying perspectives is taken on the work of professional social workers.

In addition to the expectations listed here for you as a new professional social worker, several other organizations outside your university and agency also place a great emphasis on the practicum as one of the highlights of social work education. Both the Council on Social Work Education, the accrediting body for all social work programs in the United States, and the National Association of Social Workers, the professional organization of social workers in the United States, value the practicum as integral to quality social work practice and a hallmark of social work education. Both organizations share a commitment to both students and their eventual clients and view the practicum as a way of ensuring the following:

- *Basic competency* for BSW graduates
- *Advanced competency* for MSW graduates
- *Quality services* to clients and client systems
- *Accountability* to the profession of social work
- *Accountability to the organizations* and institutions for whom graduates work
- Continual and ongoing *enhancement of social work knowledge and practice*

> ▶ Watch this video produced by the National Association of Social Workers about the professional activities in which a variety of social workers engage every day. What competencies do you think they need to do their jobs? www.youtube.com/user/socialworkers

Most students find the practicum to be a very positive and meaningful experience, but occasionally the practicum can fall short of expectations. The quality of every practicum experience can be enhanced if students are provided with guidance in identifying and making use of learning opportunities. A practicum structure that helps students to examine and analyze their settings in ways that build on their prior classroom learning is of critical importance. In addition, some of the most meaningful learning occurs as a result of having to deal with unexpected events and frustrations during the practicum. This book is designed to be a tool to structure, support, and maximize the time spent in practicum because the next step is real-world social work.

> ? Assess your understanding of background and context by taking this brief quiz.

As you work toward actual social work practice, you will come to recognize that professional experiences such as practicum require you to *strike a balance* in a number of areas. In order to ensure a positive learning experience and minimize the chances of having negative experiences, you should think of the practicum as a bridge and a balance between the following concepts:

- The *academic learning* you have experienced in school and the *real-life application and integration* of this learning with actual clients
- Your *professional responsibility* to serve your clients and your *role as a student* who has much to learn
- Your own *professional goals* and the *expectations of your school and agency*
- *Structuring your practicum* for maximum learning and *remaining open to unplanned* experiences

GUIDANCE AND DIRECTION

Three major factors will determine the overall quality of your social work practicum experience:

- *Your motivation to learn*, including your career goals, the level of effort you are willing to put into this experience, your level of openness to learn about yourself, and your motivation for selecting social work as a career

- *Your capacity to learn*, including your strengths, limitations, learning style, experiences upon which to build, academic ability, and ability to integrate theory and practice
- *Your opportunity to learn*, including adequate time to devote to the practicum, your ability to minimize distractions from other parts of your life, the availability of experiences in your agency, and the presence of mentors and supervisors

Social workers acquire many skills needed to play various social work roles, develop competence at all levels of practice, and design interventions based on a broad range of perspectives, theories, and models. This is a very high professional expectation. You will not be expected to possess these skills at the outset of your practicum, but will be taught, trained, monitored, and supervised as you acquire them through the process described in the second workbook activity at the end of this chapter. The table in the workbook section of this chapter represents the process of skill building through increasingly challenging levels of learning, including didactic classroom learning, rehearsal of skills, observations of others performing the skills, attempts to develop the skill under supervision, reflection on performance, successive attempts at performing the skill, ongoing skill development, and advanced skill performance. Not only do practicum students use this process as they develop skills, but professional social workers also go through a similar process each time they acquire a new skill. Refer to this table often throughout your practicum experience to help you see the progress you make.

Ethical and Professional Behavior

Practice Behavior Example: Make ethical decisions by applying the standards of the NASW Code of Ethics, relevant laws and regulations, models for ethical decision-making, ethical conduct of research, and additional codes of ethics as appropriate to context.

Critical Thinking Question: What are the ethical implications of a student providing services to real clients?

As you watch this short but powerful video of social worker Bobby LeFebre's poetry slam performance, consider the passion that he brings to his work. How does his passion, experience, and commitment to the welfare of others compare to your reasons for entering the profession? www.youtube.com /watch?v=Uw5qLiQERBg

Assess your understanding of guidance and direction by taking this brief quiz.

Self-Assessment of Practice Strengths: A Workbook Activity

Social workers are committed to taking a strengths perspective on their clients, helping them to address their problems and enhance their social functioning by building on their strengths. A strengths perspective can also be invaluable to social workers themselves when evaluating their own work. By applying the strengths perspective to your own abilities and professional growth, you can use your strengths and assets as building blocks for the professional skills you will need. The following exercise will help you take a strengths perspective on yourself as you begin practicum and again when you have completed it.

Instructions: Assess yourself in the following Practice Strengths table, checking whether you have these strengths now, believe they are in progress, or do not yet possess them. Take note of the most significant strengths that you bring to the practicum. Identify the strengths needed for practice but that you do not yet possess. Think about how you can acquire these strengths through practicum learning experiences. You will be prompted to assess yourself again at the completion of your practicum using this tool. Hopefully you will recognize significant professional growth in all areas from the outset of your practicum to its completion.

Practice Strengths	Pre-Practicum Self-Assessment			Post-Practicum Self-Assessment		
	Yes	In Progress	No	Yes	In Progress	No
Motivation to Learn						
1. Open to new learning experiences						
2. Willing to assume new responsibilities						
3. Open to developing self-awareness and professional competence						
4. Adequate time and energy to devote to the practicum						
5. A sense of "calling" to the profession						
6. Committed to using supervision						
Attitudes and Values						
7. Empathetic, caring, and concerned for clients						
8. Personal values, beliefs, and perspectives that are compatible with the agency's mission						
9. Personal values, beliefs, and perspectives that are compatible with the NASW *Code of Ethics*						
10. Committed to achieving social justice						
11. Respectful of diversity among clients and communities						
12. Nonjudgmental toward clients and colleagues						
General Work Skills						
13. Writing skills (reports, letters, professional records, using technological tools)						
14. Able to process information quickly, understand new concepts, and learn new skills						
15. Able to receive and utilize supervision and feedback for professional growth						
16. Able to organize, plan, and effectively manage time						
17. Able to meet deadlines and work under pressure						
18. Able to follow through and complete tasks						
Social Work Skills						
19. Able to listen, understand, and consider varied views, perspectives, and opinions						
20. Able to communicate verbally with a variety of people and groups						
21. Able to make thoughtful and ethical decisions under stressful conditions						
22. Assertive and self-confident in professional relationships with clients and colleagues						

Practice Strengths	Pre-Practicum Self-Assessment			Post-Practicum Self-Assessment		
	Yes	In Progress	No	Yes	In Progress	No
23. Able to identify a need and formulate a plan to meet that need						
24. Able to solve problems creatively and effectively						
Knowledge						
25. Self-awareness of how one's values, beliefs, experiences impact work and other persons						
26. Knowledge of how laws, rules, regulations, and policies of agency impact practice						
27. Knowledge of assessment tools, methods, and techniques						
28. Knowledge of theories and models of social work						
29. Understands the process and steps of planned change						
30. Knowledge of how the community context impacts agency function						
Prior Experience Related to Practicum						
31. Experience in setting similar to agency						
32. Experience with clients or client systems similar to those served by agency						
33. Experience applying theory to practice						
34. Experience working with professional teams						
35. Experience playing social work roles						
36. Training in professional skills related to those needed in practicum						

Skill Building Across Your Social Work Career: A Workbook Activity

Examine the following table and consider how the professional levels of practice build upon each other over time. Think about how each domain of skill building evolves over time for social work students and practitioners alike.

Skill-Building Domains	Levels of Practice			
	BSW Student	**MSW Student**	**Entry-Level Practitioner**	**Advanced Practitioner**
Level of experience in using a skill or practice behavior	First attempt in using a skill	Building on previous experience in using a skill	Using a skill for entry-level practice, independently but with supervision	Using a skill for advanced practice, independently while teaching the skill to others

(continued)

Skill-Building Domains	Levels of Practice			
	BSW Student	MSW Student	Entry-Level Practitioner	Advanced Practitioner
Learning context of professional development	Classroom and practicum as learning context	Classroom, practicum, and previous experience as learning context	Agency practice as context for professional development	Agency practice and leadership role as context for professional development
Value base of professional development	Identification and acquisition of professional and personal values	Deepening understanding and use of professional values	Ongoing examination, development, and use of professional values	Advanced development, use, and teaching of professional values
Theory base of professional development	Understanding and beginning application of orienting/explanatory theories and practice theories	Understanding, critiquing, and application of orienting/explanatory theories and practice theories	Application of orienting/explanatory theories and practice theories and measuring the effectiveness of practice theories	Application of orienting/explanatory theories and practice theories, measuring the effectiveness of practice theories, and theory building
Evaluation of professional development	Supervisor and faculty evaluation with self-evaluation encouraged	Supervisor and faculty evaluation with self-evaluation encouraged	Supervisor evaluation with self-evaluation required	Self-evaluation, peer review, self-evaluation required, and expectation to evaluate others

Suggested Learning Activities

- Conduct a cursory examination of each chapter in this book. Note the topics addressed and how the content is organized. Try to identify the links between chapters, since they are designed to build on each other.

- Collect the textbooks you used in your social work courses and use them to help you integrate your classroom learning with your practicum experience.

- Read your school's practicum manual. Pay special attention to descriptions of what is expected of the practicum student.

- Ask your field instructor if there is a job description for social work practicum students. If there is, read it carefully to understand what your agency expects.

- Carefully examine the practicum evaluation form and specific criteria that will be used to evaluate your performance so you can see what level of performance will be expected by your university social work program.

- Talk to former students who have completed a practicum in your agency. Ask them for advice and guidance on what to expect and about learning opportunities available. Also ask if they have any suggestions for you that will enhance your practicum.

- Listen carefully to other students in your practicum seminar. Are their concerns similar to or different from yours? What can you learn from hearing about their practicum experiences, and what can you share with them that will enhance their learning?

Suggested Readings

Baird, Brian. *The Internship, Practicum, and Field Placement Handbook: A Guide for the Helping Professions.* 7th ed. Boston: Pearson Education, 2014.

Barker, Robert. *The Social Work Dictionary.* 5th ed. Washington, DC: NASW Press, 2003.

Berg-Weger, Marla, and Julie Birkenmaier. *The Practicum Companion for Social Work: Integrating Class and Field Work.* 3rd ed. Boston: Allyn and Bacon, 2011.

Birkenmaier, Julie A., and Marla Berg-Weger. *The Practicum Companion for Social Work: Integrating Class and Field Work.* 3rd ed. Boston: Pearson Education, 2011.

Grobman, Linda May, ed. *Days in the Lives of Social Workers: 58 Professionals Tell "Real Life" Stories from Social Work Practice.* 4th ed. Harrisburg, PA: White Hat Communications, 2011.

Grobman, Linda May, ed. *The Field Placement Survival Guide: What You Need to Know to Get the Most from Your Social Work Practicum.* 2nd ed. Harrisburg, PA: White Hat Communications, 2011.

Mizrahi, Terry, and Larry Davis. *The Encyclopedia of Social Work.* 20th ed. Washington, DC: NASW Press and Oxford University Press, 2010.

Royse, David, Surjit Singh Dhooper, and Elizabeth Rompf. *Field Instruction.* 6th ed. White Plains, NY: Longman, 2012.

Sheafor, Bradford, and Charles Horejsi. *Techniques and Guidelines for Social Work Practice.* 9th ed. Boston: Allyn and Bacon, 2012.

Sweitzer, H. Frederick, and Mary A. King. *The Successful Internship: Transformation and Empowerment in Experiential Learning.* 4th ed. Florence, KY: Cengage Learning, 2014.

Implementing a Learning Plan

CHAPTER PREVIEW

This chapter offers a framework for understanding how a practicum *learning plan* can help to structure and enhance the *integrative learning experience* and in so doing get your practicum off to a good start. It outlines a set of *generalist competencies*, which serves as a template for a learning plan, and highlights the professional *competencies of the Council on Social Work Education*, both of which shape the practicum. It provides an introduction to *using supervision* and training for professional growth and allows for reflection on how your reaction to supervision parallels the reaction of clients to assessment, intervention, and evaluation. It explains the process of *integration of theory and practice*, which is a fundamental goal of practicum experiences. Finally, it offers a *tool to monitor the development of professional skills and behaviors*.

Good practicum learning experiences are usually the result of a carefully planned learning experience. For the most part, a good practicum experience is one that has been well conceived and outlined. However, you may also have some very valuable unplanned learning experiences. Overall, you will increase your chances of success if you design a clear learning plan, but will also do well if you watch for opportunities to participate in learning opportunities that present themselves along the way. You may also have some challenging and possibly even negative experiences, and although you might wish to avoid negative learning experiences, they may very well be powerful teachers. Focusing simultaneously on learning and actual social work practice will be discussed in this chapter.

BACKGROUND AND CONTEXT

Beginning a practicum is similar to starting a new job because it is a time of both excitement and uncertainty. There are many new people to meet and much to learn, and the first few weeks can feel overwhelming. Entering an unfamiliar organization is something like entering an unfamiliar culture where you encounter a set of norms, rules, and customs you do not yet understand but will be required to learn. It is common to feel some anxiety about your knowledge and skills and to wonder if you will be able to perform competently. There are a number of concrete steps you can take now to make certain that your practicum gets off to a good start.

As you begin your practicum, it is important to list your *desired outcomes for learning* and then identify and arrange activities and experiences that will help you reach those goals. As you plan your practicum experience, it is important to include experiences that will help you acquire the professional competencies identified by the profession. The competencies of the Council on Social Work Education provide a guide for developing your learning plan, as do the *Generalist Social Work Competencies* identified in the following section of this chapter.

A plan for learning will incorporate educational goals and anticipated outcomes from three sources: the university school of social work, the practicum agency and its field instructor, and the student. These goals for each of these stakeholders will usually fall into three categories: *knowledge, skills, and values*, all of which contribute to your competency as a social worker. For example, skill grows out of knowledge and professional values. Likewise, the possession of social work knowledge and values is of little use unless they both are expressed in action. Finally, knowledge and skills can be used to harm or manipulate clients unless guided by an ethical value base of services to clients.

Social work *knowledge* is an understanding of professional terminology, facts, principles, concepts, perspectives, and theories. No doubt you have spent many hours learning about individuals and families, communities, research, and social policy. All of this knowledge will be used in the practicum as you learn to apply it in real-life situations. In addition, much new knowledge about practice will be gained if you apply yourself to not only observing but also working hard to understand what is being done in your agency and why.

Social work *skills* are the behaviors of practice. They are the techniques and procedures used by social workers to bring about desired change and enhancement of the social functioning of clients or in social systems with which clients interact. For the most part, skills are learned by watching and following the lead of skilled practitioners. Your

Ethical and Professional Behavior

Behavior: Use reflection and self-regulation to manage personal values and maintain professionalism in practice situations.

Critical Thinking Question: As you gain the knowledge required for practicum, how can reflection on your personal values help you enhance that knowledge?

practicum experience will afford you the opportunity to acquire and enhance your social work skills.

A *value* is a strong preference that is rooted in one's deepest beliefs and commitments, and that affects one's choices, decisions, and actions. Social work values (e.g., service, social justice, and integrity) are usually combined with social workers' personal values and hopefully are consistent with them. Acquiring, honing, and blending social work knowledge, skills, and values will help to establish the *three foundations of practice* you will need for professional practice. Practicum will undoubtedly be a time for you to clearly understand what your values are, and you will also begin to see how your values may at times be in conflict with the values of others, including the values of your clients.

Watch this video demonstrating professional demeanor and behavior. What interpersonal skills are needed for social workers to appear genuinely professional to clients?

The curricula for BSW programs and the first year of MSW programs are built around the concept of *generalist social work practice*. Thus, the practicum is expected to reflect a broad range of experiences in order to prepare for generalist practice. Both BSW and MSW students must learn the generalist skills of practice and may also move into practice that is specialized in a particular way. The practicum can provide broad experiences in generalist social work as well as more focused experiences, which prepare graduates for a practice specialization. The second year of MSW programs allows for additional emphases, sometimes beyond generalist practice. Even if your program has specialties or emphases in the second year, generalist competencies form the basis for all social work practice. Thus, it is incumbent upon students to make certain that they prepare themselves as generalists.

Assessment

Behavior: Select appropriate intervention strategies based on assessment, research knowledge, and values and preferences of clients and constituencies.

Critical Thinking Question: As you learn to assess clients and client systems, what might be the challenges of designing interventions based on your assessment, client preferences, and research knowledge?

The *generalist perspective* is a way of viewing and thinking about the processes and activities of social work practice. It is a set of ideas and principles that guides the process of planned change at all levels of practice, works in a wide variety of settings, and helps select appropriate social work roles. One of the unique characteristics of the generalist social worker is the ability to *adapt his or her approach to the needs and circumstances of the client or client system*, rather than expecting the client to conform to the methods of the professional or the agency. The generalist avoids selecting an intervention method or approach until he or she has *collaborated with the client* to complete a careful assessment of the client's concern or problem. The generalist designs interventions only after having considered *various ways in which the client's problem or concern can be defined, conceptualized, and approached*. Finally, the generalist is prepared to draw on and use a *wide range of intervention techniques and procedures* and is not bound to a single theory or model.

Keeping the earlier definition of generalist social work in mind, study Table 2.1, which lists seven *generalist competencies* common to all entry-level practitioners and most advanced practitioners. The table provides a *rationale for the use of each generalist competency* in social work and a list of *specific skills* required for the demonstration of that competency.

Table 2.1   Generalist Competencies for Social Work Practice

Generalist Competency 1		
Competency Description	**Rationale for Competency**	**Skills Related to Competency**
The generalist social worker practices at multiple levels (micro, mezzo, and macro) both separately and simultaneously and moves between systems and levels of practice based on client/client system needs, resources, and likelihood of success to enhance social functioning and facilitate social change.	The generalist social worker practices at multiple levels because of the complex nature of social problems, and because social functioning, social change, and social justice are supported by interventions at all levels of practice.	Uses interpersonal helping skills, communication skills, relationship building, and interviewing. Engages in coordination, group facilitation, advocacy, education, consulting, and mediation. Engages in planning, community development, program management, research, social policy formation, and administration.
Generalist Competency 2		
Competency Description	**Rationale for Competency**	**Skills Related to Competency**
The generalist social worker plays a broad range of professional roles individually and simultaneously to promote social justice, enhance social functioning, and promote social change. Generalist social workers may play several roles in any given situation, and can move between these roles as needed.	The generalist social worker plays a broad range of professional roles because of the variety of client/client system needs and resources, as well as to enhance social functioning, promote social justice, and promote social change at multiple levels of practice. The generalist social worker sees the connections between professional roles and understands the importance of using them prescriptively, matching roles with need.	Selects social work role based on client/situation needs, conceptualization of the location of the problem being addressed, and targets for change. Plays roles at all levels of practice, including some roles specific to one level of practice and others that can be played at all levels of practice.
Generalist Competency 3		
Competency Description	**Rationale for Competency**	**Skills Related to Competency**
The generalist social worker uses a variety of discreet yet interacting lenses, conceptual frameworks, and paradigms to guide practice, including the strengths, ecosystems, and diversity perspectives.	The generalist social worker understands that clients, groups, organizations, communities, and social systems cannot be understood in isolation, and that understanding the interaction between these entities is essential for effective interventions.	Incorporates a variety of professional perspectives into all phases of the helping process. Uses professional perspectives to identify targets for enhancing social functioning and improving the fit between clients and social systems.

(continued)

Table 2.1 *continued*

Generalist Competency 4		
Competency Description	**Rationale for Competency**	**Skills Related to Competency**
The generalist social worker uses a variety of orienting/explanatory theories to guide practice, including social systems theory, human development theory, group theory, organizational theory, community development theory, social movement theory, and social development theory.	The generalist social worker understands the development of individuals, families, social systems, groups, organizations, and societies in order to comprehend the social conditions faced by clients and to implement effective interventions.	Incorporates orienting/explanatory theories into all phases of planned change at all levels (engagement, assessment, planning, intervention, and evaluation).

Generalist Competency 5		
Competency Description	**Rationale for Competency**	**Skills Related to Competency**
The generalist social worker uses a variety of practice theories and models to guide practice and address client needs and resources, including task-centered casework, crisis intervention, client-centered casework, empowerment model, family systems model, mutual aid model, structural model, organizational development model, community organization model, and social change model.	The generalist social social worker must use practice theories and models to design individualized interventions that are empirically based, grounded in best practices, methodologically sound, creative, and matched to the situation at hand. These theories and models provide practitioners with a versatile repertoire of techniques, help them avoid limiting themselves to a single approach, and afford the opportunity to combine approaches for effective interventions.	Incorporates practice theories and models into interventions at all levels of practice based on client need and resources. Combines practice theories and models creatively to address multiple social issues faced by clients and client systems.

Generalist Competency 6		
Competency Description	**Rationale for Competency**	**Skills Related to Competency**
The generalist social worker, in partnership with client systems, uses the planned change process of assessment, planning, intervention, termination, and evaluation at all levels of practice.	The generalist social worker uses the planned change process to enhance social functioning and promote social change because a sound assessment creates the basis for an intervention plan that can be implemented and evaluated based on identified goals and objectives.	Engages clients, builds productive professional relationships, assesses client problems and strengths, designs sound intervention plans, implements effective intervention plan, and evaluates outcomes.

Generalist Competency 7		
Competency Description	**Rationale for Competency**	**Skills Related to Competency**
The generalist social worker is guided by the National Association of Social Workers (NASW) *Code of Ethics*, incorporates social work values into interventions at all levels, and uses a process for ethical decision making and resolving ethical dilemmas.	The generalist social worker understands how personal and professional ethics and values underlie codes of conduct, client choices, community development, societal attitudes, definitions of social problems, development of social policy, and research.	Incorporates social work and client values into all interventions. Uses NASW *Code of Ethics* in ethical decision making and to resolve ethical dilemmas.

The Educational Policy and Accreditation Standards of the Council on Social Work Education (2015, 3–7) also identify the following professional *competencies* for social workers:

1. Demonstrate ethical and professional behavior
2. Engage difference and diversity in practice
3. Advance human rights and social and economic justice
4. Engage in practice-informed research and research-informed practice
5. Engage in policy practice
6. Engage with individuals, families, groups, organizations, and communities
7. Assess individuals, families, groups, organizations, and communities
8. Intervene with individuals, families, groups, organizations, and communities
9. Evaluate practice with individuals, families, groups, organizations, and communities

The list of *generalist competencies* in Table 2.1, in combination with the *Core Competencies of the Council on Social Work Educational Policies and Accreditation Standards* (2015, 3–7), can guide the structure of your practicum. Work to identify ways in which you can acquire those competencies considered vital to the practice of social work. A discussion of these competencies is woven into this book in multiple ways, showing you how they are acquired over time and in a variety of ways. Work to integrate them into your professional repertoire. Remember that *acquiring competencies is a process* that begins in practicum and continues throughout practice. Social workers are continuously expected to learn new skills; refine existing abilities; be innovative practitioners; commit to professional development; and engage in reflection, supervision, and evaluation.

As you begin this exciting practicum experience, remember that *initial experiences are pattern setting*. If the first days and weeks of contact with a new student are positive for a field instructor and other agency staff, that field instructor will likely conclude that the student can be trusted and given responsibilities. If, on the other hand, these first contacts give the field instructor cause to doubt whether the student is capable and responsible, he or she may hesitate to assign meaningful work to the student. It is good to anticipate how you as a student might be perceived by the field instructor and what he or she might be thinking and feeling about your presence in the agency. Your field instructor may have some of these thoughts about supervising students, including you:

- "I look forward to having a student. Practicum students usually have a lot of enthusiasm, and they tend to look at the work of this agency from a fresh perspective."
- "The student can do some of our work, because we're understaffed and overworked."
- "This student better catch on quickly, because I am too busy to provide a lot of supervision."
- "I worry about students overstepping their bounds. I don't want to clean up any messes."
- "I hope this student is ready for a taste of reality."
- "I like having students here because their questions encourage me to think critically about what I do and why."
- "I remember how important practicum supervision was to me, and I want to pass this good experience on to another student."

Practicum students have varied and sometimes ambivalent reactions to the challenges of the practicum. They feel both excited about learning from a mentor and anxious about being observed and evaluated. If these ambivalent reactions describe you as you begin your practicum, this is normal. This is also very similar to the experiences of a client when entering a professional relationship with a social worker. Clients are likely to be ambivalent as well, so remember this when you experience varying emotions and reactions. Honestly identifying your own positive and negative reactions to supervision will **help you become more empathetic to your clients**. Understanding your own responses to supervision can help you understand what it is like for clients to be supervised and evaluated. Understanding your reaction to being closely supervised can help you become empathetic to clients who may feel scrutinized and criticized.

Practicum students need to shift from the university focus on professional education to the agency focus on professional training. Faculty members of social work programs that provide *professional education* emphasize the learning of general knowledge, theory, and broad principles that can be applied in many practice settings. Professional education encourages discussion, debate, and the consideration of alternative ways of assessing and responding to a problem or situation. It is related to the mission and purpose of the social work profession and focuses on learning outcomes.

By contrast, agency administrators and supervisors are concerned with training that emphasizes the learning of policies, procedures, and skills specific to their agency. *Professional training* is designed to teach what the agency has established as the standard or typical approaches to given practice situations. This training is agency-specific and related to the mission of the agency. It is measured through work outcomes rather than through learning only. Because these approaches reflect agency purpose, policy, and procedures, they are generally to be followed rather than challenged. Respectful questions about agency practice and policy will be well received, however. Hopefully you will integrate the broad knowledge obtained from the academic world with the specific training provided within the agency.

▶ After watching this video, discuss with your field instructor how maintaining roles and boundaries is an example of professional behavior.

All social agencies have what is often called an *office culture*. This term refers to the general ways of operating that are based on the agency's history, values, theoretical underpinnings, morale, policies and procedures, and staff interactions. Hopefully the office culture is positive and optimistic, because this will allow you to see an organization at its best and learn how a healthy, learning, and functional organization operates. Some disagreement, conflict, and power struggles are inevitable in organizational life, however, and these will soon become apparent to you. You need to be aware that aligning yourself with one side or another in these conflicts can undermine the success of your practicum.

All organizations, including human services agencies, have a political dimension, which is referred to as *office politics*. This term refers to the undercurrent of power dynamics created by factors such as conflict between various factions within an organization, uneven distribution of power between those in various levels, personal ambition, individuals or groups jockeying for greater power, and efforts to lobby on behalf of a certain opinion. Larger organizations have more complex internal office politics than smaller organizations. Even though office politics are normal and difficult to avoid, if you become caught up in these power struggles and conflicts, learning opportunities may be closed and some agency staff may withdraw their support. As a general rule, the larger and more political an organization, the more active is the office grapevine. Rumors, gossip, and speculations are common within organizations having many bureaucratic layers and are especially frequent during times of uncertainty, conflict, and rapid change. Participating in agency gossip can be another major pitfall for you.

Recognize that there are both *formal and informal aspects to the structure and function of your practicum agency*. The official policies and procedures, the formal organizational chart, and the chain of command all serve to describe the work of your agency, show who is responsible for what, and provide written guidelines for employees. The informal workings of the agency, however, may differ greatly from what is shown in organizational charts or policy manuals. You may discover that official titles and actual job descriptions do not match, that those with official power may not be the ones to whom others look for guidance, and that exceptions may be made to official policies under certain circumstances.

> **?** Assess your understanding of background and context by taking this brief quiz.

GUIDANCE AND DIRECTION

As you prepare your *learning agreement* in light of generalist competencies and core competencies of the social work profession, work to incorporate learning experiences that will help you develop these competencies. Your supervisors understand what you must learn to become a competent generalist social worker, which is why they are included in developing your learning plan. University social work programs include the competencies they want students to acquire in the learning agreement formats. Learning agreements are *working documents* that are modified throughout the practicum as additional learning needs are identified and new learning opportunities arise. Your plan should be exciting and ambitious to stretch and expand your knowledge and skills. It must also be realistic given your practicum setting, your abilities, your prior experience, and the time available to you.

Each of us has a unique *approach to learning* or *an individual learning style*. As you develop your plan, consider your preferred method of learning. For example, you may be inclined to jump into the middle of an activity or opportunity because you learn best by doing. Perhaps you learn best by first observing others and then trying your hand at the activity after processing what you have observed. Maybe you need to first understand the theory or rationale behind an activity before you are ready to take action. No one learning style is best or most effective in all situations. In fact, it is important to remember that real-life experiences from which you will learn, including those in practicum, will not all be presented in a manner that suits your own learning style, so work hard to be able to venture into learning in ways that may be new to you.

Ethical and Professional Behavior

Behavior: Use reflection and self-regulation to manage personal values and maintain professionalism in practice situations.

Critical Thinking Question: What personal and professional values do you bring to the practicum? What reflective practices will you engage in to manage both your personal and professional values?

Include in your plan the experiences and activities that will help you to *integrate theory with practice*. This is your opportunity to see how theory supports practice, and in what ways it does so. Classroom concepts and ideas should come alive during the practicum, and you will be expected to integrate what you learned in the classroom with the real-life experiences in your practicum. Reflect on what you learned in the courses you have taken, and bring that knowledge to bear in your practicum experience. Develop an awareness of the beliefs, values, and theories behind your decisions and your selection of an intervention. Seek exposure to social work practice and programs based on various beliefs about how, when, and why people and social systems are able to change. All of these learning goals will help you bring theory and practice together, and you will begin to see how learning and actual skills are actually related.

Even though your practicum learning experience will be specific to your practicum agency, remember that you are developing *knowledge and skills that can be generalized to other social work settings*. Secure a *breadth of experience* by building a wide variety of experiences into your practicum, but also find ways to gain *depth of experience* in your particular area of interest. By doing so, you will prepare yourself for work in another setting while immersing yourself in practice issues about which you care deeply. Tell your field instructor that you want as full and broad an experience as possible in order to prepare yourself for practice.

When you put your goals for learning into words on your learning agreement, describe your desired outcomes for learning in ways that permit the *monitoring and measurement of your progress*. However, also recognize that many important learning outcomes are inherently difficult to quantify and measure, such as developing a commitment to social work values, growing in self-awareness, acquiring self-confidence, and using a variety of perspectives and theories. Describe your desired outcomes as precisely as possible, but remember that not everything will be fully measurable. It is better to describe outcomes in general and imperfect ways than to not mention them at all, even if you have a hard time showing how you will measure them. Consider how your attempts to measure your learning could parallel your clients' attempts to demonstrate their growth to those with whom they are working. Your struggle to grow and to measure that growth will hopefully increase your sensitivity to your clients' hard work and potential frustration with not being able to demonstrate their progress.

Once you have completed your plan and it has been approved by your field instructor and faculty supervisor, follow it. Review it often and modify it as needed, but resist the temptation to abandon a part of the plan simply because it calls for a learning opportunity that is difficult to arrange. Do everything possible to *arrange and obtain the experiences* you need to advance your learning. Become assertive in asking for meaningful learning experiences. If you need help to arrange these because of agency reluctance to offer them to you, ask your faculty supervisor to advocate on your behalf.

As you formulate your learning plan, give careful thought to your *individual professional plans* for the next five years. For example, if you are a BSW student hoping to go on to graduate school, what can you do during the practicum to prepare yourself for graduate study or to increase your chances of being accepted into graduate school? If you expect to enter the job market immediately after graduation, what can you build into your plan that will prepare you for the job you seek? What specific licensing or certification may be required for you to practice social work in your state or to become certified in a specialty area? If you are an MSW student, what learning goals can you set for yourself that will adequately prepare you for advanced practice?

Diversity and Difference

Behavior: Present themselves as learners and engage clients and constituencies as experts of their own experience.

Critical Thinking Question: Because it is important to learn how to work with diverse clients and co-workers, how can you learn from both?

In addition to the formal learning plans you develop, consider using a *professional journal*. This exercise can help you in many ways. A journal can document your progress in learning, show your professional growth over time, allow you to express your doubts and questions without necessarily sharing them with your supervisors, and offer you the chance to reflect on the very personal nature of your work. Many students report that journal keeping is very useful because it serves as a written record of growth that is encouraging and reinforcing, particularly when viewed over time and in retrospect. A journal can include a listing of what you have accomplished, a description of what you have learned, your questions about your experiences, and your personal reactions to what you have seen and done. Reviewing your journal over time will help you to see your own *personal and professional growth*.

In addition, be alert to learning experiences that become available to you unexpectedly during your practicum, and find ways to integrate these experiences into your learning plan. Do not be surprised if much of what you actually learn during your practicum was not anticipated and thus could not have been written into your plan. Expect and learn to appreciate surprises. For example, your agency's funding may be drastically cut, and you may end up working in a different unit or service area. Your field instructor may take another job and you will have to adjust to a successor with a different supervisory style. Although such experiences can be stressful, they can also be valuable learning opportunities. They will certainly teach you to be *flexible and open to new experiences*. You can also gain invaluable perspective on how agencies and the social workers in them cope with change and stress, capitalize on funding or policy shifts, and turn problems into opportunities.

During your practicum, it is possible that you may learn some things that are surprising or even discouraging. For example, you will probably discover that not all clients are motivated, that some are difficult to like and respect, and that some will not make use of needed and available services. You will probably learn that client, agency, or social changes can be slow; that social problems are more complex than you realized; that you must be skillful in the art of politics; and that not all professionals are competent and ethical. Your faculty supervisor can help you gain perspective on such matters that might be disappointing to you, so be sure to share these experiences and observations with him or her.

Your field instructor will be paying attention to how you begin the practicum. First impressions have a powerful impact on personal and professional relationships, so it is vital that you make a favorable first impression on your field instructor and the other staff members in your practicum agency. Make a deliberate effort to get the practicum off to a good start. No doubt you want to be assigned tasks early in the practicum so that you maximize your learning from the outset. There are a number of reasons why a practicum supervisor will feel confident about assigning challenging responsibilities to a student. To make these assignments, the field instructor must trust the student and believe that he or she is capable of doing the work and not likely to make significant mistakes. Very often, the practicum supervisor makes this decision on the basis of early patterns observed in the student's ordinary behavior. Thus, you should display the following desirable learning and work behaviors:

Learning Behaviors

- Demonstrate your *enthusiasm for learning* and applying your knowledge in the agency.
- Inform your field instructor of your *prior work and volunteer experiences* to help him or her better understand your abilities.

Demonstrate Ethical and Professional Behavior

Behavior: Demonstrate professional demeanor in behavior; appearance; and oral, written, and electronic communication.

Critical Thinking Question: In what ways can you demonstrate your professionalism through your learning and work behaviors?

Diversity and Difference

Behavior: Present themselves as learners and engage clients and constituencies as experts of their own experiences.

Critical Thinking Question: Professional practice requires the ability to engage with diverse populations. How can you structure your practicum so that you learn from clients very different from yourself?

- Demonstrate *initiative* and a willingness to take on responsibilities and assignments.
- Take all *assignments seriously*, no matter how trivial and unimportant they may seem.
- Keep your *field instructor informed* about what you are doing, why you are doing it, and what you plan to do next on all assigned work.
- Consult with your field instructor immediately if you encounter a *problem or difficulty*, especially if it has legal ramifications or might create an agency public relations problem.
- Be a good listener and be *attentive to your field instructor* and to other staff members during supervisory conferences and staff meetings.
- Show your ability to *use constructive criticism* of your work, skills, and attitudes.
- *Ask questions* that reveal a desire to learn and understand your work, but avoid asking in a manner that appears to challenge or criticize the agency.
- When being trained, *pay attention*, take notes, and ask questions to minimize the chances that you will have to ask for explanations later.
- *Volunteer* to take on tasks that are not attractive to regular agency staff.
- Make *friendly overtures* to agency staff members other than your field instructor.
- Work to *build relationships* and get along with a variety of different people.

Work Behaviors

- Prepare all *letters, reports, and client records* with great care, according to the agency's prescribed format, and in a timely manner.
- Meet expectations for *timeliness*, including meeting all deadlines, being on time for all scheduled appointments and meetings, and remaining on the job for all the hours you are expected to be in the practicum agency.
- If you must make a *change in your work schedule*, or if you discover that you will not be able to keep an appointment, contact your field instructor immediately and work out an alternative plan.
- Be *well prepared for all meetings* with your field instructor and for agency staff meetings.
- *Read agency manuals* and other materials and become familiar with your agency's mission, programs, policies, and procedures.
- Do your best to *understand a new assignment or responsibility* the first time it is explained to you, and ask for clarification when needed rather than pretending you understand.

- Assume *responsibility for your mistakes*, seek supervision about them, and commit to learning from these experiences.
- Keep your desk and work space *neat and organized*.
- Pay attention to your *personal grooming, and dress* appropriately for the practicum.
- Do not engage in *gossip*; spread rumors concerning other agencies or professionals; or criticize other students, agency staff, clients, or other agencies in the community.
- Be extremely careful *to protect your clients' rights to privacy* and the confidentiality of agency records.

As you enter the *office culture* and observe the *office politics* of your agency, make thoughtful decisions about how you can respond in ways that will protect your practicum experience and avoid offending others. Here are some general guidelines for you to consider when dealing with office culture and office politics:

- Carefully *observe how staff members interact*, maneuver, and use their power.
- Be cognizant of the *official lines of authority* and to the power relationships inherent in the chain of command as described by the agency's organizational chart. Follow the chain of command to avoid confusion and possibly putting your practicum in jeopardy.
- Do not jump to conclusions concerning who is most valued and respected within the agency and who has the most *power and influence*. Power relationships are often more subtle and complex than they appear at first. Consequently, your first impressions may be erroneous.
- *Cultivate relationships* with those in the agency who command the respect of most fellow professionals and the support staff and who are respected and valued by their administrative superiors.
- Do not align yourself with someone in the agency who has a *reputation* for being a complainer or a troublemaker or who has little loyalty to the agency.

Every organization has *unwritten rules*, and it is likely that no one will think to tell you about them until after you ask about or have broken one. For example, you might be breaking a rule if you bring food or drink to a staff meeting, or if a certain report is submitted late even though it is permissible to be a little late on other types of reports. The best way to learn about these informal rules and procedures is to observe the work of others in the agency and ask why things are done a certain way.

As a student, it is important to learn how the process of *integrating academic content and actual practicum experiences* works effectively and sometimes does not work as expected. You are likely to recall and use your academic learning, and you may encounter situations which were never covered in classes. You may find that what you have learned in the classroom and

Practice informed Research (OR) Research-informed Practice

Behavior: Use practice experience and theory to inform scientific inquiry and research.

Critical Thinking Question: How can your observations of intervention outcomes be used to engage in research about the effectiveness of your work?

? Assess your understanding of guidance and direction by taking this brief quiz.

what works in theory and in rehearsal may not work as easily or effectively in real-life situations. Instead of concluding that theory is not useful at all, consider the numerous factors which impact whether or not a particular theory works in real people's lives. Real practice is more complicated than classroom examples, and it is important to learn how to *anticipate what will influence intervention outcomes*. For example, real life is messy, people do not change in a linear fashion, there are many unknowns at the outset of an intervention, and each client or client system is unique. Figure 2.1, Contributors to Intervention Outcomes, demonstrates some of the most important factors that may account for positive or negative outcomes in interventions. This includes client, social worker, and contextual variables. These contributing factors, although briefly described, may also account for outcomes in professional social work practice beyond the practicum.

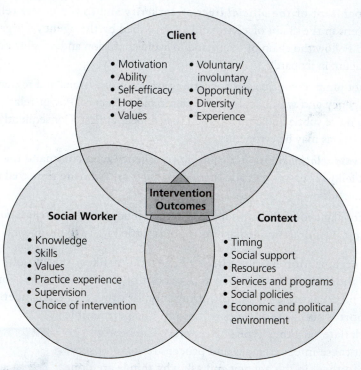

Figure 2.1
Contributors to Intervention Outcomes
This figure demonstrates the interacting and overlapping nature of these contributors to intervention outcomes. Remember that many of these factors will contribute to how well you and your clients do, and use this figure to examine why interventions you engage in are effective or ineffective. Use this information as a foundation to Chapter 14, which covers the planned change process.

Planning to Learn: A Workbook Activity

Your responses to the following questions will help you identify desired outcomes for your practicum and prepare a plan that can guide and enhance your professional growth. Respond honestly and with as much precision as possible.

1. What skills and knowledge are most needed by social workers in the agency? How can you design practicum experiences that will help you acquire them?

   _____

   _____

2. What orienting/explanatory theories (those that explain human development and behavior, family systems, group dynamics, organizational development, community development, and social development) will you try to apply in your practicum? See Chapter 14 (Planned Change Process) for a definition and listing of orienting theories. Consult with your field instructor as to which theories they use to understand individuals, families, groups, organizations, and communities.

   _____

   _____

3. What practice theories and models (those that provide guidance in developing interventions) will you try to apply in your practicum that address the needs of clients and client systems? See Chapter 14 (Planned Change Process) for a definition and listing of practice theories and models.

   _____

   _____

4. Reflect on the differences between the following terms that describe the levels of learning and performance based on this learning. Ask your faculty supervisor to give you an example that shows how these terms describe the levels of learning and performance. Work to reach the higher levels of learning as you proceed through your practicum.

   Understand _____
   ⇩
   Utilize _____
   ⇩
   Analyze _____
   ⇩
   Integrate _____
   ⇩
   Synthesize _____
   ⇩
   Critique _____

Self-Monitoring of Competency Building: A Workbook Activity

Instructions: This tool highlights the stages of competency building for social workers. Micro, mezzo, and macro social work skills can all be monitored using this tool. It also shows the professional areas in which students can monitor themselves, including knowledge, skills, and values. Use it to critically analyze and discuss the ongoing process of your skill development. Discuss the concepts presented in this tool with your field instructor, and ask him or her to help you through the stages of building your competency through observation, monitoring, and evaluation.

Stages of Competency Building	Knowledge	Skills	Values
Preparation ⇩	How do I know what skills to use?	What social work roles are indicated?	What ethical issues need to be addressed?
	What orienting theories apply in this situation?	How can I learn to use a practice model?	How do I tell my clients I am a student?
	What if I don't know what to do?	How will I know if I am being effective?	Is it ethical to practice on clients?
Initial attempt ⇩	What orienting theories apply?	What helping skills are needed in this case?	Can I employ the practice model needed?
	How can my client's goals be included in the intervention?	Can I employ the practice model?	Can I trust my judgment?
	What do my client's behaviors tell me?	How can I use my assessment to guide me?	Is it acceptable to adjust the model as the intervention proceeds?
Reflection and adaptation ⇩	What knowledge do I need that I do not possess now?	What should I do differently next time?	Am I able to focus on my client's issues rather than my own?
	How can I learn about evidence-based models?	How can I perform less mechanically?	How would my client define success?
	How can I prepare for the next time?	How can I evaluate my professional growth?	How can I get better at ethical decision making?
Refinement of competency ⇩	What is the best way to get feedback?	How can I individualize treatment plans?	Will this work with diverse clients?
	What will I need to know to work in more challenging situations?	How can I enlist client involvement?	What biases or stereotypes have I become aware of?
	What continuing education is required of social workers?	How can I work with unmotivated and involuntary clients?	What does the NASW *Code of Ethics* say about competency?

Suggested Learning Activities

- Work with a group of students to brainstorm possible tasks, activities, and projects that might be pursued in your practicum agency as a way of expanding learning opportunities.

- If your agency cannot provide all of the learning experience that you need, ask your field instructor to help you gain that experience by working several hours each week in another agency.

- Review your school's practicum evaluation form to better understand what you are expected to learn during the practicum and how you are expected to demonstrate that you have acquired specific knowledge and skills.

- If you have a specific career goal such as chemical dependency certification, school social work certification, social work licensing, or a graduate degree, identify the requirements for this goal and seek practicum experiences related to that goal.

- Ask social workers in your agency what they wish they had known or were able to do when they started their social work position. Find ways to learn this while in practicum.

- If at any time you feel disappointed with your practicum experience, discuss this concern with your field instructor. Do not delay or avoid this discussion and let your negative feelings build up inside.

Suggested Readings

Baird, Brian, N. *The Internship, Practicum, and Field Placement Handbook: A Guide for the Helping Professions.* 7th ed. Boston: Pearson Education, 2014.

Commission on Accreditation. *Educational Policy and Accreditation Standards.* Alexandria, VA: Council on Social Work Education, 2015.

Kolb, David. *Learning-Style Inventory.* Boston: McBer and Company Training Resources Group, 1981.

Sheafor, Bradford, and Charles Horejsi. *Techniques and Guidelines for Social Work Practice.* 10th ed. Boston: Allyn and Bacon, 2014.

Learning from Supervision

©VALENTINT/FOTOLIA

CHAPTER PREVIEW

This chapter provides information on the nature, functions, and context of *professional supervision*, including a variety of styles, perspectives, and approaches to supervisory activities. It shows how students can *purposefully and intentionally use supervision* when integrating theory and practice for the first time, as well as to ensure ongoing professional growth. The stages of practicum from both a student and supervisory point of view are presented, accompanied by recommendations for supervision. Additionally, the *forms and types of supervision* commonly used by field instructors are described.

Since the quality of your practicum is closely tied to the nature and quality of the teacher–student relationship you develop with your field instructor, it is advisable that you approach that relationship from a professional point of view. Learning from a skilled and caring supervisor can enrich a practicum experience and provide a positive model of staff interaction. Learning about the roles, responsibilities, and approaches to supervision will be of great help to you as you plan your practicum. Professional social workers routinely use supervision to ensure the quality of their work and to provide a structure for ongoing professional growth. The practicum provides this same experience for students.

BACKGROUND AND CONTEXT

Making full use of professional supervision requires a good understanding of the purpose and functions of supervision within an organization. The word *supervision* has its roots in a Latin word that means "to look over" or "to watch over," and this describes the overall purpose of supervisory practice. Supervisors definitely monitor the work of those they supervise and also go beyond that to educating, directing, and supporting their supervisees. All of this supervisory effort is expended with the ultimate goal of providing the highest quality of services possible, with the additional goal of preparing students for professional practice.

Functioning as a supervisor in a social service agency can be a very *challenging responsibility*. It is a job that requires sensitivity, skill, common sense, commitment, good humor, and intelligence. Supervisors are mediators and conduits between line-level social workers and higher-level agency administrators. They frequently represent the agency in its interactions with other agencies and the community. In addition, they are often faced with the challenging tasks of responding to the concerns and complaints of clients who are dissatisfied with the agency's programs or with the performance of a social worker or other staff member. The responsibility of supervisors to clients, staff, funding sources, and administrative officials is a broad and demanding expectation. It is good to remember that supervising students is only one aspect of their job.

Ethical and Professional Behavior
Demonstrate

Behavior: Use supervision and consultation to guide professional judgment and behavior.

Critical Thinking Question: How can you learn about how your supervisor deals with internal and external issues your practicum agency faces? Who else can be an example of such professionalism?

Although being a supervisor can be demanding, it can also be a satisfying job, especially for those who understand and appreciate the teaching aspect of supervision. Watching a new social worker or social work student learn and develop on the job can be a rewarding and inspiring experience. That is one reason why many busy agency supervisors choose to serve as field instructors to social work students. Hopefully your field instructor is highly motivated to teach you about social work practice because he or she wants to give back to the profession.

Kadushin and Harkness (2002) identify three functions of supervisory practice: the administrative function, the supportive function, and the educational function. The *administrative function of supervision* focuses on the assigning, monitoring, and evaluating of services. This includes such responsibilities as recruiting, selecting, and orienting new staff; assigning and coordinating work; monitoring and evaluating staff performance; facilitating communication up and down within the organization; advocating for staff; serving as a buffer between staff and administration; representing the agency to the public; and encouraging needed agency change. Additional administrative tasks include the monitoring of written documentation, coordinating work assignments, monitoring efficiency and effectiveness, and ensuring that services are evaluated and improved over time. This also necessitates that supervisors work between levels of staff and administrators and interface with the funding sources and other agencies that have influence over the way the agency works.

The *educational function of supervision* focuses on providing formal and informal training and orientation and arranging for formal in-service staff training. Basically, the supervisor is responsible for ensuring that staff members receive all of the initial training needed to perform well in their positions. In addition, the supervisor is responsible for recognizing training needs and providing ongoing in-service training. To properly educate employees, supervisors must keep abreast of the professional development of their employees, review their work and the documentation of their work, and oversee the work of employees with specific clients and interventions (Kadushin and Harkness, 2002).

The *supportive function of supervision* focuses on sustaining staff morale, cultivating a sense of teamwork, building commitment to agency goals and mission, encouraging workers by providing support, and dealing with work-related problems of conflict and frustration. It also includes the modeling of excellence, the building of trust between supervisors and supervisees so that professional growth can occur, the facilitation of the professional reflection process, and helping supervisees develop self-awareness necessary for practice. This aspect of supervision is extremely important in human services agencies in which stress and burnout can be common risks. The supervisor must strive to create a work environment that is conducive to the provision of quality services to clients, while also supporting staff who may at times feel stressed or unappreciated (Kadushin and Harkness, 2002).

Engagement

Behavior: Apply knowledge of human behavior and the social environment, person-in-environment, and other multidisciplinary theoretical frameworks to engage with clients and constituencies.

Critical Thinking Question: What are the commonalities between how your supervisor engages with you and how you will engage with your clients?

Watch this video that advises new supervisors about learning their role. How can this help you understand some of the challenges that supervisors may face? www.youtube.com /watch?v=6nBFS_A300Y

Your field instructor will be concerned with these three functions as they relate to practicum students. He or she will pay attention to whether you are performing the work of the agency in an appropriate manner and in keeping with agency policy and procedure. He or she will be sensitive to your fears and insecurities and to the fact that you have personal responsibilities in addition to those related to the practicum. Your field instructor will want to do everything possible to facilitate your learning, but, in the final analysis, his or her primary obligation must be to the agency's clients or consumers and to the agency that serves those clients rather than to your learning.

There are many *types of supervision*, all of which serve an important purpose, and all of which are valuable in specific ways. Each type of supervision addresses a certain need or situation, and it is recommended that you engage yourself whenever possible in as many forms of supervision as you can, as each one teaches differently and uses different approaches. You may receive the following types of supervision and teaching, all of which provide the opportunity for professional development:

- *Individual supervision* (regular meetings between field instructor and student)
- *Group supervision* (meetings between field instructor and a group of students or employees)

- *Peer supervision* (meetings of a group of social workers who assume responsibility for providing guidance and suggestions to each other)
- *Formal case presentations* (meetings at which social workers describe their work on a specific case and invite advice and guidance on how it should be handled)
- *Ad hoc supervision* (brief, need-based, unscheduled meetings to discuss a specific question or issue)
- *Virtual supervision* (computer, e-mail, or live Web-based supervision)
- *Observation* (watching social workers practice and discuss with supervisor)
- *Role playing* (rehearsal of skills in which student takes on client or social work role)
- *Modeling* (demonstration of a technique during supervision or actual intervention)
- *Clinical supervision* (discussion of and reflection on interventions, ethics, techniques, and professional use of self)

Social workers who assume the role of field instructor have specific *ethical obligations* because they assume responsibility for the quality of work and outcomes of those they supervise. Ethically, they must have knowledge and skill in the areas in which they provide supervision. They are expected to evaluate the performance of those they supervise, use effective and fair methods of supervision, and help supervisees gain knowledge and skills. They must also take care to manage the supervisory relationship, while maintaining professional boundaries and avoiding dual relationships, both of which can complicate and undermine the supervisory relationship.

Your field instructor will no doubt take these obligations seriously; thus you can expect that he or she will treat the supervisory relationship in an ethical and *professional manner*. Occasionally certain behaviors by a field instructor may prompt your school's faculty supervisor or practicum coordinator to reevaluate the suitability and appropriateness of using that person as a supervisor for students. This may include lack of time to supervise and not being available to students. At times, supervisors may lack genuine interest in supervising students, resulting in minimal commitment to teaching and mentoring. Hopefully you will not encounter a supervisor who is incompetent or unethical, but it is possible. If your field instructor exhibits any of these behaviors or attitudes, consult with your faculty supervisor or practicum coordinator to determine a course of action in order to ensure the quality of supervision available to you.

Social workers have a number of *legal obligations* when taking on the responsibility of field instructor. Those obligations are based on the principle of *vicarious liability*, which means that a supervisor may be held liable for the potentially ineffective or unethical actions of those he or she supervises. In their role as trainers, mentors, and supervisors, field instructors must do whatever they can to make sure that students avoid making decisions and taking actions that could be considered unprofessional in some way. This includes *malfeasance* (commission of an unlawful or wrongful act), *misfeasance* (commission of a proper act in a way that is injurious or wrongful), or *nonfeasance* (failure to act in accordance with one's responsibility).

Further, field instructors and students are also held to the concepts of *standards of care* (the type, level, and specific type of treatment or intervention that is indicated and appropriate for a specific client with a particular condition) and *standards of practice* (professional expectations for individual social workers that are based on what has been

Research-informed Practice

Behavior: Use and translate research findings to inform and improve practice, policy, and service delivery.

Critical Thinking Question: What questions can you ask your supervisor about what evidence-based or best practices are used in your agency?

? Assess your understanding of background and context by taking this brief quiz.

termed a reasonableness standard, which is the manner in which an ordinary person who is reasonable and prudent would have acted under similar circumstances). Beyond this, supervisors seek to promote *evidence-based practice* (practice supported by research demonstrating its effectiveness) and *best practices* (practice deemed to be the highest quality and suitability for a particular client base).

Supervisors have a variety of *supervisory styles* or preferred ways of doing their jobs, all of which will affect student experiences in the agency. No one style or approach is necessarily better or more right than others. Varying styles are more or less effective depending on the nature of the work to be done and the level of training and experience of those being supervised. Table 3.1 illustrates the various approaches to supervision to which the student will generally need to adapt.

Table 3.1 can be useful in understanding your field instructor's individual style and approach to supervising your work. Although supervisors will do their best to help you learn and grow, their other obligations are also important, and they may not be able to supervise you exactly as you wish. It is thus important to adjust to various styles of supervision.

Table 3.1   Supervisory Styles

Supervisory Style	Supervisory Behaviors
Orientation to work	Emphasizes the process of interventions
	Emphasizes the outcome of interventions
	Emphasizes both process and outcome
Attention to detail	Focuses on detail of work
	Focuses on broad mission and leaves details to others
	Focuses on both detail and broad mission
Delegation of work	Delegates work when necessary
	Delegates work easily
	Delegates work depending on situation
Monitoring of work	Monitors work closely to avoid mistakes and problems
	Allows supervisee autonomy and assumes success
	Monitors work depending on situation
Use of power	Retains power over supervisees and their work
	Shares power with supervisees and empowers them
	Uses power depending on situation
Functions of supervision	Fulfills administrative, educational, and supportive functions of supervision
	Fulfills one or two functions of supervision more than other functions
	Fulfills function of supervision required by situation

GUIDANCE AND DIRECTION

Because social work is challenging and sometimes stressful, and because your work directly affects clients' lives, you will need guidance, direction, support, and feedback from your field instructor. Both students and experienced social workers use supervision to help them deal with challenging situations, provide performance feedback, and give support. *Learning to use supervision for professional development* is an important part of your practicum that can teach you the immense value of supervision to you, the agency, and your clients.

Strive to use supervision in a purposeful, intentional, and responsible manner. Arranging a *regularly scheduled supervisory meeting* time each week will help you avoid the difficulties of struggling to arrange a different meeting time each week. Prepare for each meeting and do not expect your field instructor to do all of the talking. Bring questions, observations, and requests for input and feedback to the meeting. Use this time to examine your performance and explore new ideas.

Intervention

Behavior: Develop mutually agreed-on intervention goals and objectives based on the critical assessment of strengths, needs, and challenges within clients and constituencies.

Critical Thinking Question: What parallels do you see between a client and social worker setting goals for intervention and a student and supervisor setting goals for learning?

The conscious building of professional social work skills and competencies is directly related to the *conscious use of professional supervision*. This is why social work programs and practicum agencies collaborate so closely in the design and implementation of practicum programs. Both entities understand the developmental stages of professional growth, and because of that they choose to have other experienced social workers lead students through the process of *integrating theory and practice*. It is the responsibility of both the supervisor and the student to discuss certain topics in supervisory sessions. This will assist students to engage in a *reflective process* that enhances the acquisition of professional skills and practice behaviors. Students who actively engage in the supervisory relationship will gain much knowledge about practice and about themselves.

You and your field instructor will discuss many things during your scheduled time together, and two main categories of supervision will become apparent. The first of these is *supervision about your interventions with clients*. Following is a list of questions that will arise in discussions about interventions. The second category is *supervision about professional development*, and a list of discussions questions about that area is also included below. Look forward to discussing these questions with your supervisor, as this stage of your education is a unique opportunity to integrate theory and practice.

Supervisory Discussion of Client Interventions

- What *professional role* is expected of you in a particular practice situation?
- What determines the most *appropriate level of intervention*?
- What *theories* help to explain the development of individuals, families, groups, organizations, communities, and societies?
- What *theories* help to explain the etiology of a social problem or condition?
- What *theories and models of practice* help to guide the development of an intervention plan?

- What is the process of *matching client need with an intervention plan*?
- What is the role of *practice wisdom* in interventions?
- What is the role of *intuition* in interventions?
- What is the role of *social work research* in interventions?
- How can *diverse clients* be served in a culturally competent manner?
- What can be *learned from mistakes*?
- How can *academic information be applied and adapted* in real-life situations?

Supervisory Discussion of Professional Development

- How can you *acquire basic and advanced skills* in practice?
- How can you maximize your *learning style* to grow professionally?
- How can you use *supervision over a professional career*?
- Why is it important to gain *generalist skills* to address social problems?
- What can *clients teach us*?
- How can *professional growth* be measured?
- What skills and practice behaviors can be *transferred between fields of practice*?
- What *level of performance* will be expected for BSW- and MSW-level practice?
- When is a social worker *ready to supervise others*?

Take these questions with you to supervisory sessions with your field instructor and engage in professional conversations about them over time. It is good to learn how to proactively utilize supervision for both consultation on interventions and for professional growth while you are a student. Continuing to use and give supervision to others is an *element of sound social work practice*. Expect your field instructor to ask some very pointed, thorough, and thoughtful questions in order to learn about and monitor your work in the agency. Supervisors ask these questions in order to be of support to you and to ensure that clients are well served. They will help you analyze your performance, understand why an intervention was successful or not, and develop your critical thinking skills. In regard to specific cases you have been assigned, the following questions may be addressed in order to help you reflect and purposefully grow professionally. They are grouped together in the phases of the helping process in Table 3.2.

A supervisor is expected to give both instruction and feedback, and you will increase your chances of success if you seek and are open to input about yourself and your work. You may be anxious because your field instructor will be evaluating your performance in an ongoing way and at the end of your practicum. This reaction is certainly understandable, and in many ways is parallel to what clients feel when they are being monitored by social workers. However, in order for you to develop your knowledge and skills over time, your field instructor should evaluate your performance in an ongoing and continuous manner and you should accept this monitoring and evaluation in an open and nondefensive manner.

You will receive feedback, suggestions, and constructive criticism during all phases of your practicum so that you can continue to grow professionally. If this is not happening, discuss the matter with your field instructor and ask for an ongoing critique of your *performance in the use of the planned*

Human Rights and Justice

Behavior: Engage in practices that advance social, economic, and environmental justice.

Critical Thinking Question: As you set specific learning goals, how can you use supervision to help you understand how your agency advances human rights?

change process. Your supervisor may use questions similar to those in Table 3.2. These questions, as well as your answers to them, will help your supervisor understand your level of knowledge, reflection, skill, and ethics. In addition, you can expect that this evaluation will be based on direct observation of your work by your field instructor or other social workers, your verbal or written descriptions of your work and learning, feedback from clients, and observations and input from social workers in the community who have worked with you.

As you begin your practicum and take on new responsibilities, you may be afraid of making a serious mistake or in some way hurting your clients. Such worries are to be expected. In fact, your field instructor will become concerned if you do not have these concerns, because that could mean that you are overconfident or that you do not understand the seriousness of your situation. Do not hesitate to express your fears. Your field instructor can help you with these fears and help prepare you for any tasks assigned to you. Take heart in the knowledge that most beginning student errors tend to be those related to being tentative and not doing enough rather than actually doing harm to clients. Over time, social

> After watching this social worker's use of supervision regarding her concerns about a client, what did you learn about how you could bring concerns about your clients to your field instructor?

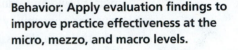

Evaluation

Behavior: Apply evaluation findings to improve practice effectiveness at the micro, mezzo, and macro levels.

Critical Thinking Question: How can you use your supervisor's questions about the effectiveness of the planned change process used with your clients to gain practice skills?

Table 3.2   Supervisory Questions Regarding the Planned Change Process

Phase of the Planned Change Process	Supervisory Questions Related to the Phase
Engagement	Was the client voluntary or involuntary?
	What skills did you use to engage the client in the planned change process?
	What problem(s) were identified?
	What was the client's level of motivation?
Assessment	Was the client voluntary or involuntary?
	What skills did you use to engage the client?
	What problems were identified?
	What strengths were identified?
	What was the client's level of motivation?
Intervention	What responsibilities did the client assume?
	What responsibilities did you assume?
	What theories guided your intervention?
	What evidence or research guided you?
Evaluation	How did you monitor and measure progress on achieving the goals and objectives?
	To what degree was the intervention a success?
	What did you use to measure outcomes?
	Did the client/client system view the intervention as successful?
	How was termination handled?

workers' growing competence will allow them to practice confidently and, at necessary points in time, with boldness.

Your field instructor will likely view any *errors or omissions* that you make not as mistakes only, but also as ways to learn and grow in your work with future clients and in more challenging future situations. Hopefully you will learn to observe, critique, evaluate, instruct, and affirm your own practice based on the constructive feedback given by your field instructor. This will teach you the value of ongoing self-monitoring of the effectiveness of your work in addition to the value of supervision.

Supervision is an *interactional process* that in many ways parallels the social worker–client relationship and the helping process (Shulman, 1992). In order to help you improve your performance, your field instructor will employ many of the techniques that you and other social workers use in working with clients such as offering guidance and support, providing feedback, recognizing strengths, and confronting when necessary. If you have the opportunity, watch your supervisor model the techniques with you that are also effective with clients, focusing on how they help you grow by being open to teaching and feedback. However, since supervision is not counseling or therapy, if you need counseling for personal issues or those related to your practicum, seek counseling from a professional other than your field instructor.

Students tend to move through several stages during their practicum experience, including *orientation, exploration and skill building, and beginning competency*. Your field instructor will provide specific types of help at each stage, helping you move forward as a professional. As you become more knowledgeable and competent, your field instructor will use different strategies of supervision with you. As you move through the practicum, be conscious of the shifts in your experiences outlined in Table 3.3.

Table 3.3   Stages of Practicum: Student and Supervisor Experiences

Stage of Practicum	Student Experiences	Supervisor Experiences
Orientation stage	**Approach to Supervision**	**Approach to Supervision**
	Enthusiastic, excited, anxious, unsure, overwhelmed, confused, ready, motivated, confident, worried about making mistakes, hesitant to be observed	Motivated to teach, hopeful that student will be competent, challenged to find time to supervise student
	Responsibilities	**Responsibilities**
	Participate in orientation and training, become familiar with agency staff and programs, attend agency meetings, visit other agencies, develop learning plan	Provide orientation and training, offer guidance and direction, provide encouragement, assist in selection of learning activities, support initial attempts at practice behaviors, identify student competencies and limitations
Exploration and skill-building stage	**Approach to Supervision**	**Approach to Supervision**
	Less anxious, more realistic, motivated, growing in confidence, willing to be observed, motivated by successes, learning from mistakes	Confident in allowing more student autonomy, aware of student strengths and limitations and need for supervision

Table 3.3 *continued*

Stage of Practicum	Student Experiences	Supervisor Experiences
	Responsibilities Take on responsibilities, implement learning plan, develop professional skills and knowledge, integrate theory and practice, gain exposure to all facets of agency practice, gain experience in all levels of practice, play variety of social work roles, identify strengths and address limitations	**Responsibilities** Monitor completion of learning activities, provide instructive and corrective feedback, help build on experiences, assist student in integrating theory and practice, help student assume more challenging tasks
Beginning competency stage	**Approach to Supervision** More confident in skills, increased insight, self-aware, motivated for professional position	**Approach to Supervision** Confident in student as entry-level practitioner, affirming of student competence
	Responsibilities Identify own professional growth needs, experienced in most aspects of practicum experience, need less supervision and direction, identify tasks independently, integrate theory and practice, and refine skills	**Responsibilities** Help student refine skills, assign broad range of tasks at all levels of practice, expect autonomous performance, help student generalize learning to other settings and populations

It is possible that tensions and conflicts may arise in your ***supervisory relationship***. For example, you may feel that your field instructor does not devote enough time to you and your learning needs. You may believe that your field instructor is too controlling or not structured enough. The two of you may have very different personalities. Perhaps you and your field instructor differ in terms of gender, race, ethnic background, or age, and at times these differences affect your relationship and work. If you have a conflict or difficulty with your supervisor, talk about it. Do not avoid the problem or circumvent your field instructor. You will be expected to find ways to deal with these issues, both now and in any future work environment. If the problem cannot be worked out with your field instructor, consult with your faculty supervisor.

Assess your understanding of guidance and direction by taking this brief quiz.

Exercise caution on developing a ***dual relationship*** with your field instructor. He or she is to be a supervisor, not a friend or a counselor. Although there can be an element of friendship between students and supervisors, this can also be problematic when supervisors need to provide feedback and students need to be able to accept it. If personal problems arise during your practicum, do not ask or expect your field instructor to provide counseling. If you need such services, arrange to receive them in another way.

Recall what you learned in this chapter by completing the Chapter Review.

Professional Standards for Supervision: A Workbook Activity

There are a number of governmental and professional standards for supervision in social work practice. Review the standards for supervision in the following two areas and discuss with your field instructor and faculty supervisor.

1. Supervision requirement for social work licensing in your state
    *   Who is considered an approved supervisor for social workers seeking licensing (i.e., degree, training in supervision, practice experience)?

    _____

    _____

    _____

    *   How much supervision is required, with what frequency, and on what topics?

    _____

    _____

    _____

    *   How is supervision documented and included in applications for licensure?

    _____

    _____

    _____

2. NASW (National Association of Social Workers) Best Practices in Supervision
    *   What responsibilities does a social work supervisor assume?

    _____

    _____

    _____

    *   What aspects of supervision are covered by the NASW *Code of Ethics*?

    _____

    _____

    _____

    *   How does the supervision in your agency compare with NASW Best Practices?

    _____

    _____

    _____

Preparing for Supervision: A Workbook Activity

Use the following guide to prepare yourself for supervisory sessions. It provides you with sample questions you can use for professional development and encourages you to seek supervision in the administrative, educational, and supportive facets of supervision described in this chapter.

Administrative Supervision

What orientation will be required before I am assigned clients and tasks?

Who will assign tasks to me?

Is it possible to work with other staff members besides my supervisor?

What are the required and preferred methods of communication within the agency?

What do I need to know about agency structure, function, and chain of command?

Educational Supervision

What training opportunities are available to me?

Is it possible for me to attend in-service training?

Are there any webinars, videos, or other training I can use on my own?

How can I learn to perform the tasks required of me?

What practice models are used primarily in the agency?

How will you coordinate with my faculty supervisor about my practicum?

How can I get feedback on my writing and documentation?

Supportive Supervision

How important is self-care in this agency?

What is the best way to deal with my anxiety about my work?

Who should I talk to when I am struggling or unsure about what to do?

How can I identify my professional strengths and build on them?

How can I prevent burnout, compassion fatigue, and secondary traumatic stress?

Suggested Learning Activities

- Present a case you are working on at a peer supervisory session, asking for input from other social workers.
- If appropriate and feasible, work with a variety of social workers, supervisors, and managers in your agency so that you can observe differing supervisory styles.
- Ask your field instructor how your agency provides support to its employees, such as through an employee assistance program and continuing education.

Suggested Readings

Aasheim, Lisa. *Practical Clinical Supervision for Counselors: An Experiential Guide*. New York: Springer Publishing Company, 2011.

Association of Social Work Boards. *An Analysis of Supervision for Social Work Licensure: Guidelines on Supervision for Regulators and Educators*. 2013. Retrieved from https://aswb.org/wp-content/uploads/2013/10/supervisionjobanalysis.pdf

Baird, Brian N. *The Internship, Practicum, and Field Placement Handbook: A Guide for the Helping Professions*. 7th ed. Upper Saddle River, NJ: Prentice Hall, 2014.

Kadushin, Alfred, and Daniel Harkness. *Supervision in Social Work*. 4th ed. New York: Columbia University Press, 2014.

National Association of Social Workers. *Code of Ethics*. Washington, DC: NASW Press, 1999.

National Association of Social Workers and Association of Social Work Boards. *Best Practice Standards in Social Work Supervision*. 2013. Retrieved from http://www.socialworkers.org/practice/naswstandards/supervisionstandards2013.pdf

Pecora, Peter, David Cherin, Emily Bruce, and Trainidad de Jesus Arguello. *Strategic Supervision: A Brief Guide for Managing Social Service Organizations*. Los Angeles: Sage Publications, 2009.

Sheafor, Bradford, and Charles Horejsi. *Techniques and Guidelines in Social Work Practice*. 10th ed. Boston: Allyn and Bacon, 2014.

Shohet, Robin, and Peter Hawkins. *Supervision in the Helping Professions*. 4th ed. Columbus, OH: Mayfield Publishing, 2012.

Shulman, Lawrence. *Interactional Supervision*. 3rd ed. Washington, DC: NASW Press, 2010.

Weinbach, Robert. *The Social Worker as Manager: A Practical Guide to Success*. 7th ed. Boston: Pearson Education, 2015.

4

Personal Safety

©GSTUDIO GROUP/FOTOLIA

CHAPTER PREVIEW

This chapter describes the potential dangers of social work practice and offers ways in which social work students can practice safely by identifying the *sources and types of danger* most often encountered in social work practice, becoming familiar with potential dangers and risks in practicum, and informing themselves of agency policies and procedures that can *reduce risk and protect staff and clients*. It also familiarizes students with *precautions and preventive actions* that can reduce the risk of being harmed and provides guidance on steps and actions that can be taken to *de-escalate threatening situations and deal with violence when it happens*.

When dealing with clients in stressful personal situations, social workers sometimes find themselves involved in emotional encounters laden with the potential to undermine the safety of both clients and social workers. Although social workers see themselves as helpers and expect most clients to be cooperative, at times they find themselves in situations in which they must deal with clients who are angry, emotionally volatile, and threatening. Violence toward social workers is often due to client frustration with human service systems; cutbacks in services; increased levels of crime, drug use, and violence in society; and antiauthority or antigovernment attitudes on the part of clients. In light of potential threats and attempts at violence toward social workers, it is of the utmost importance that students learn how to avoid such danger and deal with it should it actually occur.

In addition to the physical dangers associated with certain circumstances and types of practice, exposure to job-related danger can lead to **negative outcomes** for social workers such as anxiety, low morale, burnout, family stress, cynicism, and high job turnover rates. As a social work practicum student, you must be cognizant of the dangers you face so that you do not experience physical or emotional assaults. You need to exercise certain precautions so as to reduce risks to your safety. Moreover, you must know what steps to take when you encounter a dangerous situation rather than assume that you are not in danger or that you can handle situations without training and consideration of specific guidelines and recommendations.

BACKGROUND AND CONTEXT

Although social work practice occurs in the context of potential danger, it is possible to prevent violent incidents from occurring, as well as to reduce the threat and potential of harm. Knowing the sources of possible harm will help greatly, as will understanding how to react when threats occur or when they are imminent. This section summarizes the various sources of harm, including high-risk settings, certain social work practices and interventions that can present danger, and potentially dangerous clients.

Certain **high-risk settings** present more risk to social workers than others. Examples of such settings include child protection agencies, corrections programs, forensic units of psychiatric hospitals, shelters for the homeless population, and residential facilities for youth who may be aggressive and impulsive. These settings are potentially dangerous because some of those served may have tendencies toward the use of violence. However, remember that any practice setting can be threatening because client–worker interactions often involve emotionally charged situations and concerns. Even clients with no previous history of violence or high-risk behaviors can, under certain circumstances, pose a threat to social workers.

After watching this video about the work to make safety training mandatory for social workers in Massachusetts, reflect on the challenges to institutionalizing such safety training. www.youtube.com /watch?v=bmldqOs8yFY

Certain **social work practices and interventions** have a greater likelihood of placing the social worker at risk than others. Examples of such activities include the initial investigation of child abuse allegations, the involuntary removal of a child from a parent's home, protection of a victim of domestic violence, outreach to youth involved in gang activity, home visits with clients on probation or parole, intervention with drug- and alcohol-involved clients, transporting clients who do not wish to be moved, behavioral management of persons with certain forms of brain injury, and the monitoring of clients in correctional settings. In these situations, social work actions can be perceived by clients as threatening or coercive. This may result in heightened emotion or defensiveness on the part of clients and an inclination to use violence.

Social workers who work with **potentially dangerous clients** face the difficult challenge of remaining humane, open, and accepting of clients while also being alert to the possibility of danger or attack. It is important not to view every client as a potential threat, but it is also very crucial to recognize a client who might be a threat. Although any client may have the potential to be of danger to social workers and practicum students, it is good to anticipate the possibility of heightened emotion, unregulated behavior, extreme stress, and history of violence. In order to anticipate possible danger in your practicum, consider the following examples of specific clients who may present a threat:

- A client with a *previous history of violence* or threats
- A parent reacting to the *removal of a child* from their home
- A client engaging in an *illegal act* that is discovered by a social worker
- An *involuntary client* being transported to a secure facility
- A client being seen in a follow-up visit who is *angry about a previous encounter*
- A client with a mental illness involving *paranoia, delusions, or hallucinations*
- A client *under the influence of substances*, which lower inhibitions
- A client in *withdrawal from substances*, which can lead to violent behavior
- An involuntary client who does not respect or *resents the authority of professionals*
- A client with a *lack of impulse control*
- A client with *post-traumatic stress disorder* experiencing hyperarousal due to perceived threat by a social worker
- A *perpetrator of partner violence* who wants to know the whereabouts of their partner
- A client who possesses and is not afraid to use *weapons such as firearms*

Research-informed Practice

Behavior: Use and translate research findings to inform and improve practice, policy, and services delivery.

Critical Thinking Question: What does the professional literature tell us about the factors that put social workers at risk for violence by clients?

Engagement

Behavior: Apply knowledge of human behavior and the social environment, person-in-environment, and other multidisciplinary theoretical frameworks to engage with clients and constituencies.

Critical Thinking Question: What aspects of social work practice and the way social agencies provide services could contribute to strong emotional reactions by clients?

In addition to the threat of physical violence, social workers in some settings experience frequent *verbal abuse* due to the nature of their work and the clients they serve. Because most of these threats do not result in actual violence, social workers may become complacent about actual risk. They may come to view verbal threats as part of their job, mistakenly assume that their clients are usually bluffing, and consequently fail to take reasonable precautions. Some social workers erroneously believe that because they have been trained in basic helping skills, they will always be able to talk their way out of a dangerous situation. These overly confident workers may *underestimate the risk to themselves*, believe that they do not need special training in how to respond in truly dangerous situations, and thus put themselves at higher risk. It is important that practicum students learn to take their personal safety very seriously. They must be made aware of potentially dangerous situations, helped to identify such situations themselves, trained in all agency policies regarding violence prevention, become knowledgeable about how to report negative experiences, supported when unsure of themselves, and provided with supportive services in the event of a threat or actual form of violence.

 Assess your understanding of background and context by taking this brief quiz.

GUIDANCE AND DIRECTION

Probably the most important idea regarding social work safety is that much violence toward social workers can be prevented if they understand the *stages of potentially violent incidents* and how to intervene at each phase of escalation. Many dangerous interpersonal psychosocial situations are the result of tensions that have grown and intensified over a short or long period of time. It is vital to understand the phases of escalation, clients' needs and feelings during each phase, and what actions or interventions by the social worker might reduce the tension and level of risk. Before learning the specifics of prevention and response, think about the following *principles of promoting safety*:

- There is potential for harm in *any setting or client encounter*.
- Certain practice situations and clients present *higher risk than others*.
- The potential for harm can be *anticipated* in some cases.
- The potential for harm can be *reduced* with effective approaches.
- *Different approaches* need to be used at different levels of escalating threat.
- *Ineffective responses* to threats can actually increase the risk of harm.
- *Safety training* is necessary for all social workers and practicum students.
- *Agency safety policies* are necessary and must be reviewed, updated, and followed.
- Reducing the potential for harm requires a *dual focus on interactions with clients and the design and management of the environment* and context of these interactions.
- Clients use threats and violence when other *forms of communication fail them*.
- Past behavior is the single best *predictor of future behavior*.
- The *attitude and approach of the social worker* play a role in either controlling or provoking threatening behavior.

How can the tips shown on this video be incorporated into your practicum setting to promote social work safety?
www.youtube.com/watch?v=2leLuzA77yM

It is vital to *intervene as early as possible* in high-risk situations in order to prevent escalation and eventual loss of control by the client. Remember that clients who may threaten violence are likely experiencing a myriad of emotions. Depending on the situation, they may feel afraid, judged, threatened, lonely, without hope, wronged, misunderstood, overwhelmed, frustrated, without power or recourse, or vengeful. A genuine attempt by the social worker to understand the emotions of people who are extremely upset may be helpful in defusing or de-escalating potentially dangerous situations.

Think of all potentially violent situations as having *five general stages*. These include *high-risk situation, escalation, threats, violence,* and *postincident*. It is vital to understand that in each of these stages, distinct goals and approaches to managing the situation are to be used. Hopefully such situations can be prevented, defused, or resolved without actual violence, but in some circumstances actual violence occurs. The goal of de-escalation in such situations is to resolve the threat before it moves from one stage to another. Social workers may be harmed physically or emotionally, and there are real cases of social workers losing their lives in extreme circumstances. Table 4.1, Dealing with Potentially Violent Situations, outlines the stages of potentially violent situations and recommends approaches to be taken at each stage in order to prevent harm. In addition to these guidelines, agencies have their own specific policies regarding actions to be taken.

Table 4.1   Dealing with Potentially Violent Situations

Stage of Incident	Client Emotions	Client Behavior	Goal	De-escalation or Intervention Approaches
High-risk situation ⇩	Stress, anxiety, fear, anger	Client in control of own behavior but exhibits unusual behavior	Prevention of violence	Recognize potential for high-risk situation to escalate Use active listening and empathy to allow the client to be heard and work toward resolution of concerns
Escalation of emotion and potentially violent behavior ⇩	Escalation of emotions and irrational thought	Verbal venting or unusual quietness Client control over own behavior lessening	De-escalation of violence	Assess potential for violence Utilize nonthreatening, respectful, and calm responses to client statements and behavior Avoid arguing and challenging client Seek solutions satisfactory to client
Threats ⇩	Feeling attacked, disrespected, vulnerable, mistreated, unheard	Verbal attacks, intimidation and threats of physical violence Client control over own behavior being lost	Dealing with threats	Set limits in speech and behavior Develop potential escape plan Avoid giving orders or returning threats Call for assistance
Violence ⇩	Extremely angry, sees no alternative to violence	Threatening actions, actual violence Client control over own behavior lost	Dealing with violence	Use self-defensive measures If safety cannot be ensured, leave or escape Cooperate with responding law enforcement or others who arrive to assist
Post incident	Remorse, release of tension, need for containment	Client exit or social worker exit	Review of incident	Consult with supervisor and administrators Document the incident Provide critical incident debriefing and support as needed

Building on this information provided, review Table 4.2, Approaches Tailored to Specific Client Threat, and consider how an understanding of any *specific client threat* can lead to specific social work approaches to reducing client threats. Depending on the intense emotions felt by clients and their specific situations, distinct and individualized approaches will be effective. This information is an example of learning how to use your interactional skills with clients in very challenging situations.

Table 4.2   Approaches Tailored to Specific Client Threat

Threat	Approaches
Client with a history of threats or violence	Consult agency records prior to meeting with a potentially violent client to inform yourself. Notify colleagues when planning to meet a client with a history of violence.
Angry client	Provide the client as much privacy as possible without compromising your own safety. Allow the client to vent angry feelings and maintain a calm and confident attitude. Do not touch or stand above the client and give him or her personal space.
Fearful client	Recognize that fear can turn to aggression. Acknowledge client emotion and provide reassurance if possible. Speak and act in ways that lessen the client's need to fear you.
Client with escalating emotion and behavior	Recognize physical signs of emotional escalation such as rapid breathing, teeth grinding, dilated pupils, loud speech, clenched fists, and threatening movements. Reduce threatening stimuli to de-escalate emotion and threat. Increase structure and boundaries to de-escalate emotion and threat.
Client under the influence of substances	Identify the level of client impairment. Identify the extent of inhibition due to substance use and remember that reasoning with the client may be ineffective due to impaired judgment.
Clients with access to weapons	Assure the client you intend no harm. Remember that weapons may be kept in kitchens or bedrooms. Remember that any object can be used as a weapon.
Client threatening you with a weapon	Do not attempt to disarm a client with a weapon. Do not endanger yourself by remaining in the situation and use any escape route available.
Client involved in illegal activities	Recognize that you are a threat to the client and what you have seen. Find a reason to exit the situation.
Client who makes you uncomfortable	Trust your instincts and assume that you have a built-in unconscious mechanism that can recognize danger more quickly than your rational thought processes. Utilize predetermined excuse to leave or seek help.

Table 4.3 provides guidelines for *anticipating and managing potential agency-based dangers*, identifying situations that might put you at risk, preventing or dealing with risky situations, resolving violent situations should they arise, and managing the aftermath of threats and actual violence that do occur. Discuss these dangers and the approaches to dealing with them with your agency field instructor, making certain that you understand your practicum agency policies. Observe whether these approaches are utilized or not in your agency, and whether any improvements could be made in agency structure and function that might

Engagement

Behavior: Use empathy, reflection, and interpersonal skills to effectively engage diverse clients and constituencies.

Critical Thinking Question: What interpersonal helping skills can you use to decrease the chances that you will be involved in dangerous situations with clients?

Table 4.3   Anticipating and Managing Potential Agency-Based Dangers

Dangers	Approaches
Exterior of office	Ensure that the exterior of the agency and parking area are well lighted.
	Make entrances and signs friendly, clear, and inviting.
Environmental stimuli	Keep waiting rooms and offices clean and create a pleasant and inviting physical environment.
	Avoid unkempt or impersonal appearance that may convey disrespect to clients and generate frustration and hostility.
Agency policy regarding acceptable behavior	Post a statement in waiting rooms and in other prominent places explaining that alcohol, drugs, and weapons are not allowed in the building.
	Post a statement that security officers or police will be called and legal action may be taken when clients become threatening.
Quality of services	Provide services in a timely and professional manner to reduce client frustration.
	Avoid waiting lists when possible and reduce waiting periods for eligibility determination or services.
Meeting space	Designate a specific office or room for meeting with potentially threatening or violent clients.
	Select a room that is easily and frequently observable by others.
Policies and protocol	Develop policies on how staff members are to assess danger and respond, including bomb threats, hostage taking, and hazardous materials management.
	Develop policies on when and how to seek police assistance, including a written agreement with local law enforcement agency.
	Review and revise policies as needed.
Staff training	Provide training for all staff on personal safety, including repetition of training over time.
	Rehearse and provide drills to reinforce staff understanding and ensure effective response.
Identification of high-risk clients	Devise record-keeping systems that use color codes or other markings to identify clients with a history of threats or violence.
	Share information with all staff, especially when staff members are new to the agency.
Safety measures and devices	Install call button in each office.
	Utilize code words and phrases for letting others know that help is needed.
Reporting and documentation	Encourage all staff to report threats or attempts of violence.
	Maintain a log of all threats so staff can identify those clients who present a risk.
	Review actual incidents to determine the effectiveness of agency response, and make revisions as necessary to protect staff.

(continued)

Table 4.3 *continued*

Dangers	Approaches
Legal actions	File criminal charges against those who harm or threaten physical injury to either staff members or their family.
	Develop agreement with law enforcement and court system to enlist their support for agency policy.
Staff support	Provide counseling, emotional support, time off, and other services to lessen the effects on the staff member and family.
	Offer critical incident debriefing support to all staff, even those not involved in an incident.

reduce potential risk for harm. Inquire about training available to you, and ask about which situations in your agency may have the potential for violence.

Table 4.4 describes the *potential dangers of home visits* as well as approaches to dealing with those dangers. These approaches apply when planning a visit, entering a home, conducting a home visit, and utilizing escape strategies.

Table 4.4   Anticipating and Managing Home Visit Dangers

Dangers	Approaches
Preparing for a home visit	Learn as much as possible about a potentially dangerous home, its occupants, and its neighborhood.
	Seek the assistance of another social worker or law enforcement if necessary.
	Assign two staff members for potentially dangerous home visits.
	Inform your agency of the time and place of all home visits.
	Unless there is a good reason to visit a home unannounced, call ahead to schedule a visit.
	Consider meeting a client in a neutral location unless the home needs to be visited.
	Educate yourself about drugs and illegal drug labs so that you can recognize the dangers inherent in entering such a place.
Entering a home	Enter a home only after identifying any signs of risk, including sounds of violence.
	Check in with your agency when you arrive, during your home visit, and when you leave.
Managing a home visit	Be aware that weapons may be kept in bedrooms and that kitchens contain knives and other potential weapons.
	Do not sit in a chair or couch from which you cannot quickly get to your feet. A hard and movable chair could be used as a shield against a threat.
	Watch for hazardous materials such as those in a methamphetamine lab and for objects such as syringes and chemicals.
Escape plan	Have an escape plan ready in case you need to flee, including an escape excuse.
	Identify possible escape routes.
	Park your vehicle in a way that allows for quick escape if necessary.
	Keep your vehicle in good running order and full of fuel so you do not become stranded.
	If you are being followed, go immediately to a police or fire station or to a public place.
	Do not go to your home if you believe someone is following or watching you.
	Wear shoes and clothing that permit running.
	Carry a means of calling for help (e.g., cellular phone, emergency signal).

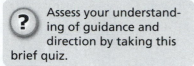

? Assess your understanding of guidance and direction by taking this brief quiz.

V Recall what you learned in this chapter by completing the Chapter Review.

Reducing the Risk of Harm: A Workbook Activity

Responding to the following questions will help to identify, understand, and utilize agency policies and procedures regarding potential threat.

1. What training is provided in your agency to help social workers prevent and deal with threatening or violent clients or situations?

_____

_____

2. What agency policies and procedures are in place to ensure personal safety and reduce risk to agency employees and clients?

_____

_____

3. What high-risk clients or situations are you likely to encounter in your practicum? How will you prepare yourself to deal with them?

_____

_____

4. Have any employees in your agency been threatened or harmed by clients? If yes, describe the circumstances that gave rise to the incident and how it was handled.

_____

_____

5. Is it possible that agency policies or environment could contribute to client frustration? If so, what changes do you recommend?

_____

_____

6. Does your agency have a formal, written agreement with law enforcement authorities detailing when they are to be called for assistance?

_____

_____

7. Are there any clients or situations that frighten you? If so, how can you deal with your concerns and fears?

_____

_____

8. Does your agency have an incident reporting system for documenting threats and violence toward workers?

_____

_____

9. What services does your agency provide to workers who are threatened, injured, or traumatized by threats or violence (e.g., counseling, critical incident stress debriefing, or support groups)?

_____

_____

Suggested Learning Activities

- Invite a local police officer to offer guidance on how to reduce risk in and around your agency.

- Interview experienced social workers and ask for their advice about reducing personal risk based on their experiences.

- Role-play situations that illustrate each of the stages of potentially violent situations described in this chapter.

- Educate yourself on the specific safety issues faced by your agency (e.g., methamphetamine abuse, use of restraining orders).

- Attend training offered by your agency on safety.

- Determine what services (i.e., counseling or legal services) would be offered to you or others in your agency should you experience a threat or actual incident of violence.

Suggested Readings

Birkenmaier, Julie, and Marla Berg-Weger. *The Practicum Companion for Social Work: Integrating Class and Field Work*. 3rd ed. Boston: Allyn and Bacon, 2011.

Newhill, Christina E. *Client Violence in Social Work Practice: Prevention, Intervention, and Research*. New York: Guilford Press, 2004.

Sheafor, Bradford, and Charles Horejsi. *Techniques and Guidelines for Social Work Practice*. 10th ed. Boston: Allyn and Bacon, 2014.

Weinger, Susan. *Security Risk: Preventing Client Violence Against Social Workers*. Washington, DC: NASW Press, 2001. www.socialworkers.org/practice/naswstandards/safetystandards2013.pdf

5

Communication

©PHOTOBEE / FOTOLIA

CHAPTER PREVIEW

Professional communication, which is at the heart of social work practice, is the focus of this chapter. Information on *interpersonal communication* with clients is provided, including its use with resistant clients. *Organizational communication* with colleagues and supervisors is highlighted, including oral and written communication. Principles of and guidelines for *electronic communication and social media* are detailed in terms of their uses, cautions about potential pitfalls, connections with social work ethics, and recommendations for agency policies.

The effective use of *following and furthering techniques* in social work practice is central to success. These techniques are used intentionally at specific *phases of the planned change process*. *Resistant and involuntary clients* present unique challenges in communication, which can be addressed through the use of effective communication techniques. *Written and electronic forms of communication* both play an important role in social work as well. In order to ensure that communication at all levels and between all parties is effective, a sound understanding of the purposes of various types of communication is needed. In addition, communication skills must be developed, and the ethical and legal aspects of communication must be understood. This chapter is designed to assist students in developing essential communication skills.

BACKGROUND AND CONTEXT

Communication of all types serves many purposes in professional social work practice, depending on the task at hand. As a result, it needs to be

- *Intentional* (purposeful and based on careful thought)
- *Judicious* (based on good judgment, prudent)
- *Matched to client needs* and resources (tied to assessment of client and client goals)

Understanding the importance of effective communication is the prerequisite for actually becoming a skilled communicator, which is the goal of both the student and lifelong practitioner.

There are a number of specific *effective interpersonal communication skills*, which when used with clients, colleagues, or others have a positive impact on the professional relationship. These skills can deepen and strengthen the working relationship and enhance outcomes. There are also a number of specific *ineffective interpersonal communication skills* that have a negative impact on the professional relationship. These ineffective interpersonal skills can undermine and weaken the working relationships and reduce the chances that outcomes will be positive.

Therapeutic techniques for use with clients, including those taught in social work practice courses, can be acquired and honed in the practicum. Hopefully they will become actual professional competencies with additional experience over time. The following list of communication techniques is divided into two overall categories common to most communication. Viewing your communication with clients based on this categorization will be helpful to you as you think about what type of technique is indicated in various situations.

Following techniques
- These techniques are used primarily in the *engagement and assessment phases of the planned change process*.
- They focus on developing rapport, trust, and a foundation for effective interventions.

Furthering techniques
- These techniques are used primarily in the *intervention and evaluation phases of the planned change process*.
- They help clients make progress, reach goals, enhance their functioning, develop insights, make sustainable changes, and view interventions as successful.

The intentional utilization of both following and furthering techniques, often in combination with each other, will increase the chances that interventions will be successful. Table 5.3 in the guidance and direction section of this chapter identifies and defines the techniques that fall under these two categories. It also demonstrates how specific techniques are most useful at particular points in the helping relationship and what purposes they serve in enhancing communication.

Clients who are *resistant, unmotivated, or involuntary* present unique challenges to effective communication, and social workers must develop skills with clients in these categories. Effective communication with reluctant clients requires a clear understanding of the possible underlying reasons that clients could be reluctant or unwilling to engage with social workers. Social workers who view such clients in a respectful manner and use specific approaches with them are more likely to be successful, as will their clients.

Written communication is an important form of organizational communication and takes as many forms as it has purposes. Documenting one's work through the use of intake instruments, assessments, treatment plans, case notes, discharge summaries, and court documents are all common in practice with individuals and families. Organizational written documentation includes memos, reports, minutes of meetings, letters, contracts, grant proposals, employee manuals, online materials, policies, and procedures. At the community, research, and social policy levels of practice, writing takes the form of needs assessments, interagency agreements, surveys, questionnaires, program evaluation, client feedback, policy briefs, and written testimony for legislative proposals. Although developing skills in all forms of professional communication is a major undertaking, competence in professional writing begins in the practicum, where numerous opportunities to learn writing skills present themselves. Students can observe, read, and emulate a wide variety of written materials and thus acquire skills in writing under close supervision.

Electronic communication in social work is a central feature of contemporary practice for many reasons. Computers, the Internet, websites, cellular phones, social media, faxes, blogs, and social work "apps" provide opportunities for enhanced effectiveness and creative service delivery. Electronic communication is efficient, providing quick and sometimes immediate access to information, other professionals, and clients themselves. Electronic communication allows social workers to reach numerous people simultaneously with needed information and reduces the need for travel to central locations for meetings and training sessions. There are also *potential pitfalls* in the use of electronic communication, many of which have implications for client outcomes, relationships with clients, legal aspects of practice, and ethical dimensions of practice.

Engagement

Behavior: Apply and communicate understanding of the importance of diversity and difference in shaping life experiences in practice at the micro, mezzo and macro levels.

Critical Thinking Question: How does diversity impact communication between social workers and clients? What can you do to enhance your ability to communicate with those very different from you?

Assessment

Behavior: Social workers collect, organize, and critically analyze and interpret information from clients and constituencies.

Critical Thinking Question: How can effective following techniques that are used in the engagement and assessment phase of the planned change process improve assessments? How will this result in good intervention plans?

What can you learn from this video demonstration of verbal and written communication skills that you can apply to clients facing complex situations and potential interventions that they may not fully understand?

? Assess your understanding of background and context by taking this brief quiz.

GUIDANCE AND DIRECTION

Because you have been trained in interactions with clients and client systems, consider first the ways in which you can hone your interpersonal communication skills. Table 5.1 illustrates the major *effective interpersonal communication skills* you will need

Table 5.1 Effective Interpersonal Communication Skills

Effective Communication Skill	Positive Impact on Professional Relationship
Active listening	• Enhances accurate understanding • Communicates intent to understand
Building rapport	• Establishes effective working relationship • Provides foundation for intervention
Taking turns	• Demonstrates interest in two-way communication • Promotes balanced exchange between persons
Clarity of expression	• Increases mutual understanding • Reduces time spent trying to understand
Nonjudgmental response	• Promotes trust and openness • Communicates good faith
Genuineness	• Demonstrates real intent to communicate • Promotes trust and openness
Listening to underlying messages	• Shows desire to understand what is not communicated • Deepens level of understanding
Use of open-ended questions	• Promotes power of listener to select response • Deepens sharing
Paraphrasing	• Demonstrates understanding • Communicates motivation to understand
Nondefensive attitude	• Reduces misunderstandings • Allows for increased honesty
Seeking common ground	• Encourages deepened communication • Reduces defensiveness and divisiveness
Respect	• Promotes reciprocal respectful response • Fosters ability to understand diverse viewpoints
Fostering dialogue	• Communicates desire to understand • Promotes exchange of ideas
Seeking mutual understanding	• Provides foundation for action • Demonstrates willingness to clarify
Checking for accuracy	• Demonstrates desire to understand • Promotes precision for sender and receiver
Self-awareness	• Reduces chance of misinterpretation • Promotes conscious use of self
Allowing adequate time	• Reduces chances of misunderstanding • Demonstrates motivation to hear and understand
Structuring physical environment	• Reduces environmental barriers to communication • Increases opportunity for effective communication
Matching language	• Reduces misunderstanding due to language barrier • Enhances understanding by tailoring terminology
Managing emotions	• Lowers potential interference of emotions • Promotes mutual exchange
Summarizing	• Consolidates communication for sender and receiver • Allows for effective end of communication session

to develop, as well as the *impact* of the use of these skills on others. Review this list and make specific plans to develop these skills by intentional practice. Pay particular attention to the positive impact these skills can have on the working relationship.

Try to understand exactly how the skilled use of these techniques results in enhanced communication and perhaps enhanced outcomes. Table 5.2 describes a number of *ineffective interpersonal communication skills* and illustrates the *impact* of these negative techniques on intervention outcomes. These positive skills can also be applied to your work with colleagues, supervisors, and other professionals, as good communication with them resembles positive communication with clients in many ways. These ineffective interpersonal communication skills are potential pitfalls in communication with colleagues as well as clients.

It is not uncommon for students to wonder how they will know *which techniques to use* in communicating with clients. When integrating what

This video demonstrates the use of active listening skills, which are described in Table 5.1. How does this demonstration of communication skills help you understand the impact that they might have on your work with clients and colleagues? www.youtube.com /watch?v=0eHxNdIyo7g

Table 5.2 Ineffective Interpersonal Communication Skills

Ineffective Communication Skill	Negative Impact on Professional Relationship
Dominating conversation	• Discourages mutual communication • Demonstrates lack of interest in understanding
Rushing rapport	• Assumes trust without establishing relationship • Suggests a hidden agenda
Interrupting	• Demonstrates lack of respect for speaker • Lowers chance for mutual understanding
Sending unclear messages	• Reduces clarity of content • Reduces chance of accuracy in receiving
Responding judgmentally	• Reduces desire to share more • Reduces sender's expectation of being understood
Sending mixed or confusing messages	• Reduces accuracy of understanding by listener • Lowers chance that mutual goals will be reached
Missing cues	• Suggests lack of interest in message • Reduces level of understanding
Missing underlying messages	• Results in surface-level understanding • Demonstrates lack of interest in what is not said
Using closed-ended questions	• Reduces opportunities for deepened responses • Results in factual and limited responses
Not allowing adequate time	• Communicates disinterest in allowing adequate time • Reduces chances of mutual understanding
Failing to check for accuracy	• Bases understanding on inaccurate information • Suggests disinterest in message sent
Assuming	• Closes off genuine inquiry • Results in limited and distorted understanding
Defensive attitude	• Reduces sender's motivation to communicate • Reduces receiver's ability to hear message
Trying to prove a point or win an argument	• Suggests that communication is one-sided contest • Discourages response
Failing to show respect	• Shuts down open communication • Reduces trust
Environmental barriers	• Provides limitations and barriers to communication • Demonstrates lack of commitment to communication

Table 5.2   *continued*

Ineffective Communication Skill	Negative Impact on Professional Relationship
Asking excessive why questions	• Builds listener defensiveness • Increases respondent need to justify response
Failing to match language	• Increasing chance for misunderstanding • Demonstrates inability to connect with listener
Lacking genuineness	• Reduces honest response by listener • Demonstrates lack of interest in understanding
Experiencing information overload	• Interferes with communication task • Reduces ability to send and receive messages
Lacking observation skills	• Misses opportunity for enhanced understanding • Misses what is left unsaid
Misinterpreting	• Distorts understanding • Results in flawed intervention
Stacking questions	• Confuses listener • Results in inadequate responses
Asking leading questions	• Intimidates listener • Pushes respondent toward a certain response

Diversity and Difference

Behavior: Apply self-awareness and self-regulation to manage the influence of personal biases and values in working with diverse clients and constituencies.

Critical Thinking Question: How can you combine cultural sensitivity and effective communication skills to design effective intervention strategies at all levels of practice?

you have learned in the classroom setting into your experience with real people, it is helpful to place *helping techniques* into the two broad categories mentioned previously, and to connect them to their use in specific *phases of the planned change process*. Think of how the helping relationship with clients is established (engagement phase), facilitates an understanding of client situations (assessment phase), allows for work and progress (intervention phase), and terminates when complete (evaluation phase). Work hard to tie your understanding of this dynamic relationship with clients to specific communication techniques. This will help you know what technique is indicated at certain stages of your relationship with clients. There is no magical or universally effective response that works in all situations, and there is no way of phrasing questions and speaking with clients that works for all clients. Communication with clients is both an art and a science, and the skilled social worker will not only understand what is likely to work but how to use helping techniques somewhat prescriptively with clients based on their needs, strengths, and responses.

Following techniques are those that are used to engage clients in the initial phases of the helping relationship, and that can be used to engage clients enough that they will begin to trust the social worker and participate somewhat openly in the assessment process. They are used to let clients know that you are genuine in your desire to understand their situation as they see it and that you want to hear their story. They are designed to create the possibility of an ongoing helping relationship that will move through the stages of the helping process.

The establishment of a professional relationship provides the foundation for the use of *furthering techniques*, which are those used to move the relationship and the client forward toward meeting their goals in the actual intervention and evaluation phases. These techniques are employed to help clients feel supported, be challenged when this might be needed, develop insight into their own situation, recognize their progress, and move through the intervention. Using furthering techniques before a foundational relationship is established can be counterproductive because clients may not have fully engaged in the actions required in the treatment plan or intervention. Remember also that following techniques are carried into the intervention and evaluation phases as well, since clients need to believe they are understood and heard throughout the planned change process.

Table 5.3 describes the major following and furthering techniques used by social workers, and highlights how they can be used within the respective phases of the helping process. Use this table to help you think about what techniques will help your clients based on where they are in the stages of the planned change process. Remember that following techniques are not restricted to the first two phases of the planned change process, and that furthering skills might also be used in the assessment phase.

Not all clients become involved with social services agencies voluntarily. Some may be *resistant, hostile, or perhaps involuntary*. Communication with such clients presents specific challenges to the new social worker or practicum student. Understanding *possible reasons for the reluctance of clients* to engage in assessments and interventions will provide insight into how to adapt your communication skills to effectively engage these clients to the degree possible. Even for voluntary clients, working with social workers can be uncomfortable, intrusive, and even humiliating. Resistant clients will likely experience these reactions and more. Being required to share very personal struggles, concerns, and sometimes even failures with a professional they do not know can make clients very resistant to engaging in the helping process.

The practicum will require that you combine a number of concepts and ideas as you develop your communication skills. First of all, integrate the information provided earlier in this chapter about effective and ineffective communication skills with your understanding of how following and furthering techniques are used within the planned change process. Next, consider how client feelings, reactions, level of motivation, and inability to exercise choice and self-determination will help you determine how to relate to them. Understanding clients' emotional reactions to being required to participate in assessments and interventions is essential to knowing over what points and issues it is possible to build rapport, connect, and potentially engage in a working relationship.

Working effectively with resistant clients is partially due to a social worker's ability to use *anticipatory empathy* and address clients' aversion to social work interventions. Clients who do not want to work with you may appear or be angry, passive, sarcastic, hostile, quiet, and even threatening. Resistant and involuntary clients actually need more understanding and more support than voluntary clients in some important ways.

Table 5.3   Following and Furthering Techniques in the Planned Change Process

Engagement Phase

Following Techniques		Purpose of Techniques
• Active listening • Empathy • Open-ended questions • Rapport building • Use of genuineness		• Show interest in understanding client • Help the client feel heard/understood • Empower client to tell story • Develop helping relationship and trust • Convey real concern

Assessment Phase

Following Techniques		Purpose of Techniques
• Active listening • Empathy • Open-ended questions • Rapport building • Clarification • Seeking concreteness		• Assess client need and resources • Support client emotions and beliefs • Encourage the client to assess situation • Encourage the client to share information • Obtain clear understanding of situation • Help clients move from generalization to concrete ideas and experiences

Intervention Phase

Furthering Techniques		Purpose of Techniques
• Paraphrasing • Prompts • Focusing • Contracting • Interpretation • Reflection of content and meaning • Reflection of feeling • Confrontation • Cognitive restructuring • Reframing		• Convey understanding • Encourage sharing • Help the client focus until progress is made • Set expectations of the client and social worker • Help gain insight in thoughts and behavior • Help the client recognize issues • Help the client recognize emotions • Point out client need to change • Assist the client to change thoughts and beliefs • Assist the client to view situation differently

Termination and Evaluation Phase

Furthering Techniques		Purpose of Techniques
• Encouraging • Summarizing • Evaluating • Closing		• Assist the client to maintain progress • Highlight helping process and gains made • Help the client measure outcomes and effort • Terminate the relationship

Because they may find themselves without choice in the matter, they are likely to experience one or more of the following reactions:

- Fearful of judgment, lack of control, and forced participation
- Fearful of the consequences for not cooperating
- Angry and resentful at being required to accept services
- Apathetic toward the prospect of change that may be required

- Ambivalent about fully engaging in services
- Confused about expectations
- Unmotivated even if problems are acknowledged
- Resistant to intervention that does not make sense to them
- Limited self-efficacy with regard to ability to change or complete treatment
- Overwhelmed and paralyzed by what is required of them
- Embarrassed, ashamed, or guilty about failures perceived by others
- Powerlessness to object or refuse to participate
- Hostile or belligerent toward authority figures
- Passive or uncooperative

It is understandable why people who have little or no choice about engaging in interventions might have these feelings and reactions, and the first **key to communicating well with resistant clients** is to acknowledge and appreciate this dynamic. Some clients may never cooperate, see the need for change, or honestly engage in treatment plans; but their resistance or ambivalence may be lessened when social workers are genuinely empathetic about such clients' emotions. Acknowledging that such reactions are to be valid for clients, expected, and expressing empathy about having to engage in services will at least help clients know that their reasons for resistance have validity and that they are being heard.

Clients may have had previous negative or coercive experiences with social workers, and these experiences are likely to impact the effectiveness of treatment plans. Clients may also have had deeply harmful personal experiences that have resulted in negative coping skills. Experiences such as childhood abuse, sexual assault, early life trauma, loss, addiction, or mental illness may result in limited ability to effectively engage in interventions or to even talk about the need to do so. These experiences may result in **barriers and obstacles to establishing positive working relationships**, including client defensiveness, distorted thinking, false bravado, denial, minimization, projection, inability to recognize one's own problems, ineffective coping skills, sarcasm, and manipulative interactional patterns. Seen as strengths by the social worker, these results of negative life experiences can be reframed by the social worker as what clients needed to do to cope with or escape such experiences. Recognizing these as strengths and letting clients know that you see they have endured much will promote positive communication.

Interventions with resistant clients have a higher likelihood of success if the following guidelines are followed. These guidelines are based on the same social work values surrounding interactions with voluntary and motivated clients, but require **additional communication skills**. Utilizing anticipatory empathy, which is preparing yourself to think about how clients may feel, will serve you well in dealing with clients who are not motivated to work with you.

- **Share power** and **offer choice** whenever possible.
- Encourage clients to **say what they want**, do not want, and hope for.
- Remember the **details of clients' lives** from session to session.
- **Treat clients respectfully** even if they are uncooperative or disrespectful.
- Use a **clear, concise communication style**.
- **Avoid becoming defensive** when clients communicate negatively, because client behavior is often a result of overwhelming emotion and not a personal attack on you.

- *Suspend disbelief* about clients' ability or willingness to tell the truth.
- Know that *one emotion may mask another*, as when a fearful client reacts in anger.
- *Be truthful and honest* about what is possible and what is not, and what the positive and negatives outcomes might be.
- Be careful to *treat clients fairly*.
- *Avoid making assumptions* or judgments about clients because they are resistant.
- *Customize interventions* whenever possible to empower clients.
- *Recognize all efforts* made by clients.
- *Ensure transparency* in plans, record keeping, and sharing of information with others.

As described earlier, *written communication* is a vital part of social work practice. Remember that all forms of written communication, including client case records or documents about an organization, have a *specific purpose* and must meet a *professional standard*. For example, written records are used to document services offered, make decisions based on social workers' recommendations, record progress or lack of it, provide rationale for a proposal, confirm verbal agreements, record decisions, demonstrate the use of best practices, address legal requirements, and may be required by licensing or accreditation organizations. With this in mind, follow these guidelines in your written communication:

- Understand who your *audience* is, what they need to know, and how they want the information presented so it is readable for the purposes of the document.
- Use the *documentation format* required by your agency.
- Recognize that you may need to make several *revisions* in your writing, and seek to incorporate feedback into your revisions.
- Use *professional language*, but do not overuse jargon.
- *Avoid slang and language that could be judgmental*, derogatory, biased, disorganized, speculative, or ambiguous and that could be interpreted in more than one way.
- Use *direct, clear language* rather than vague and tentative words.
- Check for *accuracy* of all statements made, using factual and objective wording.
- Make sure that overall records are *comprehensive* and include all required elements.
- Complete all required documentation in a *timely manner*.
- Understand agency policies about making *corrections to client records*, and avoid any action that could be viewed in retrospect as falsification of records.
- Assume that all records might be *subpoenaed* and write accordingly.
- Make sure that overall records are *comprehensive* and include all required elements.
- Remember that records may be *read by someone in your absence* or after your practicum is completed, and you will have no opportunity to explain or clarify what you wrote.
- Make *copies* of all written communication that is sent out of the agency.

You may wonder *how much detail about clients is required*. A good guideline for this question is to include enough detail to bring the issue to life for anyone reading it, but not to overwhelm the reader with unnecessary and extraneous information. Every written word should help to convey meaning, and each one counts toward that purpose. When writing about programs or client systems, remember to be clear, convincing, and attuned to the needs, requirements, or motives of the readers. There are many subtle components to written communication, so do not leave written statements open to misinterpretation. There is much at stake for clients whose lives and experiences are being written about, and social workers' assessments and recommendations can have major positive or negative impacts on their clients' lives. There is also much at stake for agencies in regard to their record keeping, report writing, accreditation documents, grant proposals, and annual reports, so make certain that you understand this when you begin to write on behalf of your agency.

There are a number of *legal guidelines for written communication*, and you need to learn and abide by them, especially in regard to electronic communication. Because electronic record-keeping systems are used to store a wide variety of very personal information about clients, be very aware of *confidentiality of client records* and learn to anticipate potential *breaches in confidentiality* that could occur when sharing information between agencies because client records need to be protected, and electronic breaches in confidentiality can result in *cyber liability*. Learn what can be shared and what cannot. Learn when and how to use *releases of information*, which record clients' permission and approval to share information with other professionals or agencies that may need this information. Be cautious with the use of *electronic forms of communication* such as computerized client database information, faxes, voice mail, and e-mail, so that client confidentiality is always guarded and is electronically locked so that only those who are involved have access to the information. Even though clients waive some of their rights to confidentiality in order to be eligible for third-party payments for services, this does not mean that they understand the degree to which their confidentiality may be compromised.

Clients have the *right to see and obtain copies* of any documentation about them. They are partners with the agency in the services they are offered, including when they are involuntarily involved. Because of this, it is important to consider what to enter into the formal record and to use factual, nonjudgmental language. *Informed consent* means that clients understand the impact of what they are signing or agreeing to, and it is often the social worker's responsibility to advocate for clients, making sure they truly do understand and agree. Abide by all agency policies as well as state and federal regulations about the sharing and protection of client information.

> **Demonstrate Ethical and Professional Behavior**
>
> **Behavior: Use technology ethically and appropriately to facilitate practice outcomes.**
>
> **Critical Thinking Question**: In what ways can the guidelines in Table 5.4 help social workers communicate in ways that are considered ethical?

Remember that each form of communication can be very helpful to social workers and other entities that serve clients, but also potentially very harmful to clients if confidentiality is compromised.

Table 5.4 presents guidelines regarding electronic communication of many forms and can supplement any guidelines, policies, or requirements of your agency and your university. While reading and considering these guidelines, think about your own privacy and protection and make decisions that will serve to protect you. Think also about what is best for your clients and your agency.

Table 5.4 Guidelines for the Use of Electronic Communication

Telephone and Text Messages

- Use separate professional and personal telephone numbers.
- Avoid checking cell phone messages when meeting with clients.
- Avoid taking telephone calls when working with clients if possible.
- Send text messages to clients only for professional purposes.
- Word text messages to clients or colleagues in a professional manner.
- Disable automatic location setting on cell phones to protect against clients who may monitor your whereabouts.
- Do not give your personal phone number to clients.

Web Presence

- Use agency website to describe mission and services as outreach to potential clients.
- Refrain from excessive political and personal content on website.
- Use blogs to provide education and resources for clients on topics of relevance.
- Use podcasts to provide education and resources for clients on topics of relevance.

Social Media

- Remember that social media postings can become public.
- Protect yourself and your privacy by using privacy settings.
- Recognize that privacy settings are not universally effective and secure.
- Refrain from posting comments about your work and your clients.
- Consider the impact of personal photographs on your professional image.
- Consider the impact of personal postings on your professional image.
- Do not engage in social media with clients.
- Respect client privacy by not viewing their profiles and postings on social media.

E-mail

- Remember that e-mail can be forwarded to people other than those who were intended to receive them.
- Remember that e-mail cannot be entirely deleted.
- Use professional communication skills in e-mails to clients and colleagues.
- Remember that e-mail can be misinterpreted.

Fax

- Protect client confidentiality by restricting staff access to only those who need to see them.
- Abide by HIPAA requirements in sending and receiving faxed messages.

Computer-Based Live Communication

- Conduct electronic meetings professionally.
- Conduct electronic client sessions professionally.
- Supplement electronic sessions with actual personal contacts with clients.
- Utilize live electronic communication for individual, family, and group interventions.
- Utilize live electronic resources to provide and take advantage of professional training.

Social Work "Apps"

- Familiarize yourself with and use smart phone "apps" focusing on client education and support.
- Utilize "apps" to supplement client sessions and for client assignments between sessions.

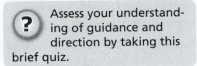

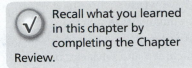

Developing Communication Skills: A Workbook Activity

Using Table 5.2, "Effective Interpersonal Communication Skills," and Table 5.3, "Ineffective Interpersonal Communication Skills," consult with your field instructor about the use of both positive and negative communication skills with your clients. Ask your field instructor to provide you with feedback on the following:

1. The effective communication skills you possess and how you can build on them:

_____

_____

_____

2. The ineffective communication skills you need to work on:

_____

_____

_____

3. The ways in which effective communication promotes successful outcomes:

_____

_____

_____

4. The ways in which ineffective communication threatens successful outcomes:

_____

_____

_____

Suggested Learning Activities

- Ask your field instructor to show you examples of both well-written and poorly written letters, memos, reports, and case records. Examine these materials and observe how writing style, organization, and choice of words affect their quality.

- Rewrite a report you have written (three to five pages in length), reducing its length by half so that you have to identify what essential message is to be included and what can be removed. Eliminate any unnecessary words. Shorten your sentences. Eliminate all repetition of content.

- Seek opportunities to make a presentation to your agency or a community group.
- Ask your field instructor to help you develop your own communication style, building on the skills you have, and what you need to do to become a more effective communicator.

Suggested Readings

Baird, Brian N. *The Internship, Practicum, and Field Placement Handbook: A Guide for the Helping Professions.* 5th ed. Upper Saddle River, NJ: Prentice Hall, 2011.

Falender, Carol, and Edward Shafranske. *Casebook for Clinical Supervision: A Competency-Based Approach.* Washington, DC: American Psychological Association, 2008.

Knapp, Mark. *The Sage Handbook of Interpersonal Communication.* 4th ed. Thousand Oaks, CA: Sage Publications, 2011.

Knapp, Mark, and John Daley. *Interpersonal Communication.* Thousand Oaks, CA: Sage Publications, 2010.

Ross, Johanna. *Specialist Communication Skills for Social Workers: Focusing on Service Users' Needs.* New York: Palgrave Macmillan, 2011.

Sidell, Nancy. *Social Work Documentation: A Guide to Strengthening Your Case Recording.* Washington, DC: NASW Press, 2011.

Sidell, Nancy, and Denise Smiley. *Professional Communication Skills in Social Work.* Boston, MA: Pearson Education, 2008.

Thompson, Neil. *Effective Communication: A Guide for the People Professions.* Basingstoke: Palgrave MacMillan, 2011. www.ncss.gov.sg/documents/documentation_record_keeping_guide5.pdf

6

Organizational Context of Practice

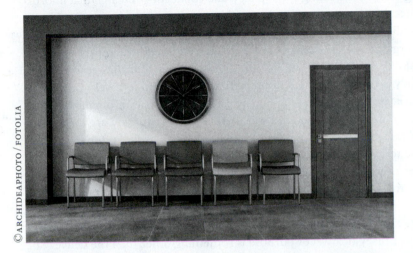

©ARCHIDEAPHOTO / FOTOLIA

CHAPTER PREVIEW

This chapter focuses on the *organizational context of practice*, providing information on *formal* and *informal structure* of agencies, *practice hypotheses* upon which agencies build their programs, and the *culture and climate* of social agencies. It also lists the *contextual factors* surrounding agency operation and the organizational tasks necessary for agency effectiveness, relevance, and sustainability. Also featured are the potential positive or negative *impact of organizational characteristics* on clients and the ways in which organizations communicate formally and informally with their client base.

Throughout history, social work has been an agency-based profession. The daily activities and decisions of a social worker are heavily influenced by the nature and purpose of the organization that employs him or her. A majority of social workers are employed by agencies, and they provide their services within an organizational context. Given this reality, you must examine and understand your practicum agency mission, goals, structure, funding sources, and level of effectiveness in order to use your organization as a foundation for your practice.

BACKGROUND AND CONTEXT

Knowing that the word *agency* refers to an organization authorized or sanctioned to act in the place of someone, on behalf of others, or in response to a particular social problem helps draw our attention to what agencies can and should do. Acting on behalf of others can mean supporting clients in their social functioning, advocating for individuals and groups who cannot act on their own behalf, providing substitutive services that clients are unable to provide adequately for themselves or their families, planning and developing programs, developing and implementing social policy, and conducting research that informs social work practice. It is important to understand much about your agency in order to work effectively within it.

The type of organization in which your practicum is situated will impact what you learn, what you do, and how you do it. You may be working in a *public agency* created by a legislative body at the federal, state, county, tribal, or community level. You may be placed in a *private nonprofit agency* established by private individuals or organizations to meet an identified social need or address a social problem. Perhaps you are doing your practicum in a subcategory of private nonprofit agencies known as the *sectarian* or *faith-based agency*. The term *membership agency* is used to describe an agency that derives some of its budget from membership fees and in which members are involved in setting policy. In contrast to a public agency or a private nonprofit agency, a *for-profit agency* is a business corporation that sells a set of services and is designed and operated to yield a profit for investors and stockholders. Finally, your agency may be a *host setting* in which the organization's primary mission or purpose is something other than the delivery of social services.

Research-informed Practice

Behavior: Use and translate research findings to inform and improve practice, policy, and service delivery.

Critical Thinking Question: What empirical evidence is there to support the theoretical approach of your agency?

Public agencies are often mandated by law to provide certain services and are funded by tax revenue. Private for-profit agencies focus on both providing services and making a profit for owners and stockholders, as opposed to private nonprofit agencies that focus only on providing services and not making a profit. Sectarian agencies are guided by particular religious beliefs and foundations for the provision of their services, and membership organizations serve their members. Host agencies provide services other than social services and include social workers in their interdisciplinary teams.

A typical social agency is designed and structured to provide one or more social programs in *response to particular social problems*. A social program is an organized and planned activity designed to accomplish one of the following:

- *Prevention of a social problem* (stopping a problem from developing, such as programs working to block child abuse or racism)
- *Enhancement of social functioning* (improving social functioning when no significant problem exists, such as programs that provide parent training or respite care)
- *Remediation of an existing problem* (addressing an existing problem such as child abuse, unemployment, or delinquency and providing services to those impacted by it)

Social agencies also fall into several categories based on their strategy to achieve their mission and purpose. They tend to use one or more broad *strategies* to achieve their purposes:

- *Socialization* (assisting and encouraging people to understand, learn, and abide by the norms of society for their own benefit and that of the family or community)
- *Social integration* (encouraging and helping people to interact more effectively with other individuals and with the social systems or resources they need in order to function effectively and cope with problems)
- *Social control* (monitoring and restricting those who exhibit self-destructive or dangerous behavior)
- *Social change* (expanding the number and types of life-enhancing opportunities available to people, taking actions that will improve the environment in which people must function, and taking actions necessary to reduce or eliminate negative and destructive forces in their social environment)

Many human services agencies are quite *bureaucratic*, especially public agencies. Bureaucratic agencies have a direct impact on clients and the social workers who work in them. The characteristics of a bureaucracy follow:

- A clear *chain of command* in communication and assigned authority
- An *organizational structure* consisting of a vertical hierarchy with numerous units, each of which has a designated leader responsible for that unit's operation and who has authority over those working in the unit
- A set of *written rules, policies, and guidelines* that outline procedures to be followed in performing work
- Clear *eligibility guidelines* that regulate the provision of services
- *Standardized policies and programs* geared toward equal treatment to clients
- *Division of labor* giving employees a specific job and job description
- *Centralization* of power and communication channels
- *Supervision* of each employee's work
- An emphasis on *formal communication*, written documentation, and record keeping
- A higher level of *job security* than that which exists in nonprofit organizations

Some agencies have developed less bureaucratic structures in an effort to be more responsive to clients and to their ever-changing environments. They often use *feminist, partnership, and empowerment principles*; seek to involve their clients in the work of the agency; promote shared power and decision making at all levels; develop flexible guidelines and approaches; and strive to individualize and customize their interventions and services. As a general rule, these agencies are more flexible than bureaucratic organizations and provide a less stressful environment for the social workers working for them in terms of adhering to policies and procedures. Agencies that operate on these principles often are private, smaller organizations that do not need the structure of bureaucracy in order to be efficient or to provide equal services to all clients.

Social agencies base their services on an integration of beliefs, available data, goals, objectives, approaches, and anticipated outcomes. They are based on what you have learned as *conceptual frameworks for practice*. A conceptual framework is an organized way of thinking about practice that provides a foundation for all interventions. Knowledge and ideas about clients and about social work practice are organized into a variety of conceptual frameworks. The broadest of these conceptual frameworks are *professional perspectives* (i.e., strengths perspective, diversity perspective, ecosystems perspective). You have learned that it is important to use these perspectives as lenses to understand your client systems, but also that these perspectives are broad. They do not meet the definition of a theory, which is an explanation or hypothesis about social phenomenon. Theories can be tested so that they can be used to understand clients and client systems and also they can be used with confidence that they have been shown to be effective.

Orienting or explanatory theories are specific types of conceptual frameworks that explain how and why people and families develop, what aspects of the social environment impact social functioning, what explains social problems, and how the social issues they address can be explained. These are used by agencies as assumptions and understandings about clients and the social environment of which they are a part. They may have been validated through empirical study and provide a general understanding of how people, families, groups, organizations, and communities function. Agencies also use *practice theories and models* that are in keeping with their mission, goals, and objectives. These theories and models provide specific guidance on what interventions will be used and what actual strategies will be employed. They are also based on an understanding of clients and client systems These models will hopefully be well matched to the clients served and supported by evidence of efficacy.

Think of your agency's goals as *practice hypotheses* about how their services and programs will address social problems and what sort of outcomes they expect. Hypotheses identify expected *outcomes*, which can be short-term results, longer-term changes, and even large-scale outcomes at the community level. Hypotheses exist at all levels of practice, such as the examples given in Table 6.1.

Table 6.1   Practice Hypotheses at Micro-, Mezzo-, and Macro Levels

Micro-Level Practice	Sample Hypotheses
• Practice with individuals • Practice with families	• Child neglect can be reduced by targeting and serving teen parents. • Elder abuse can be prevented through caregiver support, respite, empowerment of older adults, and family therapy.
Mezzo-Level Practice	**Sample Hypotheses**
• Practice with groups • Practice with organizations	• Mutual aid groups can help members deal effectively with addictions by providing peer support and understanding. • Program improvement is the result of environmental scanning, use of best practices, and evaluation of services.
Macro-Level Practice	**Sample Hypotheses**
• Community practice • Policy practice	• Effective community organization is driven by the perspectives and motivations of citizens involved in the social issue being addressed. • Social policy development is impacted through collaborative efforts between advocacy groups and those most impacted by such policies.

Be alert to the fact that all organizations have both a formal and informal structure. The *formal* or *official structure* of an agency is described by organizational charts, policy and procedure manuals, the official chain of command, and documents that explain the structure and function of various organizational units. The term *informal structure*, sometimes referred to as the *shadow structure*, refers to various networks of employees and unofficial channels of communication that operate through unwritten but universally understood rules. This informal structure is sometimes described by staff as the way the agency really works. This informal structure often becomes apparent only after working in the agency for an extended period of time.

An agency's informal structure is that framework and set of guidelines that allow for some *flexibility and individualization of services* for clients and that recognize the need to adapt services for diverse clients. This informal structure allows staff members to give input through informal channels when needed and adapts decision-making procedures as needed. It includes frank behind-the-scenes discussions among staff members that may not shared with the public. Informal structure may also be used to describe the influence of key staff members who may not possess official power, but are listened to and looked to for guidance and wisdom.

The term *organizational communication* refers to the somewhat impersonal exchange of messages and information between the various levels, departments, and divisions of an organization and also between the organization and various individuals and groups outside the organization. Compared to other types of communication, communication within an organization tends to be more formal and more often in written form. Moreover, the nature and flow of information within an organization is strongly influenced by lines of authority and the chain of command.

Effective organizational communication promotes the organization's overall mission, efficient functioning, clarity of roles, and the provision of services to individual clients. Organizations that develop strong communication networks and policies understand that inherent in every agency function is an opportunity to develop and maintain positive communication. This includes practices such as the following, which involve both oral and written communication:

- *Supervisory sessions*, which require the ability to provide direction and support as well as seek direction and training
- *Employee feedback and performance evaluations*, which necessitate providing and receiving constructive feedback
- *Staff and committee meetings*, which are productive when policies are clear, input is solicited and valued, and agency problems and strengths are openly discussed
- *Team building*, which develops trust, negotiation skills, and working toward common goals
- *Training* of employees, board members, and volunteers, which clarifies expectations, addresses policies and procedures, and teaches new skills in working with clients

In addition to intra-agency communication, agencies engage in both *formal and informal forms of communication with their clients* through their written materials, web presence, physical environment, quality of services, policies, staffing levels, and

Policy Practice

Behavior: Assess how social welfare and economic policies impact the delivery of and access to social services.

Critical Thinking Question: What legislation and social policies shape or dictate the work of your agency?

Table 6.2   Organizational Values Demonstrated to Clients

Organizational Dimension	Organizational Value Demonstrated
Clear mission	Vision of and commitment to clients
Well-trained, effective staff	Commitment to quality services, competent staff, and ongoing learning
Effective programs and services	Commitment to program evaluation and quality improvement
Eligibility requirements	Inclusion and access
Physical setting	Dignity, respect, and access
Standardization of services	Equality and nondiscrimination
Individualization of services	Client-centered focus
Safety policies	Security and protection
Written and electronic materials	Access, readability, and commitment to outreach
Practice theories and models	Evidence-based practice
Funding levels	Quality and availability of services ensured
Policies and procedures	Clarity, organization, and fairness
Client input	Respect, dignity, and inclusion
Place in continuum of care	Collegiality, cooperation, and commitment to seamless services

professional knowledge and skills of the social workers it employs. Consider how the dimensions of organizations that are listed in Table 6.2 indirectly send messages to clients about the values of the organization. The policies, processes, and structures of organizations hopefully signal or even clearly inform clients that they are valued, respected, and entitled to quality services.

Organizational climate and organizational culture are other terms used to describe the way organizations function. Organizational climate refers to the "tone" of the agency and includes relationships, level of teamwork, morale, communication, and the level of mutual support among employees. Organizational culture refers to the values of the agency that impact its programs and are the underpinnings of the services provided. Both climate and culture are important influences on the agency's effectiveness, workplace environment, and satisfaction of both employees and clients.

Because it is important that agencies grow, change, improve their services, and respond to emerging trends and social problems, they must become what have been described as *learning organizations*. Learning organizations seek to maintain relevance, work toward best practices, continuously evaluate their services, anticipate needed improvements, and base their growth on sound information and a commitment to their mission.

▶ Watch this video about innovative social work practice in an uncommon setting. Based on what you learned from Table 6.2 about how organizational policies and practices communicate their values to clients, reflect on this example and what values about clients this type of social work exemplifies. www.youtube.com /watch?v=oOeBLhs5Jko

? Assess your understanding of background and context by taking this brief quiz.

GUIDANCE AND DIRECTION

Your practicum agency will be a *learning laboratory* in which you will develop professional social work skills, observe other social workers providing services, and learn how agencies are organized and structured to address social needs and problems. You will begin to understand how organizations are organized, administered and managed; learn about the common problems of organizations; and see how to work effectively with others within an organizational context.

Work to learn about your *agency's history*, why and when it began, and how it has evolved over time. Inquire about how and why your agency may have modified its original mission, changed its structure, and adapted to a shifting community and political context. This will help you understand how agencies survive within an ever-evolving environment and continually adjust and adapt their efforts to address the changing social problems and needs on which they focus.

Ask your field instructor about *external forces* that shape or limit your agency, such as funding priorities and sources, community attitudes, client feedback, regulatory bodies, political pressure, and research findings. Ask how much influence internal forces such as staff suggestions, changes in personnel, and staff morale have on the agency and its programs. Learn what contemporary, current external forces influence the focus, work, and effectiveness of your agency.

Agencies are *always changing*. Notice how shifts, increases, or cuts in funding cause changes in the services that can be provided. Observe how public attitudes and political forces shape the ways in which your agency functions. Your agency may go through some significant changes during your practicum. For example, it may even experience a crisis in funding, be negatively evaluated by an outside source, or be required to change significant portions of its program because of financial or political forces. You may even observe the birth of a new agency, or perhaps the dismantling of one that has lost its support or outlived its usefulness. You will learn about the dynamic nature of human services organizations if you closely observe the functioning of your own agency and that of others in the community.

As mentioned earlier, your agency will use one or more specific *perspectives, orienting theories, or practice theories* in the design and provision of its services and programs. Determine what those conceptual frameworks are and why they were chosen. For example, does your agency use the strengths, ecological, or diversity perspective? Does it base its programs on its understanding of social systems theory? Does your agency use a family preservation or family reunification approach to intervention? Does it invest its resources in prevention, early intervention, or rehabilitation? Is the approach therapeutic or correctional? Does your agency hire generalist social workers or those with specializations in certain fields of practice? Does it work toward social change and social justice? Does your agency provide holistic services or does it specialize? Review courses you have taken and books you have read to help you understand why a particular approach was chosen by your agency to address the problem or concern identified. Consider what other

Human Rights and Justice

Behavior: Engage in practices that advance social, economic, and environmental justice.

Critical Thinking Question: What human rights does your agency commit to in its work, and what social justice issues does it address?

Diversity and Difference in Practice

Behavior: Apply and communicate understanding of the importance of diversity and difference in shaping life experiences in practice at the micro, mezzo, and macro levels.

Critical Thinking Question: What groups of clients might potentially feel positively or negatively about your agency and why?

theoretical approaches might also be used to enhance, replace, or improve existing services.

Become familiar with your *agency's methods of evaluating its programs and services*. Find out how your agency assesses its effectiveness, determines whether it is honoring its mission and reaching its goals, measures client or community satisfaction, and decides whether it is making a difference. Your agency may use formal or informal methods of evaluation, process or outcome measures, and collect quantitative or qualitative data. Ask your field instructor whether he or she thinks these approaches or evaluation tools are valid and adequate. Ask what methods he or she would ideally recommend to evaluate services provided enough time and money were available. Further detail on organizational evaluation methods is provided in Chapter 15, Evaluation of Practice.

Agencies regularly reexamine their program effectiveness, review their mission and goals, adjust their objectives, and engage in *strategic planning* for the future. This is done to maintain focus on the mission and vision of the organization; shift priorities in light of changing political climates, community need, or financial resources; and continuously search for better ways to serve those to whom they are committed. If you have the opportunity to become involved in such efforts, count yourself fortunate to be allowed to participate in the agency's work to redefine itself or improve its services.

Agencies may do this work through staff retreats involving a review of history and mission, and as a result identify new ways to meet their goals. They can then engage in strategic planning, identify strengths and needs, and clarify opportunities and barriers. Agencies that are most effective in the long run are those that stay current, adjust priorities as needed, build on past success, measure their effectiveness, and look to the future. Watch for these qualities in your organization. Think about what makes an organization strong and able to serve its clients well.

It is vital to understand **how an agency is perceived by its clients**, including clients' view of the agency's openness, effectiveness, and ability to address their needs. Observe the ways in which your agency works to maintain links to clients, opens itself to client feedback, and works in partnership with client groups, especially diverse populations. In the end, clients are best served by learning organizations that continue to value their input and continually work to improve services. Agencies that grow, thrive, sustain themselves, and provide measurably effective programs and services must work hard to achieve these outcomes.

Effective organizations, their leaders, and their staff members must continually work in coordination with entities outside the agency boundaries, accurately assess the multiple contexts of agency practice, and recognize that they are part of a much larger social system made up of interacting parts. This is often referred to as *environmental scanning* and includes being knowledgeable about and able to incorporate an understanding of the following *contextual factors* into their work on behalf of those they serve. Consider the immense challenges that all agencies face in understanding all of these contextual factors and integrating them into their mission and operation of everyday activities.

Watch this video about a social worker recognized for her work to make agencies more sensitive to and effective with people with disabilities. Reflect on the responsibilities of social work agencies to ensure access to all individuals, and consider what organizations must do to make this possible.
www.youtube.com/watch?v=QtWcWkT2HUY

- Current and projected *client needs*
- Current and projected *social problems*
- *Expectations* of clients, communities, funding sources, and other agencies
- *Values* of clients, communities, funding sources, and other agencies
- *Political economy*, which impacts funding, program focus, and client need
- Social, cultural, and political *forces for change*
- Social, cultural, and political *forces for the status quo*
- External *barriers* to service delivery
- Current and emerging *social policies*
- Current and emerging social work *research* on agency-related social problems
- Current and emerging *practice models*, including evidence-based practice
- Emerging *best practices* in agency's field of practice
- *Cultural changes* in the social environment
- Professional *standards* for practice
- External issues regarding *regulations*, licensing, and accreditation
- *Continuum of services* addressing social issues in the community

In order for agencies to be considered effective, growing, and in touch with social needs and the most appropriate ways to address those needs, they must become what are called *learning organizations*. A learning organization is one that adapts as needed and desired, continuously works to improve its approach and outcomes, customizes its work to client needs, and regularly redesigns itself as necessary. Again, this is no easy task, but it is necessary for organizations to remain relevant, stable, and sustainable. To that end, learning organizations must engage themselves in the following organizational tasks:

- *Scanning* of other learning organizations to learn from their successes
- Periodic *review of mission*, vision, goals, and objectives and *revision* as needed
- Commitment to remaining on the cutting edge of *emerging, evidence-based, and best practices*
- Development of *agency-specific best practices* based on program evaluation
- Development of *practice wisdom* that is integrated into policies and programs
- *Theory building, innovation*, and creative approaches to practice
- Identification of and building upon *agency strengths*
- Identification of and attention to *agency gaps* in services
- Future orientation and *planning*
- Commitment to employee *continuing education*, knowledge building, and skill development
- Adjustment in *staffing patterns* and redesign of position requirements and duties
- Diversification of *staff and administration*
- Periodic review of *agency policies and procedures* and revision as needed
- Inclusion of *client input* into program planning and evaluation
- *Team building* and *empowering of employees* to engage in program planning
- Engagement in *sustainability activities* to maintain and support agency
- Ongoing *supervision and leadership* development
- Commitment to continuous *program quality improvement*

Finally, commit yourself to understanding your agency, work to integrate yourself into the organization in a productive way, observe and participate in as many

? Assess your understanding of guidance and direction by taking this brief quiz.

V Recall what you learned in this chapter by completing the Chapter Review.

agency activities as possible, learn about its inner workings, and imagine yourself as a supervisor or administrator. This process may help you to consider, understand, and participate in the vital role of a social agency and all that is involved in keeping it effective and responsive to client needs at all levels of practice.

Agency Analysis: A Workbook Activity

Answer the following questions about your practicum agency, using the information in this chapter. Doing so will help you analyze what your agency does, why, how effectively, and in what ways. This will be the beginning of your professional skills in agency analysis.

1. What type of organization is your practicum agency? What strategies does it employ?

_____

_____

_____

2. What practice hypotheses are in place in your agency, either formally or informally?

_____

_____

_____

3. What perspectives (i.e., strengths, diversity, ecosystems) does your agency use?

_____

_____

_____

4. What features of bureaucratic organization are at work in your agency?

_____

_____

_____

5. Based on your analysis of Table 6.2, what organizational values are demonstrated to your clients?

_____

_____

_____

Suggested Learning Activities

- Attend meetings of the agency's board of directors or advisory board and consider how the topics discussed relate to the agency's mission, goals, programs, and funding.

- Find out how ordinary citizens or the general public view your agency. Speak with friends and acquaintances who know little about social work and ask what they know or have heard about your agency.

- Attend public meetings sponsored by United Way or other social welfare planning groups in order to better understand how your agency fits into the overall social welfare system.

- Accompany a client applying for services at another agency and identify attitudes reflected in how agency staff members treat clients and handle client requests.

- Visit other agencies that provide similar services to those of your agency and compare approaches and programs.

Suggested Readings

Austin, Michael J., Ralph P. Brody, and Thomas Packard. *Managing the Challenges in Human Services Organizations.* Thousand Oaks, CA: Sage Publishing, 2008.

Calley, Nancy. *Program Development in the 21st Century: An Evidence-Based Approach to Design, Implementation, and Evaluation.* Los Angeles: Sage Publications, 2011.

Cooperider, David, and Suresh Srivasta. *Appreciative Management and Leadership.* San Francisco, CA: Jossey-Bass, 1999.

Coulshed, Veronica, Audrey Mullender, David N. Jones, and Neil Thompson. *Management in Social Work.* 3rd ed. New York: Palgrave Macmillan, 2006.

Dudley, James R. *Social Work Evaluation: Enhancing What We Do.* 2nd ed. Chicago, IL: Lyceum Books, 2014.

Hasenfeld, Yeheskil. *Human Services as Complex Organizations.* 2nd ed. Los Angeles: Sage Publications, 2009.

Kettner, Peter, Robert Moroney, and Lawrence Martin. *Designing and Managing Programs: An Effectiveness-Based Approach.* 4th ed. Los Angeles: Sage Publications, 2012.

Kirst-Ashman, Karen, and Grafton Hall. *Brooks/Cole Empowerment Series: Generalist Practice with Organizations and Communities.* 6th ed. Boston, MA: Brooks/Cole, 2015.

Moxley, David. *Beyond Oversight: Developing Grassroots Nonprofit Boards for Community and Institutional Change.* Washington, DC: NASW Press, 2011.

O'Connor, Mary Catherine, and F. Ellen Netting. *Organization Practice: A Guide to Understanding Human Services Organizations.* 2nd ed. Hoboken, NJ: John Wiley and Sons, 2009.

Watkins, Jane, Bernard Mohar, and Ralph Kelly. *Appreciative Inquiry: Change at the Speed of Imagination.* 2nd ed. Hoboken, NJ: John Wiley and Sons, 2011.

Weinbach, Robert. *The Social Worker as Manager: A Practical Guide to Success.* 7th ed. Boston, MA: Allyn and Bacon, 2015.

7

The Community Context of Practice

©SERGEY NIVENS / FOTOLIA

CHAPTER PREVIEW

This chapter examines the **community context of social work** that can enhance or undermine the level of social functioning of individuals, families, and groups. This includes **resources and assets** that are valuable to individuals and families. It also focuses on problems, attitudes, and gaps that can negatively impact the social functioning of individuals and families. It describes **types of communities**, includes the functions of a community, and discusses the use of power and influence within communities. Further, it describes the range of **goals of community social work practice** and their accompanying **social work roles**. A selected number of **orienting/explanatory theories** that inform community-level practice ad presented. In addition, **practice theories/ models** used in community-level practice are shown.

The community is one of the most important **contexts of social work practice** and also one of the most **common targets of social work practice**. It is in communities that relationships are forged, **social functioning** is enhanced, **social capital** is built, **social assets** are developed, **attitudes** are shaped, and **socialization** takes place. Communities are dynamic systems that interact with the individuals, families, groups, and organizations within them as well as with the larger *social systems* that impact them, such as social policies, societal attitudes, and social movements. Because of the immense impact of communities on both clients and social agencies, it is vital to understand how communities work in order to strengthen these communities and help them develop the assets needed to meet the needs of residents through *community development* and *community organization*.

BACKGROUND AND CONTEXT

Practicum agencies exist in and are influenced by the communities of which they are a part. Because of this, it is important to study the community in which your practicum agency is located. It is obvious that agencies do not exist in a vacuum. In fact, an agency mission, programs, and operation are often a *reflection of the community's characteristics*, such as its values, politics, history, and special problems. Most of your clients live and work in this community, so it is not possible to understand your clients without understanding their wider social environment and both the positive and negative conditions and forces within that environment. If you work within an agency working on the micro level, the client assessments and intervention plans you develop must take into consideration your client's interactions with the community, as well as the resources available in it.

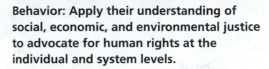

Human Rights and Justice

Behavior: Apply their understanding of social, economic, and environmental justice to advocate for human rights at the individual and system levels.

Critical Thinking Question: What community social, economic, or environmental justice issues are addressed by your agency?

Your informal **study of the community** will allow you to begin to identify unmet human needs as well as the gaps in the service network that should be addressed in order to better serve the people of the community. By gathering information about community values, history, power structure, economic base, demographics, religious beliefs, and decision-making processes, you will be able to identify those groups or individuals who have the power and influence to either facilitate needed social change or block harmful social change within the community.

As you have learned, the term *community* refers to a group of people brought together by physical proximity or by a common identity based on shared experiences, interests, or culture. There are two major types of communities: communities of interest or identification and communities of place or location. A *community of interest and identification* can be described as a group of individuals who share a sense of identity and belonging because they share a characteristic, interest, or life experience such as ethnicity, language, religion, sexual orientation, or occupation. The social work community, the business community, the LGBT community, the Native American community, the faith community, and the university community are examples of a community of interest and identification.

The second type of community, a *community of place or location*, is defined mostly by geography and specified boundaries. Such communities include neighborhoods, suburbs, towns, and cities. The boundaries of a community of place might be a legal definition, a river, or a street. They may have formal or informal names such as the south side, Orange County, the Blackfeet Indian Reservation, the university area, the west end, and the warehouse district. People living in these areas or places may share some level of identification, but typically they are more diverse in terms of values, beliefs, and other characteristics than the people of a community of interest and identification. Also, it is not uncommon for the people within this type of community to be in conflict over a variety of issues. Living in proximity to others, in and of itself, does not create a social bond and a sense of belonging. In fact, for many of your clients, the community in which they live does not provide a sense of belonging and may even negatively impact their quality of life. Within a given community of place, there may be many different communities of interest and identification.

Learning about a community takes time and effort. However, you will find this to be an invaluable and interesting experience. You will become fascinated as you begin to observe and understand the *interplay between the functioning of individuals and families and their neighborhood and community*. If your practicum agency is concerned mostly with micro level practice, you will soon see how your clients' lives are either enriched or harmed by community factors. If your organization is involved in macro level practice, you will come to understand that every community has its own complex personality and profile, and that in order to deal effectively with social problems and bring about needed social change, you must understand and appreciate that uniqueness.

Diversity and Difference in Practice

Behavior: Apply and communicate understanding of the diversity and difference in shaping life experiences in practice at the micro, mezzo, and macro levels.

Critical Thinking Question: In what ways does an agency's level of cultural competence impact its ability of provide effective services to diverse groups?

Social workers and social agencies must be knowledgeable about how power and influence are used in the community. Simply put, *power* is the ability to make change happen in some way, whereas *influence* is the capacity to increase the chances that a desired change may occur. Successful efforts to develop a new agency program, pass a new law, modify social policy, and bring about social change all depend on the skilled use of power and influence. By themselves, social workers may possess little power or influence. Thus, in order to promote social change, they must have access to and positive relationships with those individuals and organizations that have power and influence and are willing to use it on behalf of the social agency or its clients.

There are various forms of power and influence within the community context, and social workers must understand this. It is important to remember that the movers and shakers of a community (i.e., those with real power and influence) are not always the visible leaders. Many key decision makers work behind the scenes and hold no formal positions, but are capable of contributing greatly to social change. Those are the individuals with whom you will develop relationships in order to call attention to the issues you care about and to help you work toward social change. Influential people that social workers involved in community practice must engage with while undertaking effective and long-lasting community development and organization efforts include elected officials; those who control credit and loans; those who control the media and information; executive directors of corporations and owners of businesses; respected religious and moral leaders; recognized experts in their field; longtime, respected residents; natural leaders without formal power; leaders or advocacy organizations; and clients or citizens that are skilled in self-advocacy.

Communities attempt to grow, progress, and improve the quality of life for their citizens, and thus engage in a variety of activities designed to reach these goals. Many of these activities are undertaken by people who care about life within their community. This includes citizens, governmental entities, private or membership organizations, economic development groups, special interest groups, religious leaders, public employees, and many others. Social workers can build upon the motivation, energy, and resources of all of these groups of people and at times engage with them to promote their goals for quality of life, which supports social functioning. This can take the form of either community development or community organization.

> This video shows the planning phase of a community organization project in response to community members' evictions and foreclosures. How do their efforts protect and enhance the social functioning of vulnerable populations?

Those working to improve communities generally do so from a *holistic* stance that social workers would call the *ecosystems perspective*. They understand that each type of community asset will support and enhance others. Other professionals work on one facet of community life only, and spend their effort improving that area of community life. Community assets work in concert with each other by virtue of their coexistence and because one asset may be a prerequisite for another. Community assets tend to cluster together and enhance each other in the same way that community problems tend to cluster together and reduce the quality of life in those communities.

All of this work should be based on a foundation that is accurate, factual, and values based. *Community needs assessments* are often undertaken by networks of individuals and groups interested in knowing what problems need to be addressed, whether those problems are getting better or worse, the consequences of these problems, and what the community wants to be done about them. Needs assessments can be done in a variety of ways, including gathering of data from both primary and secondary sources, from individuals affected by community life, from those trying to improve it, and in both quantitative and qualitative ways. The following sources of information, in combination with each other, can provide a good understanding of the community and what its citizens want.

- *Surveys* of citizens, professionals, interest groups, and public officials
- *Interviews* with citizens, professionals, interest groups, and public officials
- *Focus groups* with interested or affected parties
- *Community or neighborhood "walks"* to visually assess needs
- *Data sources* such as the U.S. Census Bureau, chambers of commerce, labor unions, neighborhood groups, health departments, and social agencies
- *Participatory action research projects* designed to involve those who are impacted as researchers

Social indicators are measures of social conditions and social problems, including how those conditions and problems change over time and compare with similar communities. Many social indicators can be used to measure a social problem within a community. For example, the level of addiction and associated problems can be measured by numbers of arrests and convictions for alcohol-related offenses, percentage of substance-related emergency room visits, numbers of traffic fatalities due to impaired driving, rates of interpersonal violence related to substance use, counts of illegal drug sales or manufacturing laboratories, rates of bars selling alcohol to minors, and numbers of individuals seeking treatment. Taken together and understood as interactive and dynamic, such social indicators can paint a picture of social conditions and allow for social planning efforts to address them. Ask your field instructor about social indicators related to the work of your agency, and find out if the problems addressed in your agency are improving, getting worse, or staying the same.

Studying social indicators can provide information that can help to guide program improvement, service delivery systems, grant writing, and grass roots efforts to reduce social problems. Focused study of social indicators will help identify the *incidence* of a social problem (the number or percentage of people impacted by a social problem in a given period of time), *prevalence* of a social problem (likelihood of individuals or families experiencing such problems), *trends* in problems and potential societal changes, projections, *comparisons* with other locations or time periods, and the dynamic *interactions* between social problems. Public and private community organizations tend to *identify the social indicators* important to them or that they are required to address, *measure* them regularly over time, *monitor* efforts to improve conditions, and *support resources* that appear to be making conditions better.

Asset mapping is another important tool for community social work practice, which involves measuring the resources available to a community that could either be enhanced because they promote positive communities or used to address negative aspects of communities. Assets within a community fall into categories such as social, cultural, physical, environmental, financial, political, spiritual, and educational resources. Every community asset is influenced by others, and every community asset can be improved when others are improved. In addition, the lack of one community asset may prevent the development of another community asset. This could result in challenges to changing the status quo or in a decline in positive social conditions overall. Asset mapping also shows the relationships and synergy between community assets, as these assets influence each other rather than existing in a vacuum.

Following are *examples of assets*, some of which are measurable through quantitative means and some of which are not that easily measured but which are powerful just the same.

- *Sense of community* leading to *community involvement*
- Formal and informal *social networks*
- *Shared identity* that contributes to solidarity
- Acceptance of *diversity* within the community, which reduces cultural conflicts
- Access to *power and influence*, which can facilitate positive social changes
- Untapped *potential and talent* that can be mobilized to address social change
- *Physical resources* that support the development of social assets
- Attitudes that support *civic responsibility*
- *Motivation, capacity, and readiness* to grow and change that strengthen social change efforts
- *Social planning* efforts agreed to by stakeholders
- *Leadership* committed to community welfare

Become involved in work that assesses your community's assets, because these community assessment skills will be necessary in any community work. This will help you understand what a community is like at the current time, how it sees itself, what it wants for its future, what its priorities are, and what vision for the future drives current decisions. It will also help you clarify the ways in which you can become involved in community social work practice.

? Assess your understanding of background and context by taking this brief quiz.

GUIDANCE AND DIRECTION

Understanding the **community context of practice** will help you see that people are all shaped in both positive and negative ways by their life experiences. They are supported or undermined, protected or put at risk, guided or controlled, served or stressed, and encouraged or discouraged by their interactions with the individuals, groups, and organizations that make up the communities in which they live. These interactions have a profound effect on social functioning and quality of life.

Be conscious of the fact that the clients or consumers served by a social agency are members of a particular community of place and probably members of several communities of interest and identification. You need to understand the personal meaning attached to these groups by clients and the ways in which they impact clients both positively and negatively. It is possible that your clients may not perceive the community in which they live as supportive, accepting, and willing to include or support them. It is not uncommon for people experiencing stresses of life to view the community as uncaring, unresponsive, judgmental, or culturally insensitive to them, even though the residents and social agencies in the community are desirous of helping. Perceptions of community assets by clients are as important as the reality of those assets, and must be taken into consideration in any interactions with client groups.

If you have not been exposed to the negative aspects of community life as your clients may have been, acknowledge that your **privileged position** in a community may make it difficult to understand your clients' views of the community. They may not have the option to live in a neighborhood of their choice or they may lack the social skills to engage productively with others to give and gain social support. Your clients may have had significant life experiences that have shaped their attitudes toward the community, as well as toward your practicum agency.

When working directly with clients, identify their **social roles** (e.g., spouse, parent, or employee) and then consider how specific community characteristics may make it easier or more difficult for them to fulfill those roles. As you examine the **influence of a community on the social functioning of individuals and families**, consider whether your client has the benefits and opportunities listed here that support social functioning or whether he or she lacks these benefits or perceives them as unavailable to them.

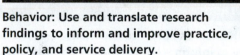

Research-Informed Practice

Behavior: Use and translate research findings to inform and improve practice, policy, and service delivery.

Critical Thinking Question: What research can you engage in that will help to inform the service delivery of citizens of your community?

- Adequate **employment opportunities** to support himself or herself and a family
- Adequate, safe, and affordable **housing**
- **Safety** when at home and in the community and protection by law enforcement and environmental policies
- **Support and empowerment** by interactions with others in the community
- **Acceptance and equitable treatment** by others in the community

- Access to public *transportation, education, and training*, and *affordable health care*
- *Political power* to influence conditions and policies that impact them

As social work students gain experience and carefully observe and participate in a given community, they often become aware of dynamics that are common to many communities. For example, be alert to the following *community dynamics*:

- All communities and neighborhoods have *social support networks and informal helpers*. However, special effort may be required to identify and access these resources for clients or social workers.
- There may be a degree of *overlap and duplication* in the functions and programs of various agencies in the community. Sometimes this duplication is unnecessary and wasteful, but in many cases the duplication is beneficial to clients and healthy for the total system of services.
- There may be *"turf" issues and conflicts* between agencies within a community, brought on in part by their competition for funding, the differences in how they define and explain problems, and what they consider to be their territory.
- An agency with the *support of powerful and influential individuals* can secure funding and gain recognition, even when its mission may be less important and worthy than that of other agencies in the community.
- An agency *without the support of powerful and influential individuals* may find it more challenging to secure funding and gain recognition, even when its mission may be more important, needed and worthy than that of other agencies in the community.

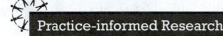

Practice-informed Research

Behavior: Use practice experience and theory to inform scientific inquiry and research.

Critical Thinking Question: How can you use your practicum experience to formulate research and program evaluation questions?

Ethical and Professional Behavior

Behavior: Use supervision and consultation to guide professional judgment and behavior.

Critical Thinking Question: How can you identify mentors in the community who will help you understand the role of community developers and organizers?

- *Negative community attitudes* toward a certain client group or a certain type of agency can be a major obstacle to developing and providing needed services to a particular group.
- Certain community *groups are better organized* and better able to act as advocates for themselves than are others.
- Communities under *economic stress* are sometimes ripe for the development of social problems and may not be able to support their citizens in positive ways.

At times, the focus of community work may be the community itself. This level of practice sees the action *community itself as the client, the target, or the focus of* intervention. When social workers engage in this level of practice, they must use their knowledge of community, communication skills, commitment to creating healthy communities, and ability to partner with others to this important work. Innovative combinations of these skills will help to enhance social functioning of clients and client systems, which is the overall goal and purpose of social work.

The *goals of community-level practice* are many, and all are based on a belief that communities are central contributors to positive and negative human development. Community assets can enhance social functioning, while community problems can negatively impact social functioning. There are two major approaches to community practice, both of which are commonly engaged in by community-level practitioners. **Building approaches** to community practice are those that identify and strengthen community assets. These approaches are based on the belief that building strong communities will result in the enhancement of social functioning.

Blocking approaches to community practice are those that identify and address community problems and gaps. These approaches are based on the belief that reducing such community problems will also result in the enhancement of social functioning. The two approaches are not mutually exclusive and in fact are often used simultaneously by community practitioners. Goals of community social work practice are given in Table 7.1. Review this information and determine which agencies in your community, including your practicum agency, work toward either or both of these goals of community practice.

A number of conceptual frameworks provide the underpinnings of community-based social work, including **orienting/explanatory theories** that attempt to explain and describe both the positive and negative development and functioning of individuals, families, groups, organizations, communities, and societies. They serve to orient social workers to what can be expected in terms of community development, how clients and their social environments interact, how social problems emerge, and what can influence development at all levels. Commonly used orienting/explanatory theories used to explain social phenomenon at the community level of practice include conflict theory, multicausal theory, political economy theory, social exchange theory, social learning theory, social movement theory, social systems theory, strain theory, structural theory, subculture theory, and others. Review each

> Watch this inspiring video about the Philippine rural reconstruction movement. In what ways do the 12 guidelines presented in the video resemble building approaches to community organization described earlier? www.youtube.com /watch?v=WtT_bpbn4Qs

Table 7.1 Goals of Community Practice

Building Goals (goals that strengthen community assets)	Blocking Goals (goals that address community problems)
Support social functioning of individuals and families	Address problems that undermine or reduce social functioning of individuals and families
Identify and enhance community assets	Identify and address community problems and gaps
Build social capital	Address barriers to building social capital
Empower individuals and groups to identify, own, and reach goals	Address barriers to community participation by citizens and impacted groups
Create community conditions that facilitate both broad and specific community development	Address community problems that impede overall and specific community development
Engage in community organization efforts directed toward building community assets	Address overall conditions responsible for community problems
Build coalitions, networks, and partnerships to effect community change	Reduce conflict, strain, and power differentials between groups
Create social change desired by community	Address barriers to social change efforts

of these theories to determine their utility in understanding your community and its development.

Practice theories/models at the community level of practice are those that build on community orienting/explanatory theories, are matched to client resources and needs, and fit with client values and perspectives. These theories and models specify what actions can be taken in intervention plans, and include particular approaches and strategies based on sound community assessments. These theories are built into intervention plans, guide the implementation of the plan, and provide opportunities to evaluate effectiveness of interventions. Commonly used community practice theories/models include the community development model, community organization model, community resilience model, harm reduction model, social change model, social development model, social justice model, social planning model, social policy development model, and structural model. Table 7.2 highlights selected orienting theories and practice theories that are commonly used by social workers. It also supplements this information with the social work roles to be played while using these models.

Social work roles played at the community level are both similar to and distinct from those social work roles played at the micro level of practice. These roles may be adapted depending on the level of practice, but have overall similarities nonetheless. Review each of these orienting/explanatory theories, practice theories/models, and social work roles, making sure that you understand the meaning of each, how they can be combined to effectively bring about community change, and what skills and practice behaviors are needed to actually implement interventions.

Watch for opportunities to *engage in community practice*. You may have the chance to participate in such activities as grant writing, community development, budgeting, self-advocacy efforts by community groups, and interagency collaborations. Reread the portions of your textbooks that refer to the roots of the social work profession, and you will be reminded of the social work profession's historical focus on community development as a way to enhance social functioning and the interplay between individual well-being and the health of communities.

Table 7.2   Orienting Theories, Practice Theories/Models, and Social Work Roles for Community Practice

Orienting Theories	Practice Theories/Models	Social Work Roles
• Conflict	• Community development	• Advocate
• Multicausal	• Community organization	• Broker
• Political economy	• Community resilience model	• Community developer
• Social exchange	• Harm reduction	• Community organizer
• Social learning	• Social change model	• Facilitator
• Social movement	• Social development	• Mediator
• Social systems	• Social justice campaign	• Networker
• Strain	• Social planning	• Policy analyst/developer
• Structural	• Social policy development	• Researcher
• Subculture	• Structural change model	• Social planner

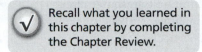

? Assess your understanding of guidance and direction by taking this brief quiz.

✓ Recall what you learned in this chapter by completing the Chapter Review.

Developing Community Practice Skills: A Workbook Activity

Refer to Table 7.1, Building and Blocking Goals of Community Practice, and respond to the following questions. The research needed to respond to these questions will help you develop skills in community practice.

Question	Response
What community problems are addressed by your agency?	
What other organizations or groups also address these problems in your community?	
Has a needs assessment been completed on these problems?	
Has an asset map been completed on resources to address these problems?	
What are the various visions for the community in regard to the problems?	
What blocking goals are in place to prevent or reduce the problems?	
What building goals are in place to strengthen community resources to address the problems?	

Selecting Community Practice Theories and Models: A Workbook Activity

Using Table 7.2, Orienting Theories, Practice Theories/Models, and Social Work Roles for Community Practice, respond to the following questions. Doing so will help you learn to select and match a community-level practice theory to the work of your agency.

1. What community practice theories are used by your agency, if any, to address the social problems it and its clients face?

2. What community practice theories are used by other groups and organizations to address the social problems?

3. What evidence exists that this community practice theory is effective?

4. What additional or different community practice theories do you recommend?

Suggested Learning Activities

- Participate in interagency committees or task groups made up of representatives of various community organizations.

- Read grant proposals and reports written by your agency to see how the agency claims to meet community needs.

- Locate and study community resource directories and historical materials to deepen your understanding of a particular social problem addressed by your agency.

- Examine census data related to the area served by your agency.
- Attend meetings of support groups whose goals are related to the problems addressed by your agency.

Suggested Readings

Daley, Michael. *Rural Social Work in the 21st Century*. Chicago, IL: Lyceum Books, 2015.

Hardcastle, David, Stanley Wenocur, and Patricia Powers. *Community Practice: Theories and Skills for Social Workers*. 3rd ed. New York: Oxford University Press, 2011.

Hardina, Donna. *Analytical Skills for Community Organization and Practice*. New York: Columbia University Press, 2002.

Homan, Mark. *Promoting Community Change*. 6th ed. Pacific Grove, CA: Brooks/Cole, 2016.

Mcknight, Joyce, and Joanna Mcknight Plummer. *Community Organizing: Theory and Practice*. Boston, MA: Pearson Education, 2015.

Roberts-DeGennaro, Maria, and Sondra Fogel. *Using Evidence to Inform Practice for Community and Organizational Change*. Chicago, IL: Lyceum Books, 2010.

Rothman, Jack, and John Ehrlich, eds. *Strategies of Community Interventions*. 7th ed. Peosta, IA: Eddie Bowers Publishing, 2008.

Rubin, Herbert J., and Irene S. Rubin. *Community Organizing and Development*. 4th ed. Boston, MA: Allyn and Bacon, 2008.

Sheafor, Bradford, and Charles Horejsi. *Techniques and Guidelines in Social Work Practice*. 10th ed. Boston, MA: Allyn and Bacon, 2014.

Wambeam, Rodney. *The Community Needs Assessment Workbook*. Chicago, IL: Lyceum Books, 2015.

Weil, Maria. *The Handbook of Community Practice*. 2nd ed. Thousand Oaks, CA: Sage Publications, 2012.

8

The Social Problem Context of Practice

©ROMAN_23203 / FOTOLIA

CHAPTER PREVIEW

This chapter defines the terms *social condition*, *social stressor*, *social problem*, *social policy*, *social problem clusters*, and *asset clusters*. Information is provided on various perspectives on, theories about, and approaches to social problems. It also proposes a variety of *social work roles* in dealing with social problems. Guidelines for analyzing social problems and their impact on client level of social functioning are provided, along with content on the *science of prevention* of social problems. Most of the agencies and organizations that employ social workers were created in response to specific social problems or needs. In order for you to understand your agency's purpose, policies, and operation, it is important to carefully examine the social problems or conditions on which it focuses its attention and resources.

BACKGROUND AND CONTEXT

The conceptualization and definition of a *social problem* is a complex process shaped by historical, political, and cultural forces as well as by existing empirical knowledge. There can be intense

Human Rights and Justice

Behavior: Apply their understanding of social, economic, and environmental justice to advocate for human rights at the individual and system levels.

Critical Thinking Question: In what ways might the social problems addressed by your agency be examples of social, economic, or environmental injustice? What human rights issues are related to these social problems?

disagreement over whether a particular social condition is even to be defined as a social problem. Even when there is agreement that a problem exists, there can be much debate over its cause, its severity, what can and should be done about it, and who is responsible for addressing it. There can also be great disagreement over whether those experiencing a social problem are to be blamed or held accountable for their situation or instead to be supported by others as they attempt to cope with or change their situation.

For example, one segment of society may view addiction and its negative impact on clients and others to be solely the *responsibility of the individual* who is addicted and not consider how genetics, social learning, mental health issues, and lack of coping skills in combination may result in addiction. Homelessness may be viewed as the responsibility of the individual by some, whereas others may see this problem as related to low wages, high cost of living, lack of health insurance, and an inadequate safety net during financially stressful times. The profession of social work examines *social problems from an ecosystems perspective*, understanding the interplay between micro and macro factors in terms of the development of a social problem.

How a social problem is defined and the predominant beliefs about its *causation* have a profound effect on the *formulation of social policies* and the *design of social programs* that are intended to address the problem. Moreover, as an understanding of the problem changes or deepens, agencies must modify their guiding principles and adapt their services and interventions to these new interpretations. Because of these challenges to defining and describing social problems, it is vital that the certain related terms be understood and differentiated from each other.

A *social condition* is a factual reality that can be observed and measured. It can be positive or negative, and may or may not rise to the level of a social problem. Examples include the fact that many marriages in the United States end in divorce, a large percentage of the homeless population is families, in some communities a majority of high school students do not graduate, and a growing number of college graduates are not able to secure a job after completing their education. These are facts, but are they actually social problems? If yes, in what way are they problems? For whom are these problems significant? Who decides that a particular condition is a problem? When does a social problem require action by the community or government? Whose values, norms, and beliefs are to be used in forming a judgment?

A *social stressor* is an event, series of events, or crisis experienced by a vulnerable individual, family, group, or community that moves the social condition to the status of a social problem. Examples of social stressors include loss of employment, medical emergencies, breakdown of social support systems, and increased costs of living. Given enough interacting social stressors without the resources, assets, or resiliency factors needed to mitigate these social stressors, the individual, family, group, or community finds itself dealing with all of the impacts of a true social problem and may be in need of informal and formal services.

A *social problem* can be defined as a social condition that negatively impacts the *social functioning of individuals or communities* and as a situation in which the welfare, values, and well-being of at least a portion of society may be compromised. A social problem is considered as such because many people believe that its existence is harmful, wrong, or immoral. Other people or groups may define a social problem as a violation of human rights or a social injustice because it prevents people or groups of people from obtaining the basic resources, guarantees, and protections deemed to be universal. Others presume that it is simply an inevitable, ongoing, predictable, and acceptable part of life that requires no special response. A social problem threatens the values, sense of morality, security, or safety of those in a community or a society and hopefully will be addressed by those who have the power and influence to bring forth collective action to develop new policies, programs, and agencies that will address this problem.

You have learned that **social functioning** is the domain of the profession of social work and that clients' ability to function in all the ways required of them is impacted by the social problems that directly and indirectly impact them. Social functioning includes the ability to fulfill desired and required social roles, meet one's own basic needs, make adequate contributions to family and community life, and achieve autonomy and satisfaction in the pursuit of one's life goals. Social problems, part of the social environment of all people, impact the ability of individuals, families, organizations, and communities to function positively and effectively. It is good to remember how the relationship between social problems faced by your clients, the social assets they have to cope with these problems, and the social support they receive from both informal and formal resources influences the lives of clients you serve. It is a large part of the context of their lives and must be factored into any effective intervention at the micro level. It is also important to note that vulnerable populations may be those most negatively impacted by social problems, especially when those social problems are severe and interconnected to other serious social problems.

Diversity and Difference in Practice

Behavior: Apply and communicate understanding of the importance of diversity and difference in shaping life experiences in practice at the micro, mezzo, and macro levels.

Critical Thinking Question: In what specific ways are minority groups more negatively impacted by serious social problems?

Because social problems do not exist in isolation and because the root causes may be related to a variety of interacting social conditions, **social problem clusters** often develop. This means that social problems tend to be associated with each other in complex ways, often in terms of **causation** or **increased vulnerability** to additional social problems. This means that one social problem can lead to another, that one social problem makes another one more likely because it increases vulnerability, or that one social problems makes another worse. At the micro level, for example, a health crisis that puts a family into medical bankruptcy will lead to family stress and may result in mental health issues such as depression, loss of financial assets, caregiver stress, and early retirement. On the other hand, when one social problem is decreased, others may be positively impacted as well. Also, positive social conditions tend to support and enhance each other.

An understanding of how vulnerability and certain risk factors impact human behavior is vital. This understanding complements what we know about how some clients are more likely to experience clusters of social problems than those with more social assets are likely to experience. The level of resilience, ability to adapt, presence of assets, and effective coping skills exhibited by individuals, families, groups, organizations, and communities all influence a client

Watch this video on the subject of posttraumatic stress disorder (PTSD) in veterans. How might a veteran with PTSD be more vulnerable to an additional cluster of social problems? www.youtube.com /watch?v=d8-eG7gYC4A or client system's well-being. Working in such client situations requires that social workers enhance and help to build client and client system strengths so that they are capable of better dealing with the crises facing them. Clients or client systems without sufficient **strengths in social functioning** will be more deeply impacted by a cluster of social problems than clients who possess an adequate number of strengths in social functioning. These assets might include client self-efficacy, hope, a realistic perspective on problems and their future, motivation and perseverance, problem-solving abilities, optimism, cognitive ability, emotional regulation skills, spiritual foundation, and physical strength and stamina.

This is not, however, to suggest that all social problems can or should be solved by individual effort and initiative on the part of those experiencing the impact of these problems, but that those who have sufficient strengths in social functioning may be in a better position to **insulate themselves from the negative impacts of the social problems** they face and even to extricate themselves from challenging situations. This grouping of strengths can be termed **social assets**, and they tend to build upon each other into **social asset clusters**. In addition, those with supportive and adequate social environments will have additional advantages when dealing with social problems. Understanding this as a social worker will help you design interventions that enhance and utilize whatever parts of your clients' social environments are positive, nurturing, and supportive. Knowing how, why, and when social assets tend to cluster together gives social workers insight into how to structure interventions. This is an **application of the strengths perspective** you have learned so much about, because interventions will **use and build upon client assets** and strengths in order to address the social problems they face.

Using the same example of a family facing a medical crisis, but one with additional social assets, it is clear to see that although the situation may be similar, a family with effective coping skills, strong social support, flexible employment situation, and respite from care-giving tasks can be less likely to be totally overwhelmed and less likely to experience financial and social collapse. One of the jobs of the social worker is to maximize and enhance the assets of struggling families. The terms **social functioning** and **social assets** also apply to groups, organizations, and communities. In mezzo- and macro social work practice, these assets are used to improve the functioning and well-being of each of these social systems.

You will be able to identify several **competing theories of causation** of the social problems addressed by your agency, each of which purports to explain why problems exist and what can and should be done about them. Different solutions or actions may be proposed, each resting on a particular set of assumptions, values, and beliefs about the cause of the problem and what interventions are necessary, feasible, and effective. There are various views of what is a viable and desirable solution, as well as how to measure outcomes and success. There will be critiques of historical and contemporary approaches based on factors such as the following:

- The reluctance to raise taxes to fund additional programs
- A view of social programs and policies as approaches that create dependency
- A belief that root causes rather than symptoms need to be addressed
- A conviction that solutions are the responsibility of individuals and families, community, or society

A comprehensive understanding of the contributors to social problems requires an examination of theories of **etiology**, often called **explanatory theories**. This understanding is also derived from a number of other factors, including empirical evidence, personal values, individual experiences or lack of experiences, and even misconceptions and biases. A partial, incomplete, or flawed explanation for the etiology of social problems will result in partial, incomplete, and flawed responses at the micro, mezzo, and macro levels. The decisions about the nature and cause of the problem are often heavily political and will reflect the views and preferences of those who have power and influence. That is why social workers must become competent in the political and social policy arena if they are to effect change in the social policies that impact their clients. This requires that social workers also

- Understand the *complex etiology* of social problems
- Articulate this understanding to *decision and policy makers*
- Persuade those with *power and influence to collaborate* in addressing the social problem
- Assume leadership in influencing *social policy formation* to effectively address the social problems.

The decisions made about which actions should be taken to address a social problem eventually give rise to specific *social policies*. Social policies, described in detail in Chapter 9 *The Social Policy Context of Practice*, are the federal, state, and local laws; statutes; and ordinances enacted to address social problems. Social policies can mandate services to be provided, enable organizations to provide services, fund programs, create unfunded mandates, set priorities for social programs, or set standards for types and quality of services to be provided. Many of the social agencies that serve as social work practicum settings have the responsibility of carrying out these social policies and designing specific programs and interventions to solve the problem.

 Assess your understanding of background and context by taking this brief quiz.

GUIDANCE AND DIRECTION

In any community or society, there is great variety in the perspectives of its members as they try to understand and explain the social problems they observe and experience. These different viewpoints will be based on personal experiences, attitudes, values, information, misinformation, and even stereotypes. You may think that some of these perspectives are uninformed or biased, but it is important to realize that the beliefs make sense and seem valid to those who hold them. Not everyone agrees that a social condition is a social problem, and not everyone agrees on the causes of social problems. Further, there is much disagreement on what social policies should be put in place to address social policies.

Although this can be confusing and may make it hard to know how to begin addressing social problems, answer the questions in Table 8.1 to gain a comprehensive perspective on a social problem that concerns you and that your agency addresses. The table provides a *social problem analysis model* that can be used to analyze any social problem. Discuss these questions with your field instructor, and try to understand how the ability to complete a *social problem analysis* using the structure and questions provided in Table 8.1 will be essential in designing interventions, programs, and organizations that will effectively address the social problems they face.

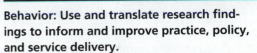
Research-informed Practice

Behavior: Use and translate research findings to inform and improve practice, policy, and service delivery.

Critical Thinking Question: What empirical research evidence is there to support the ways in which your agency approaches social problems?

Table 8.1   Social Problem Analysis Model

Agency Focus on Social Problem

- What social problem is addressed by your agency?
- How do your agency mission and programs address the social problem?
- How is this social problem related to other social problems?
- How is this social problem defined and understood?

Status of Social Problem

- What is the scope and scale of the problem?
- In recent years, has this problem worsened, stayed the same, or improved?
- How does its level of severity compare with the same problem at the state or national level?

Theories of Causation and Etiology

- What are the proposed theories of causation of this social problem?
- On what are these theories based?
- How does taking an ecosystems perspective on this social problem enhance an understanding of why it exists and persists?

Values Surrounding Social Problem

- What societal values are threatened by the existence of this social problem?
- What human rights are compromised by this social problem?
- What social justice issues are raised by the presence of this social problem?

Perspectives on Social Problem

- What groups in your community see this social problem as real and significant?
- What groups in your community do not view this social problem as real or significant?
- What other social problems are connected to the social problem, and how do they interact and impact each other?

Support of Agency Approach

- What groups in your community support your agency's work to address this social problem?
- What groups in your community do not support your agency's work to address this social problem?

Impact of Social Problem

- In what ways does this social problem impact the social functioning of your clients?
- How does this social problem impact the community?
- How would the absence of this social problem change social well-being?

Evidence-Based Practice

- What research is available on evidence-based approaches and best practices to address the social problem your agency addresses?
- What program evaluation is done by your agency to measure its impact on the social problem it addresses?

Prevention of Social Problem

- What social conditions, if enhanced, would help to prevent the social problem from occurring or worsening?
- What social conditions, if reduced or eliminated, would help to prevent the social problem from occurring or worsening?

Research and Knowledge Building about Social Problem

- What practice models addressing the social problem at the micro, mezzo, and macro levels need to be studied for effectiveness?
- What demonstration and pilot programs would you recommend in order to test emerging and promising approaches to dealing with the social problem?

The *contrasting viewpoints and the political debate* that arise from these diverse perspectives will at times result in social policy that you support and, at other times, in social policy that you see as ineffective or harmful. Remember that the democratic political process is influenced by *public attitudes, values, information, and power*. In order to influence the process of social policy formation, you will need to venture into the process of politics and use your skills to advocate for social policies that benefit those you serve. This will rarely be easy to navigate because of the strongly held beliefs of everyone involved in the issue and because those negatively impacted by existing social problems or policies may not have access to power.

As our society becomes more *diverse and pluralistic*, there will be even more diversity in how people think about social conditions and social problems. Strive to understand perspectives that are different from your own and think about how these perspectives lead to definitions and potentially different solutions. Expect increasing numbers of lively discussions, heated debates, conflicts, and sometimes stalemates between groups with very different views about what constitutes social problems and what ought to be done about them. In addition, if you wish to address social problems at the community or societal level, you will need to contribute reason, collaboration, the ability to compromise, access to reliable data, and political influence to this debate. Remember that no one perspective on why social problems exist and what should be done about them is always adequate, totally accurate, or complete. Resolve to find any common ground that can be built upon between those holding competing perspectives when addressing social problems. This will also require that you develop the political skills of listening to those with whom you disagree, compromising, and at times settling for modest gains in addressing the social problems you care about.

Perhaps the most important perspective on social problems is that of the *clients who are experiencing them*. Their personal beliefs about causation come from the world of personal experiences, and must be included in any complete understanding of social problems and what to do about them. Remember that clients who are experiencing problems firsthand may view them very differently from the way in which you view them. A situation that you or other professionals define as a problem may not seem like a problem to your client or vice versa. If you have never been poor or homeless, were not raised in an unsafe home or neighborhood, or have not been affected by racism, you may not fully appreciate the profound effects these experiences have on people. Listen sensitively to accounts of your clients' life experiences so that you can better understand their importance and the impact on their lives. It is always desirable when clients can be empowered to become involved in efforts to alleviate social problems by which they are impacted. Community organization and community development initiatives that include and at times are *led by clients* may at times be the most effective. Work to involve yourself in any such efforts available to you.

Draw on your understanding of the *ecosystems perspective* and *social systems theory* to examine how social problems develop and change over time. Identify the many factors, conditions, and circumstances that interact to create a social problem. As you gain experience, you will see more clearly how

Diversity and Difference in Practice

Behavior: Apply self-awareness and self-regulation to manage the influence of personal biases and values in working with diverse clients and constituencies.

Critical Thinking Question: What might get in the way of truly listening to and learning from others whose opinions about social problems may differ from yours?

Watch this video about the social worker of the year who worked to identify and reduce hate crimes. How would diverse people within a community setting view the concept of hate crimes differently? https://www.youtube.com/watch?v=XPAotCc2ZWc

one social problem can lead to or exacerbate others, or how several problems clustered together can overwhelm clients or communities and have devastating consequences. You will also see that *social change at the macro level* must often take place in order to enhance the social functioning of individual clients and families at the micro level.

Think critically and creatively about the *concept of prevention* and the ways in which you could become involved in preventing the social problems you are attempting to address. Ask yourself questions that will help you analyze conditions and make plans for interventions.

- What changes at the community and societal level are needed in order to prevent adverse conditions and social problems from developing in the first place?
- Do existing prevention programs appear to be effective?
- Do we have the knowledge, the resources, and the political will to launch effective programs of prevention?
- What would various solutions cost and from where would this money come?
- What are the advantages, disadvantages, feasibility, and probable effectiveness of various prevention efforts?
- Should prevention be attempted at the micro, mezzo, or macro level, or at all levels?
- What groups might oppose prevention programs and why? Can something that did not happen even be measured?

Answering these questions in order to design effective prevention efforts will require a grasp of the *science of prevention*. Effective efforts to prevent social problems are based on an understanding and use of concepts such as *risk factors and protective factors*, and the ways in which they interact to influence the development or prevention of social problems. To most students, prevention programs seem to make more sense than reacting after problems have developed, so work to understand how to design such problems. You will need knowledge about the *precursors* to problems, and how they set the stage for the development of social problems. The *causation of problems* must be understood before a prevention program is designed, and the *epidemiology* (i.e., incidence, prevalence, impact) must also be described in order to design effective prevention efforts. You will also need to know what factors are considered protective and how they *buffer, inoculate, and mitigate the social problems*. Both risk factors and protective factors cluster together, making them more powerful in either a positive or negative fashion.

During your practicum, you will most likely meet clients who are truly remarkable, positive human beings despite the fact that they grew up in very challenging or destructive social environments and experienced the impact of social problems. For reasons that we are just beginning to understand, some individuals are resilient and able to resist the negative influences of a corrosive environment. There may also have been social supports available at a variety of levels to these individuals that enhanced individual strengths and coping skills, allowing them to function well in spite of their experiences. Seek to understand why individuals respond differently to the positive and negative aspects of their social environment. Learn from your clients about the strengths and *resiliency factors* that have made it possible for them to overcome adversity.

Use Table 8.2 to consider and reflect upon the potential roles for social workers in addressing social problems by *increasing awareness of social problems*, *designing and implementing interventions and programs*, *engaging in research*, and *influencing social policy*.

Table 8.2   Social Work Strategies to Address Social Problems

Identify social problem	Social workers engage in the planned change process in order to address social problems, including the identification, naming, and highlighting of social problems so that they and others can respond. They shine a light on the existence, scope, and depth of the problem; show the negative impacts on all levels of society; explain the complex causation of social problems; standardize definitions of social problems; give voice to impacted populations; and illustrate the relevance of diversity on social problems.
Intervene to address social problem	Social workers, in collaboration with stakeholders, set goals and objectives and design programs to address social problems. They destigmatize the problem, work to shape attitudes, appeal to commonalities, clarify societal values, incorporate diverse stakeholders into intervention, and anticipate forces for change and opposition to intervention. They incorporate best practices and innovations into plans. They include impacted social systems in efforts and evaluation of outcomes and effectiveness of interventions and programs.
Conduct and utilize research on social problem	Social workers research evidence-based practices to apply to social problems, and engage in program evaluation to determine effectiveness of interventions and programs. They utilize varied research approaches, including process, outcome, quantitative, qualitative, and action research. They include client groups in evaluation. They use research results to understand causes and contributors to social problems, and disseminate this information to practitioners, social planners, policy makers, and educators.
Engage in social policy practice to address social problem	Social workers utilize program evaluation data to inform clients, stakeholders, and policy makers. They make recommendations for new policy initiatives and for policy amendments based on findings. They use an ecosystems perspective and social systems theory to impact social policy development in a holistic manner.

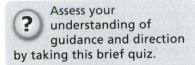

Assess your understanding of guidance and direction by taking this brief quiz.

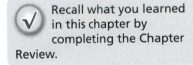

Recall what you learned in this chapter by completing the Chapter Review.

Social Problems and Social Work Responses: A Workbook Activity

Understanding the social problems addressed by your agency will help you analyze them and begin the work necessary to reduce or eliminate them. This understanding includes contributors to these problems, your agency responses to these problems, the context in which your agency works, and the research surrounding them.

Using Table 8.2 Social Problem Analysis Format, identify the major social problem(s) addressed by your agency,

and respond to questions in the table. This exercise will help you to gain skills in analyzing the problem you see addressed in your agency and will also provide a framework for social problem analysis in the future from the micro-, mezzo-, and macro levels.

Beliefs About Social Problems: A Workbook Activity

Social workers encounter numerous beliefs about social problems held by a variety of people. Those beliefs are rooted in values, experiences, observations, and informa-

tion about those problems. Engaging in conversations with people who have divergent beliefs about the social problems you care deeply about will help you clarify your own beliefs, acquire reliable information, and understand how the views of those impacted by social problems shape their beliefs.

Respond to the following commonly heard beliefs about social problems, reflecting on how your response could further discourse that might lead to deepened understanding of social problems so that they may be addressed adequately. Discussing them with fellow students and supervisors will also help you to anticipate such statements.

Common Beliefs about Social Problems

"Social problems are inevitable."

"Social problems will never be solved."

"Social problems are the responsibility of those who experience them."

"It doesn't impact me."

"It's not my problem and not my responsibility."

"Someone should do something."

Professional Beliefs about Social Problems

"One person can't do much about such overwhelming problems, so I would rather work one-to-one with clients."

"We only work on the micro level, and do not get involved in social policy."

"If I can help one person, I will be satisfied."

"It's all political."

"We do the best we can."

Suggested Learning Activities

- Attend public meetings (e.g., city council meetings) and read the letters to the editor of the local newspaper in order to better understand the various ways in which people explain the existence of social problems and the variety of solutions they propose.

- Attend the meetings of a group or organization that defines the problem addressed by your agency differently than does your agency. Try to understand the basis for their views.

- Identify and attend a self-help group that addresses the social problem your agency addresses.

Attend a meeting to see how it explains the existence of the social problem.

- Examine the *Social Work Almanac* or a similar reference book that presents national statistics on the social problem addressed by your agency and compare them with those of your area.

- Read print and electronic media descriptions of social problems. Pay attention to whether the media takes a strengths or deficit perspective on these social problems.

Suggested Readings

Eitzen, D. Stanley, Maxine Baca Zinn, and Kelly E. Eitzen Smith. *Social Problems: Census Update*. 10th ed. Boston: Allyn and Bacon, 2012.

Hardcastle, David A., Patricia R. Powers, and Stanley Wenocur. *Community Practice: Theories and Skills for Social Workers*. 3rd ed. New York: Oxford University Press, 2012.

Hoefer, Richard. *Advocacy Practice for Social Justice*. 2nd ed. Chicago: Lyceum Books, 2012.

Jansson, Bruce. *Becoming an Effective Policy Advocate: From Policy Practice to Social Justice*. 7th ed. Belmont, CA: Brooks/Cole, 2014.

Kettner, Peter M., Robert M. Moroney, and Lawrence L. Martin. *Designing and Managing Programs: An Effectiveness-Based Approach*. 4th ed. Thousand Oaks, CA: Sage, 2012.

Kinsterbusch, Kurt. *Taking Sides: Clashing Views on Social Issues*. Columbus, OH: McGraw-Hill, 2014.

Leon-Guerrero, Anna. *Social Problems: Community, Policy, and Social Action*. 5th ed. Thousand Oaks, CA: Pine Forge Press, 2015.

Mizrahi, Terry, and Larry Davis. *The Encyclopedia of Social Work*. 20th ed. Washington, DC: NASW Press and Oxford University Press, 2010.

Unrau, Yvonne A., Peter A. Gabor, and Richard M. Grinnell. *Evaluation in Social Work: The Art and Science of Practice*. 4th ed. New York: Oxford University Press, 2007.

9

The Social Policy Context of Practice

©KLUBLU / FOTOLIA

CHAPTER PREVIEW

This chapter provides a summary of *social policy practice*, including *definitions of social policy* and related terms. It presents a *typology of social policies* and describes the ideal and actual trajectories often seen in social policy formation and implementation. Also offered is a *social policy analysis framework* to be used to understand the effectiveness and efficiency of policies in addressing social problems. It also presents a *rationale and value base* for involvement in social policy practice, as well as direction in comprehending the ways in which social policies can be implemented or adapted.

Previous chapters focused on the agency context, the community context, and the social problem context of social work practice. This chapter examines a fourth context and arena for practice, the *social policy context*. The clients served by your practicum agency, the other social workers and staff within this agency, and even your practicum experiences are affected by social policy. This chapter attempts to clarify the nature of social policy by defining and distinguishing between various terms and explaining the impact of social policy on a social agency and those that it serves. Specific suggestions are offered on how you can identify and locate information concerning the social policies most relevant to your practicum setting.

BACKGROUND AND CONTEXT

The study of social policy can be exciting because it involves an examination of what we as a society believe about people and the problems they experience, about which social workers care deeply. Studying social policy also highlights what can and should be done about these problems. It forces us to carefully examine our own *assumptions, beliefs, and values*, and in the process we are sometimes surprised by what we discover about ourselves and our views. Although stimulating, the study of social policy is also a complex undertaking. For example, the analysis of a particular social policy requires students to be able to locate relevant governmental documents and legal codes; understand the legislative process; and acquire a basic understanding of the many historic, political, cultural, and economic forces that shaped the development of a particular policy.

For purposes of this chapter, *social policy* is defined as a decision made by public or governmental authorities regarding the assignment and allocation of resources, rights, and responsibilities and expressed in laws and governmental regulations. Needless to say, lawmakers and government officials formulate policies on a wide variety of topics. Thus, there are public policies on international relations, economics and the monetary system, tax structures, interstate and international commerce, military and defense, transportation, use of public lands, environmental safety, education, and the like. For the most part, social welfare policies address matters or issues related to the *social well-being* of people and the relationships between various groups within society. Thus, social policies focus on such concerns as marriage, divorce, adoption, domestic abuse, needs of older adults, juvenile delinquency, mental health, discrimination against minority groups, training and employment opportunities for the disadvantaged, economic assistance to the poor, availability of affordable housing, immigration, and other similar concerns. The term *social welfare policy* is often applied to those social policies that focus primarily on the distribution of economic, educational, and health benefits to those in need.

Policy Practice

Behavior: Assess how social welfare and economic policies impact the delivery of and access to social services.

Critical Thinking Question: How is policy practice similar to and different from planned change at the micro level?

These approaches account for the ways in which many federal and state laws and social policies have been enacted, some of which result in effective social policy, and some of which do not.

Social policies are *directly related to social problems* and are intended to address them in a way that will hopefully prevent or reduce the extent of these problems. Thus, once a social problem is identified, various groups, all with different values, belief systems, and political affiliations, begin the process of addressing these social problems. They propose laws that may actually change the social structures that contribute to or add to the social problems. Social policies often direct agencies to do what is required, perform to a certain standard, and accomplish goals within a given budget. Further, they provide the tools that are to be used to measure the effectiveness and show accountability in the use of public money.

Watch this segment of the famous "I Have a Dream" speech by Martin Luther King, Jr. What social policies arose out of the U.S. civil rights movement in response to the social problem of racism and discrimination?

Stakeholders with personal, financial, civic, or policy-making perspectives all have individual views on the need for, design of, and goals for state and federal social welfare policies. They bring their values, political beliefs, and knowledge to the process of social policy involvement. In a democratic system, everyone ideally has input into the social policies that impact him or her directly or indirectly. In reality, however, numerous forces, groups, and individuals with power and influence may have a disproportionate amount of control over that policies are enacted. The social work profession is committed to *social policies that support vulnerable populations* they serve because these groups often do not possess or exercise political power. Social workers know that to achieve success in policy practice, they must become familiar with and involved in the formation of social policies that support those they serve. Given next are the *stakeholders* impacted by and involved in the development and implementation of social policy. This list includes those who are not involved in social policy development and reform, those who are passive, and those who are actively involved for a number of reasons. Use this categorization to help you understand the variety of perspectives that will be represented in social policy work that impacts the clients of your agency and those you will serve in your career.

- *Individuals directly impacted by social welfare policy*
  - Those who are aware of the impact and are not involved
  - Those who are aware of the impact and are involved
  - Those who are unaware of the impact and are not involved
- *General public*
  - Those who support social policy and are actively involved
  - Those who do not support social policy and are resistant to its formation
  - Those who are passive and uninvolved
- *Policy makers*
  - Legislators who are informed and involved
  - Legislators who are uninformed and involved
- *Special interest groups*
  - Those who promote social policies that benefit themselves
  - Those who resist social policies that disadvantage or do not benefit them
- *Advocacy groups*
  - Those who promote the welfare of others
  - Those who speak for those without power and influence
  - Those who work to empower those impacted by social policy

Social welfare policies fall into a number of *policy categories and domains* based on their focus, intent, values, assumptions, eligibility, and funding. Work to understand the social policies that impact your clients, and use Table 9.1 to help you categorize those social policies so that you can truly understand what they are intended to achieve, and whether or not they do so effectively or at all.

Social policies are in a constant state of *evaluation and revision*. Social work policy practice is geared toward policy development and revision that is based on research evidence regarding the effectiveness, impact on social problems addressed by the social policy, and an overall rational approach. However, numerous additional variables influence how actual social policies are developed and whether or not they are revised based on

Table 9.1   Domains of Social Welfare Policy

Domain	Description
Type	Social insurance
	Health insurance
	Cash assistance
	In-kind assistance
	Public programs and services (e.g., education and public health)
Goals	Societal well-being
	Prevention of social problems
	Reduction in social problems
	Safety net
	Protection
	Remediation
	Demonstration project
Value base	Self-sufficiency
	Altruism
	Dignity
	Minimum standard of living
	Rights
	Responsibilities
	Protection
Assumptions	Social support for vulnerable populations results in self-sufficiency
	Social support for vulnerable populations results in dependency
	Social support is necessary
	Social support is unnecessary
Funding	Taxpayer-funded (federal and state budget)
	Employee and employer contributions through payroll
	Pilot program
	Pass through from federal to state government
Eligibility	Means testing
	Entitlement
	Status on a particular measure
Human rights base	Equity
	Access
	Freedom from restriction and exploitation
	Right to life
	Social justice and economic justice
Social benefits	Social well-being
	Growth
	Prosperity
	Upward mobility
	Public health
	Solidarity

sound information. Table 9.2 highlights the *ideal and actual trajectories* that often characterize *social policy formation, implementation, and revision*. In an ideal world where social policies are developed based on a comprehensive understanding of the issues involved, each of the dimensions of social policy listed in Table 9.2 would be fully developed to form an ideal trajectory of social policy development. However, social policy development rarely follows an ideal trajectory, which means that social policies are not always comprehensive, inclusive, and effective. As you learn about social policy development, consider the process using these terms. It should be noted that stakeholders will have varied opinions on what ideal trajectories of social policy development might be.

No doubt you have already learned about how large-scale societal dynamics influence social policy. This includes societal attitudes, global factors, political differences, and changes in administration at the state and federal levels. Laws are envisioned, implemented, amended, blocked, and abolished depending on what is needed, what is politically feasible, and what those possessing power achieve in passing or blocking social policy. Recent *trends in social policy* have included some of the following dynamics that you should understand and be prepared to deal with as a social worker:

- *Privatization* involves the transfer of public responsibilities and power from public control to private entities and has the potential to greatly change the ways in which services are provided, as well as what is offered.
- *Devolution* is the granting of power and responsibility from one level of government to a lower level, granting the lower level of government choice regarding what is provided and how it is provided.
- *Decentralization* shifts responsibility for programs from one central location to various regional, state, or local locations.
- *Reduction in government influence* over social welfare is a result of political and societal beliefs that government is not responsible for responding to social needs and problems, and other entities or individuals should address them instead.

Table 9.2   Ideal and Actual Trajectories in Social Policy Development

Dimension of Social Policy	Ideal Trajectory	Actual Trajectory
Value base	Societal values	Political compromise
Knowledge base	Comprehensive understanding of social problem and its etiology	Partial understanding of social problem and its etiology
Scope	Comprehensive and universal	Limited and partial
Time orientation	Timely and future oriented	Slow and crisis oriented
Stakeholder base	All stakeholders including the client base involved	Stakeholders with political power and influence involved
Empirical base	Based on facts and sound research	Based on interpretation of facts and emotion
Relationship to existing and future policy	Built upon effective policy and allows for future growth	Detached from effective policy and future orientation
Rationality	Purposeful and planned	Reactive and unplanned

Human Rights and Justice

Behavior: Engage in practices that advance social, economic, and environmental justice.

Critical Thinking Question: What local, state or federal social policies protect your clients from oppression and discrimination?

- *Rollback or reversal of social policies* happens when there is dissatisfaction with the results or philosophy of existing social policies, and a change is seen as necessary.

Although an *agency policy* is not a social policy using the definitions in this chapter, social policies do filter down to the level of a local or community agency and find their way into the agency's policy manual. At the local level, social policies have a significant impact on an agency's services and programs and on what a social worker actually does or does not do in his or her work with the clients. The *impact of social policy on agency policy* is most evident in the operation of a public agency in which one will find that many of the statements found in the manual are direct responses to specific legal codes and various governmental rules and regulations.

Social policies are a *reflection of values* and what is believed to be right and wrong, desirable and undesirable. They are shaped mostly by those who have power and influence. The formulation of social policy is basically a political process, and politics are primarily about power. The art of gaining, exercising, and retaining power in order to *influence and enact social policies* is the *goal of policy practice*. Hopefully the effectiveness of social policy implementation is monitored, measured, and evaluated, and results are shared with policy makers so that social policies can be continually improved in order to address social problems more effectively.

If social policies are ill conceived because the decision makers either do not understand the problem or have erroneous beliefs about its causes, the resulting social programs will also be flawed. Those who understand the concerns being addressed and the inadequacies of existing policies and programs have both an obligation and an opportunity to provide accurate information to the decision makers so they can develop appropriate and effective social policies. In the absence of such information, policy makers will assume that social policies are addressing the needs they were intended to address. Social workers can thus be extremely influential in not only providing needed information but also lobbying for just, equitable, and effective social policy changes.

(?) Assess your understanding of background and context by taking this brief quiz.

GUIDANCE AND DIRECTION

You may be surprised at the degree to which your work is impacted by social policy. Because of that, you need to learn about social policy so that you can take part in its formulation. Hopefully you are excited at the prospect of working at the macro level to design social policies and social programs that could improve the lives of many people. Social change and social policy development are the most efficient and instrumental ways to help large numbers of people and promote social justice. As mentioned earlier, this level of practice is referred to as social policy practice.

Depending on your practicum setting, you will need to become familiar with a range of social policy issues and concerns. You must acquire a basic or *working understanding* of the social policies that most directly influence the operation of your agency, its own agency policies, your role, and its clients or consumers. There are many arenas or fields of social policy of interest to social workers and social agencies. They include the broad areas of education, health, family life, housing, crime, mental health, violence, immigration, disability, addiction, and numerous others.

When entering policy practice, it is helpful to understand that there are several broad *types of social policies*, each of which reflects a philosophy, set of values, structure, and belief system about how society should deal with social problems. The following categories illustrate how social policies are enacted to accomplish certain goals for society.

- *Policies of social and financial support* are those intended to help or encourage people to carry out their roles and responsibilities and meet their basic needs for food, shelter, and so on. Examples include policies related to financial assistance, medical care for the poor, and subsidized housing for low-income elders.
- *Policies of protection* are those that seek to protect people from harm and exploitation, especially those who are most vulnerable. Examples are policies related to child abuse and neglect, domestic violence, landlord-tenant interactions, the frail elderly, and to groups often subjected to discrimination and oppression.
- *Policies of rehabilitation and remediation* are those intended to correct or minimize the impact of certain conditions such as serious mental illness, addiction, victimization, and trauma. Such policies offer programs and services to reduce the impact of such conditions, provide restorative justice, and improve social functioning.
- *Policies of prevention* are those that attempt to prevent certain social and health problems from developing or increasing. Examples are social policies that encourage economic development, immunizations, parent education, family planning, proper nutrition, and curfews for youth.
- *Policies of punishment and correction* are those that seek to punish and control persons who violate laws and societal norms. Examples are policies related to crime and delinquency, probation and parole, and the monitoring of convicted sex offenders.

Social policies constantly evolve as a result of changing societal needs, shifting social values, increases or decreases in financial resources available to implement policy, and, of course, political forces. You will need to keep abreast of proposed state and federal legislative changes and find ways to have *input into the political process*. During your practicum, make a special effort to involve yourself in activities that prepare you for policy practice. Look for the opportunity to participate in task forces or serve on committees working to pass a law or assist grassroots or advocacy groups seeking to change social policy. You may be able to observe and give testimony at public meetings or legislative hearings that solicit public input before social policy decisions are made.

Be aware that when social workers do not engage in the politics of forming social welfare policy and allocating funding for social welfare programs, many client needs and concerns can be overlooked by decision makers. This also means that the insights and values of the social work profession are absent from the development of social policy. Your knowledge and skills are needed in the ongoing work of social policy development, so it is vital to develop competence in policy practice. Social workers also serve in public offices, including state and federal legislatures, and it

Research-informed Practice

Behavior: Use and translate research findings to inform and improve practice, policy, and service delivery.

Critical Thinking Question: How can research inform and improve social policies that directly impact the functioning of individuals, families, groups, organizations, and communities?

This video highlights several social workers who are engaged in policy practice by serving in elected public positions. In what ways does such policy practice honor the mission and purposes of the social work profession? www.youtube.com /watch?v=yeVxtGTKcnE

would be helpful for you to research the careers of social workers in public office and the focus on social policies they pursue.

Policy practice necessitates an understanding of several areas discussed already, including social problems, their impact, and what policy approaches will actually reduce social problems and enhance the social functioning of individuals, families, and communities. The science of policy analysis is challenging, yet social workers must familiarize themselves with the dimensions of social policy analysis generally used to understand whether or not certain policies and programs are actually effective and efficient. To do this work well, you will need to develop and utilize a *social policy analysis model* or conceptual framework to guide your examination and analysis of the social policies that impact the operation of your agency and either support or undermine the social functioning of your clients. The questions listed next are the ones often addressed in the various models and conceptual frameworks used in policy analysis. Learn to view such models as tools to help you understand and assess the effectiveness of social policies that impact your work. Recognize that these frameworks will not only guide your evaluation of social policy but can also provide you with the insights needed to improve social policy.

Sources of information regarding a social policy include the original code or statute, administrative rules and regulations, and other governmental documents that describe and explain the policy. Various professional and advocacy organizations distribute reports of their analysis of social policies relevant to their particular concerns. In addition, the observations of social workers and of clients will provide insight into how a given policy affects the lives of individuals and families. The social workers in your agency will have opinions about how social policy could be improved, how it benefits or harms clients, and how it complements or conflicts with other social policies. Clients may also have insights based on their experiences with effective or ineffective social policies, so seek opportunities to learn from them and their experiences.

If you take steps to involve yourself in policy practice while in practicum, you will soon be able to understand, describe, and engage in social policy analysis. Analyzing social policies in terms of the following dimensions will help you prepare for involvement in the social policies you care most about or that intimately impact your clients. This list of questions, when answered in depth, is considered a *model of social policy analysis*.

1. Authority and auspices of the social policy (federal, state, or local law)
2. Official name and legal citation of the social policy
3. History and reasons for its development, including various societal contexts
4. Social problems addressed by the social policy
5. Stated purpose, goals, and objectives of the social policy
6. Assumptions, values, and beliefs upon which it is based
7. Key provisions, programs, and services
8. Funding source and adequacy
9. Implementation process, including agencies involved and how they interact
10. Impact on agency operation

11. Impact on clients

12. Incentives or disincentives in the policy

13. Advantages and positive impacts

14. Disadvantages and negative impacts

15. Relationship to other social policies

16. Monitoring and evaluation process

17. Measures of the effectiveness and efficiency

18. Results of evaluation

19. Gaps and needs for revision and improvement

20. Recommendations for maintaining, changing, or abolishing social policy

In addition to these dimensions of policy analysis, there are a number of additional areas that need to be examined in order to engage in what is called a *critical analysis of social policy*. This additional level of analysis identifies and shines a light on such influences as power, diversity, and who is actually benefitting from the policy and its implementation. Such an analysis would include questions such as the following:

- Who is actually involved in the actual *decision making* of policy formation?
- Who has *power* to influence policy formation?
- Which entities actually *implement policies*?
- How are *requirements enforced*?
- Who *benefits* from certain policies and how?
- Who is put at a *disadvantage* by certain policies and how?
- What trade-offs and *compromises* were made as the policy was formed and enacted?
- How were *issues of diversity addressed*, including gender, culture, ability, and socioeconomic status?
- What *special interests* were involved, including lobbyists and funders?
- In what ways would the social policy be better able to achieve its goals if *revised*?

After you have become familiar with a specific social policy and its effects, consider how it could be improved and what steps or actions would be necessary to achieve those improvements, such as changes in existing legislation, changes in administrative rules, or the creation of incentives to adhere to the policy. Commit yourself to gaining skills and competency in policy practice. To become competent, you will need to recognize *windows of opportunity for policy change*, build coalitions of those who support policies on which you are working, recognize the values inherent in policy approaches, communicate your vision of how social policies will improve societal conditions, persuade others to support your work, anticipate and deal with opposition, and garner the support necessary to be successful. Find social workers who are actively in policy practice and learn from them about how they deal with these issues.

Finally, follow these *principles for achieving social justice* through social policy practice. Over time, even as social conditions

Ethical and Professional Behavior

Research: Demonstrate professional demeanor in behavior; appearance; and oral, written, and electronic communication.

Critical Thinking Question: How can you gain access to and learn about social policies which guide practice from legislative testimony, proposed legislation, and fact sheets?

change and policies evolve, these principles will serve you well as a social worker who promotes social justice.

Description of Policy Practice

- Social policies are *social contracts* based on societal values and commonalities.
- Social policy practice is a *vital arena for social workers* because social policy strongly impacts the social functioning of individuals, families, groups, organizations, and society.

Value Base of Policy Practice

- *Human rights* are universal and should be protected through social policy.
- Social policy should be *based on values* of equity, access, dignity, worth of the individual, opportunity, and fairness.

Goals of Policy Practice

- Social policy should proactively *promote social functioning* through empowerment, client involvement, and prevention of social problems.
- Social policies should *address social problems* from all levels of practice.
- Social policy should address, *reduce, and eliminate* social problems.

Process of Policy Practice

- Social policies should be based on both *historical and future orientations*.
- *Clients, constituents, and stakeholders* must be involved in social policy.
- Social policies should be based on an *understanding of social problems* and how policies can address them.

Politics of Policy Practice

- *Windows of opportunity* for social change can be utilized in policy practice.
- Building of *coalitions* and garnering support is necessary.
- *Opposition* must be anticipated and intentionally addressed.

Evaluation of Policy Practice

- Social policies should be based on *empirical evidence* about the causes of social problems.
- Social policies should be *measured and evaluated* for the effectiveness and efficiency.

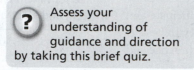

Assess your understanding of guidance and direction by taking this brief quiz.

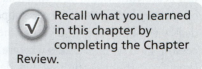

Recall what you learned in this chapter by completing the Chapter Review.

Perspectives on Policy Practice: A Workbook Activity

In order to clarify your own personal and professional perspective on policy practice, it is important to think about the following questions for yourself. It would be helpful to consider them in the context of the social problems you care most about, or the ones addressed by your practicum agency.

1. What social issues and problems do I care most about?

_____

_____

2. What social issues and problems will I become involved in as a policy practitioner?

_____

_____

3. What are my strongest held values about social policy and the role of social work in its formation?

_____

_____

4. What does it mean when there are competing theories, explanations, and even evidence about social problems and policies?

_____

_____

5. Is common ground possible among competing ideologies and political beliefs regarding social policy?

_____

_____

6. How will I deal with partial success or defeats in the promotion of social policy?

_____

_____

7. In an ideal world of my description, what social policies would be in place?

_____

_____

Preparing Legislative Testimony: A Workbook Activity

Using a social policy that impacts your agency, prepare testimony that you would give at either the state or federal level about revisions, improvements, and advances in this policy that would better address social problems, benefit those impacted, and demonstrate the effectiveness. Review your testimony with social workers and others experienced in policy practice, and seek their input on your work.

_____

_____

_____

_____

Suggested Learning Activities

- Interview a social worker in your agency about a social policy that most directly affects his or her clients and obtain his or her recommendations for improving the social policy.

- Review the National Association of Social Workers (NASW) *Code of Ethics* (1999) guidelines regarding the social worker's responsibility in the area of social policy (www.socialworkers.org).

- Read *Social Work Speaks*, which describes NASW's position on a variety of social issues. Consider how your own personal and professional positions on similar social issues are similar to or different from the NASW position.

- Attend legislative or public hearings that gather public input before a social policy is enacted or modified.

- Identify your personal position regarding a controversial area of social policy, such as abortion. Attend meetings of an organization that takes an opposing position to try to understand that perspective, including the values, beliefs, knowledge, and assumptions on which it is based.

- Invite a state legislator to discuss his or her experiences with proposing, formulating, and passing legislation.

- Use the Internet to monitor the progress of a bill before the U.S. Congress or your state legislature. For information on federal legislation relevant to social work, explore the legislative section of the website of the NASW.

- Explore the websites of organizations that monitor social policy, such as the Electronic Policy Network, Center for Law and Social Policy, U.S. Department of Health and Human Services, World Wide Web Resources for Social Workers; Professional Organization Public Affairs Division, the U.S. Congressional Budget Office, and the U.S. Congressional Record Services.

Suggested Readings

Barusch, Amanda S. *Foundations of Social Policy: Social Justice in Human Perspective*. 3rd ed. Florence, KY: Brooks/Cole, 2012.

Blau, Joel, and Mimi Abramovitz. *The Dynamics of Social Welfare*. 4th ed. New York: Oxford University Press, 2014.

Bochel, Hugh, Catherine Bochel, Robert Page, and Robert Sykes. *Social Policy: Themes, Issues, and Debates*. 2nd ed. Boston: Longman, 2009.

Caputo, Richard. *Policy Analysis for Social Workers*. Thousand Oaks, CA: Sage Publications, 2013.

Chambers, Donald, and Kenneth Wedel. *Social Policy and Social Programs: A Method for the Practical Public Policy Analyst*. 6th ed. Boston: Pearson Education, 2013.

DiNitto, Diana, and Linda Cummins. *Social Welfare: Politics and Public Policy*. 7th ed. Boston: Allyn and Bacon, 2012.

Dolgoff, Ralph, and Donald Feldstein. *Understanding Social Welfare: A Search for Social Justice*. 9th ed. Boston: Pearson Education, 2013.

Fitzpatrick, Tony, Huck-ju Kwon, Nick Manning, James Midgely, and Gillian Pascall. *International Encyclopedia of Social Policy*. Clifton, NJ: Routledge, 2012.

Gilbert, Neil, and Paul Terrell. *Dimensions of Social Welfare Policy*. 8th ed. Boston: Allyn and Bacon, 2013.

Jansson, Bruce. *Social Welfare Policy: Advancing Social Justice Through Eight Policy Sectors*. Thousand Oaks, CA: Sage Publications, 2015.

Karger, Howard, and David Stoesz. *American Social Welfare Policy: A Pluralist Approach*. 7th ed. Boston: Pearson Education, 2013.

Karger, Howard, James Midgely, and Peter Kind. *Controversial Issues in Social Policy*. 5th ed. Boston: Pearson Education, 2013.

Libby, Pat, and Associates. *The Lobbying Strategy Handbook: 10 Steps to Advancing Any Cause Effectively*. Thousand Oaks, CA: Sage Publications, 2011.

Midgely, James. *Social Development: Theory and Practice*. Thousand Oaks, CA: Sage Publications, 2013.

National Association of Social Workers. *Social Work Speaks: NASW Policy Statements 2010–2014*. 8th ed. Washington, DC: NASW Press, 2014.

Popple, Philip R., and Leslie Leighninger. *The Policy-Based Profession: An Introduction to Social Welfare Policy Analysis for Social Workers*. 6th ed. Boston: Allyn and Bacon, 2014.

Rocha, Cynthia. *Essentials of Social Policy Practice*. Hoboken, NJ: John Wiley and Sons, 2007.

Segal, Elizabeth. *Social Welfare Policy and Social Programs: A Values Perspective*. 3rd ed. Florence, KY: Brooks Cole, 2013.

van Wormer, Katherine, and Rosemary Link. *Social Welfare Policy for a Sustainable Future: The U.S. in Global Context*. Thousand Oaks, CA: Sage Publications, 2015.

10

Cultural Competence

©FLOWERSTOCK / FOTOLIA

CHAPTER PREVIEW

This chapter focuses on *cultural competence in social work practice*, including a description of cultural competence, related concepts, and a discussion of the *levels of cultural competence* of both individual social workers and organizations. Emphasis is given to both client and social worker experiences, identities, and belief systems, including their impact on *cross-cultural interventions.* The domains of social worker–client relationships that are impacted by diversity are discussed, as well as the *common misinterpretations* of difference. The challenge of engaging in *lifelong efforts to achieve cultural competence* is presented. *Guidelines for culturally competence practice* for both social workers and organizations are presented.

Social workers and social services agencies are challenged to find ways to balance the value of diversity with the value of universal human development. They must be capable of recognizing, respecting, and accommodating differences while treating all clients with fairness and equality under the law. Agencies must be thoughtful and fair in decisions about who is eligible for the services they offer and how best to allocate limited resources. They must avoid discrimination based on all forms of diversity.

BACKGROUND AND CONTEXT

Culture refers to the learned patterns of thought and behavior that are passed from generation to generation. Culture consists of the unspoken and unquestioned assumptions and ideas about the nature of reality, the human condition, and how life should be lived. Everything we do is influenced by the ways of thinking, values, beliefs, expectations, and customs that make up our culture. Much of what constitutes culture is so normal to us that we do not think of it as culture. When we encounter another culture and its assumptions and patterns of behavior, that is often the time when cultural differences and sometimes *cultural differences and conflicts become apparent*. Professional knowledge, practice, social policies, and agency policies and procedures are shaped by culture. Broadly defined, culture includes not only references to ethnicity or background, but also such variables as age, religion, level of physical ability, and gender and sexual orientation. Each of these forms of diversity shapes clients' thoughts, behavior, and worldview.

That, of course, means that every time clients and social workers engage with each other, differences related to those diverse experiences will come into play with the *potential to influence all phases of the planned change process*. It is vital to understand that cultural differences may at times emerge as the most important factors to the success of the professional relationship. These differences may be more impactful than other components of that relationship such as client motivation, social worker genuineness, client ability, and social worker skills. Knowing this, we must develop the professional ability to acknowledge and bridge cultural differences. *Cultural competence* is the ability to effectively build such bridges across cultures and to use culturally appropriate helping strategies in all phases of the planned change process.

We are all limited by *ethnocentrism*, which is the tendency to assume that one's own culture is normal and even superior, and that it is an appropriate standard for judging the beliefs and behaviors of others. We cannot avoid being ethnocentric to some degree because our own beliefs, values, and patterns feel natural and normal and seem rooted in common sense and our daily lives. These are so integral to us that it is difficult to realize there are other ways of thinking and living. We must become aware of how our culture influences our thoughts, decisions, and actions in order to avoid misunderstanding our clients and failing to recognize and respect their unique culture. Such awareness is necessary at all levels of practice from micro to macro.

Ethnocentrism leads to the possibility that we do not actually recognize the importance of cultural differences; that we view these differences as having lesser value; and that we risk developing irrelevant, ineffective, or even harmful interventions for diverse clients because we do not understand them or what would be effective for them. Further, it is even possible for social workers to blame clients for the failure of interventions on clients when it is actually the lack of cultural understanding and competence on the part of the social worker that might explain the outcome.

Apply what you have learned previous to your practicum experience about *institutional discrimination*, which includes beliefs and practices that are embedded

---

Competency: Diversity and Difference in Practice

Behavior: Apply self-awareness and self-regulation to manage the influence of personal biases and values in working with diverse clients and constituencies.

Critical Thinking Question: In light of the dynamics of ethnocentrism, is it possible for an agency to assess its own level of cultural competency?

in laws, social structures, economic systems, and governmental or organizational policy. Because institutional discrimination is often pervasive and unacknowledged, it can cause great harm to members of certain groups. Examples often given of institutional racism include policies requiring English as a primary language, those restricting access to basic services by refugees or undocumented workers, and those that disallow benefits to same-sex partners. It is also possible for social workers to engage in *unintentional discrimination* that is usually understood as behavior rooted in denial of one's own racism or stereotypical thinking. In these cases, denial of our own biases precludes an honest self-assessment and may keep us from seeing our own limitations. Remember that even unintentional acts by social workers can cause harm to the client–social worker relationship.

Clients' *membership in minority groups* may have a more significant influence on their interaction with a social worker or agency than does their membership in a specific cultural group. Minority status is not simply a function of numbers. In a given society, a particular group may be in the majority in terms of percentage of the overall population, but still have minority status because it is discriminated against. For example, even though females are slightly more numerous than males, women are often considered a minority group because they have less power and control over their lives than do men, and because they experience prejudice and discrimination based on gender. Minority status may also be tied to age, sexual orientation, disability, socioeconomic status, educational background, or religion.

If clients perceive themselves as different from others or as less powerful and more vulnerable, these perceptions have an impact on their *help-seeking behavior*, how they expect to be treated, their level of trust in a social worker or agency, and what they consider to be a useful and relevant service or program. It is also important to note that clients' membership in a minority group does not automatically mean that they are experts on their culture, able to engage with social workers from different backgrounds, or have cultural competence themselves because of their minority status. A list of *client descriptors that impact cross-cultural interventions* follows. Consider these as you learn how to work with people different from you in terms of age, ethnicity, gender, sexual orientation, or other characteristics.

- *Cultural history* including cultural conflict and its impact on client social functioning
- *Personal experiences* with stereotyping, discrimination, and oppression
- Strength of *cultural identity* and its use in daily life
- Ability to *move between cultures*
- *Disparities* in income, health, and opportunity
- *Cumulative disadvantage* over the life span due to fewer resources
- Cumulative *cultural trauma* related to discrimination or oppression
- Cultural *resources, assets, and resiliency*
- Previous *experience with social workers* and social services programs
- Beliefs about *seeking help*
- Intersection and impact of *multiple forms of diversity* in one individual or group

Many of the issues related to diversity that the social work profession addresses are at their core *human rights issues* with national and international contexts. The work you will be doing in the practicum may be very personal and individual for one client or family, but it may also be tied to the human rights issues addressed by large human rights organizations and their declarations. Recall what you have learned about the *com-*

monality between general human rights and social work values and ethics. The profession of social work is committed to protecting the human rights of all people, and a commitment to these rights may also underlie the work of your agency. Clients who are stereotyped or discriminated against may in effect be denied their basic human rights. In order to understand how your practicum experience is related to an international focus on human rights, research the mission and programs of the following organizations. Making this connection can help you to build on the strongly held values of international organizations.

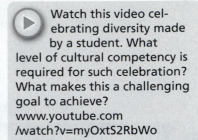

Watch this video celebrating diversity made by a student. What level of cultural competency is required for such celebration? What makes this a challenging goal to achieve? www.youtube.com /watch?v=myOxtS2RbWo

- United Nations Universal Declaration of Human Rights
- International Covenant on Economic, Social, and Cultural Relations
- International Federation of Social Workers
- Declaration of Human Responsibilities of the InterAction Council
- United Nations Convention on the Elimination of All Forms of Discrimination against Women
- United National Convention on the Rights of the Child
- Geneva Convention

Human Rights and Justice

Behavior: Apply and communicate understanding of the importance of diversity and difference in shaping life experiences in practice at the micro, mezzo, and macro levels.

Critical Thinking Question: How can a diversity perspective and a strengths perspective be used together?

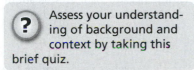

? Assess your understanding of background and context by taking this brief quiz.

GUIDANCE AND DIRECTION

No doubt you will work hard to be *culturally sensitive* and respectful of differences among people. However, you, like other people, may not always recognize your own biases, prejudices, or lack of knowledge regarding diverse groups. The practicum offers you an important opportunity for *self-examination and self-correction* in terms of such personal limitations. Seek opportunities for professional growth in cross-cultural work while you are a student, knowing that you will need to continue this learning throughout your career.

In your pursuit of *cultural sensitivity* and a desire to treat people equitably, you may believe that people are more alike than different and that treating all clients alike is fair and reasonable. However, these beliefs do not recognize the *importance and centrality of diversity* to the human experience. This may cause you to overlook unique aspects of a client's background and the powerful impact of minority status. Although it is true that people have much in common, it is also true that there are significant differences and that these can greatly affect social work practice. A balance between treating diverse people equally and yet individually based on their differences is not easy to achieve, but is an important goal. All people are entitled to be treated equally, but ignoring the differences between people can be dismissive of the centrality of culture to your clients.

Recognize the *positive experiences resulting from minority group status*, such as ethnic pride, bilingual abilities, community solidarity, extended family cohesion, and a strong sense of history. These experiences are strengths on which a professional relationship and a possible intervention can be built. Do not assume that membership in a minority group has only negative implications. Work to understand any negative experiences your clients may have had because of their minority status, such as discrimination in school, housing, or employment; inappropriate placement in foster homes; or threats and violence in the form of hate crimes. Remember that many personal problems such as depression, poverty, dropping out of school, substance abuse, suicide, and even physical illness may have some roots in the stress and inner turmoil a person feels when subjected to discrimination or oppression.

If you are a member of a minority group, you may be better able to understand the effects of prejudice and discrimination than those who are not, as well as the unique benefits that are a result of such membership. In order for you as a social worker to be objective and to perceive the uniqueness of each client situation, it is also important for you to have **satisfactorily resolved** any related personal issues, anger, and resentment related to your experiences. However, such negative experiences of personal discrimination or marginalization can also work to your advantage by providing motivation and passion for the work you may do with others who are experiencing oppression. If you have experienced discrimination because of your minority status, do not assume your minority clients will have the same experiences or conclusions about them as you have.

Practice-informed Research

Behavior: Apply critical thinking to engage in critical analysis of quantitative and qualitative research methods and research findings.

Critical Thinking Question: What evidence exists to support the effectiveness of culturally sensitive interventions with diverse clients and groups? What evidence exists to describe the impact of the use of culturally insensitive interventions?

Social work with diverse clients is complex and demanding. Stereotypical adaptations of usual social work approaches or slight changes in the agency's standard operating procedures are not likely to be effective. Rather, you will need to develop distinct, **culturally appropriate methods** that are acceptable, relevant to, and appropriate for the specific group with which you are working, and this necessitates involving them in any such steps.

Be alert to the fact that misunderstandings and misinterpretations in cross-cultural interactions can occur in many areas and situations including:

- **Spoken and written language** including words, accents, meanings, and nuances
- **Nonverbal communication** such as misunderstanding gestures, facial expressions, touch, and eye contact
- **Verbal communication** including tone of voice, word choice, turn-taking
- **Interpersonal differences** such as appropriate level of directness, assertiveness, and self-disclosure
- **Beliefs** about gender relations and appropriate touching and expressions of attraction for another person
- Judgments concerning **appearance**, appropriate dress, body ornamentation, and level of modesty
- **Views of time**, including emphasis on punctuality, use of time, and future planning
- Beliefs about **physical and personal space** and appropriate distance between people
- Ways of **learning and teaching** including giving and taking direction
- Ways of **negotiating and handling conflict** including direct and indirect communication
- Ways of **expressing emotion** such as externalizing or internalizing feelings

- *Help-seeking beliefs* and use of professional or culturally valued helpers
- Differences in *definition of family* and the involvement of family in social work interventions

In an effort to *see your agency from the perspective of diverse clients*, examine its physical environment, written materials, internal policies, and staffing patterns. Assess whether your agency is accessible to persons with disabilities. Look to see if reading material, posters, and artwork would appeal to diverse groups of people, including language adaptations and visual representations of people from a variety of backgrounds. Read agency written materials to determine if they are free of bias and whether they use inclusive language. Finally, learn if the agency staff is diverse and represents people of various ages, cultures, sexual orientations, and other backgrounds. Take advantage of any training in working with diverse populations that might be available to you as a student.

Recognize that different groups may hold very different *beliefs about the nature and cause of personal problems*. For example, some ethnic groups may view depression or physical illness as primarily a problem of spirituality (e.g., a consequence of eating a taboo food, having broken one's relationship with God, or of a lack of balance between one's spirit and body). These deeply held beliefs will significantly impact the ways in which clients may approach, seek, or accept the services of social workers and other professionals.

Seek to understand your clients' beliefs about the appropriateness of asking for help and receiving help from professionals and agencies. Members of some ethnic groups may believe that personal and family problems should not be discussed with anyone outside the family. Some may feel great shame if they must seek help from a stranger. Others may prefer to seek help from religious leaders, and some may view social workers with mistrust for historical reasons such as discriminatory agency or social policies.

Engagement

Behavior: Use empathy, reflection, and interpersonal skills to effectively engage diverse clients and constituencies.

Critical Thinking Question: How would your clients' cultural beliefs about seeking help, especially from those outside of their culture, impact your ability to engage with them?

Different groups have different ideas about what is an appropriate method of helping and who has the capacity and authority to help with or treat certain types of problems. Some people may choose to use *informal helpers and spiritual leaders*, prayer, purification ceremonies, and religious or cultural rituals rather than the services of a professional helper. You will need to learn how to work cooperatively with cultural spiritual leaders, healers, and clergy. Expect to learn from them about approaches to helping that are valued by your clients.

Remember that clients from a minority group may have had or may anticipate having negative experiences when they must have contact with social workers or social agencies, based on their group's history with those outside their group. Clients may also be fearful of interacting with social workers because they fear legal recrimination for themselves (e.g., undocumented workers or LGBT clients living in states with discriminatory practices). Their fears may be a barrier to their development of trust and their willingness to invest themselves in a professional helping relationship. Be careful not to interpret such mistrust, fear, or anger as client resistance.

Be careful when *interpreting and assigning meaning to differences* in behavior, communication, language, and ways of engaging in the helping process. For example, do not automatically interpret client quietness, reticence, or anxiety as pathology or dysfunction. Silence may mean respect or it may signal that the client does not feel understood or valued. When appropriate, acknowledge to your clients that you recognize the differences that separate you, and show your appreciation for their struggles by validating their experiences and perspectives. Remember that your level of cultural competence may be more important in your work with diverse clients than your overall knowledge and skill in social work.

Since *we use ourselves as the tool to help others*, if we are not culturally competent, the use of self is greatly compromised. Table 10.1 lists a number of beliefs

Table 10.1   Beliefs and Resulting Barriers to Cultural Competence

Belief	Resulting Barrier to Cultural Competence
"All people are alike."	Devaluing difference
"People are more like than they are different."	Devaluing difference
"It is best to be color blind."	Ignoring/dismissing difference
"As long as I care about my client, I don't need to adapt."	Naïveté about need for cultural competence
"Clients need to be bicultural."	Judgment and unwillingness to adapt intervention
"All . . . act the same."	Stereotyping and overgeneralizing
"Minority groups should forget about the past."	Dismissing individual and cultural history/ oppression
"Agency policy requires us to treat everyone the same."	Devaluing difference
"I have no biases."	Lack of self-awareness
"How can I be expected to understand all cultures?"	Defensiveness regarding cultural competency
"There is too much emphasis on being politically correct."	Dismissing meaning and importance of language
"If a client doesn't tell me something, how should I know?"	Dismissing communication differences
"These people are so amazing."	Romanticizing of diverse groups
" . . . are so resistant and unmotivated."	Inability to recognize meaning of behavior
"The reason this person is doing this is because of their culture."	Attributing too much to cultural difference
"This is how we deal with . . ."	Stereotyping and use of inappropriate intervention
"Don't be disappointed if they don't do well."	Low expectations for diverse groups, blaming client for ineffective intervention, and not recognizing client definition of success

that might be held by social workers engaged in cross-cultural practice. Statements made to clients that are based on such beliefs can be significant barriers to effective professional relationships and the outcome of interventions. Consider how these beliefs might be considered inappropriate, limited in cultural sensitivity, or offensive in working with diverse clients. Think about the list of negative impacts these beliefs might have and reflect on any of your own beliefs that might lead to similar negative outcomes.

Each of the beliefs in Table 10.1 that are held by social workers have the potential to undermine and limit the effectiveness of the professional relationship with diverse clients, showing a lack of understanding and even misinterpretation of what is said and done by clients. This lack of understanding can easily lead to inappropriate interventions and false cooperation by clients who believe they must go along with a treatment plan even if it does not fit for them. Remember that there can be a big difference between what is said and what is heard, which is because of different communication patterns. There may be questions that should not be asked because they violate cultural values and beliefs, and others that need to be asked in order to more fully understand clients' situations.

> Watch this short video on cultural humility. What are the three concepts presented as important to learning about and relating to diverse populations? https://www.youtube.com/watch?v=_Mbu8bvKb_U

Developing competence in working with diverse people and acquiring knowledge about diverse client groups required for culturally competent practice will be a long-term, even lifelong process. Relish the possibilities available to you as you venture into work with clients and communities that are very different from you. Remain aware of the limitations of your ability to understand others' experiences and your interpretations of them. Even skilled and experienced social workers cannot know the intricacies of every culture or minority group, so try to learn about the world of others in an authentic way. For this reason, it is likely true that we can never truly be culturally competent. It is also likely that believing you are culturally competent can actually present a barrier because we may stop trying to learn and develop more cultural competence skills.

Ethical and Professional Behavior

Behavior: Make ethical decisions by applying the standards of the National Association of Social Workers (NASW) Code of Ethics, relevant laws and regulations, models for ethical decision making, ethical conduct of research, and additional codes of ethics as appropriate to context.

Critical Thinking Question: Upon which NASW ethical principles is cultural competence based?

Several important motivations for engaging in *ongoing development of cultural competence* are listed here. Reflect on them to understand why cultural competence will need to be enhanced over a career, and how these reasons go to the core beliefs, experiences, and assumptions of social workers.

- Our *cultural identity* is central to all aspects of our relationships and interactions.
- Our *social reality* may be very different from that of our clients.
- The way we are *socialized* to view difference may positively or negatively impact our ability to relate to people who are different from us.
- We operate on *unconscious or conscious assumptions* about people and the world that we may not be aware of until they are challenged in some way.
- We *process information* about people based on these assumptions.
- Our *values* shape the way we view others.
- Our sense of *cultural identity* is so strong within us that encounters with diverse people may cause discomfort, fear, or judgment.

- Our *social systems and peers* tend to support our assumptions and beliefs, not challenging our views of diverse peoples' experiences.
- Our *rhetoric about being culturally competent* may not be consistent with the actual reality of our professional behavior.

Develop what is called a *dual perspective*, which is the ability to focus simultaneously on the attitudes, values, and customs of the larger society and the attitudes, values, and customs of the individual client or family. Doing this while being aware of the impact of your own values, attitudes, and customs will help you more effectively relate to diverse clients, understand how they are impacted by the larger society, and at least partially view your clients' experiences from their point of view and not just your own.

Work to develop the ability to move between your culture and that of your clients, recognizing that this can be done only partially in spite of your best efforts because of ethnocentrism. Expand your knowledge of diverse people, increasing your awareness of the impact of your own cultural identity on your work. Recognize that communication with your clients and their communication with you are both seen through personal and cultural filters. Doing so will reduce the chances of misinterpretation and inappropriate interventions, while increasing the chances that an effective professional relationship will set the stage for a culturally appropriate and effective intervention. Remember that your own position in relation to your clients may be one of privilege. If so, try to understand how clients might view you, look for commonalities while respecting difference, challenge oppression, learn from your clients, work to identify any biases, and equalize power when you can.

Agencies sometimes intentionally or unintentionally adopt attitudes, engage in behavior, and enact agency policies that reinforce stereotypes, widen the gap between social workers and clients, and eventually result in clients choosing to separate themselves from these agencies. Watch for agency attitudes, behaviors, and policies that might be uninformed, stereotypical, or culturally inappropriate. Seek out opportunities to work with diverse clients so that you can avoid adopting such stereotypes or attitudes yourself.

Honestly study yourself, other social workers, and your agency to assess their level of cultural competence. Is your agency working to serve diverse clients well and appropriately? Does it engage in the practices listed in Table 10.2 to enhance its ability to work with diverse clients? What else might it do to increase its organizational competence, given the fact that true cultural competence is probably never fully achieved by either individual social workers or social agencies? Table 10.2 illustrates a number of major practice guidelines for culturally competent practice that should be followed by both individual social workers and organizations.

Remember that social problems are likely to impact minority groups more than other groups and individuals. The *disproportionate consequences* of social problems for populations that may be underserved, underrepresented, lower in socioeconomic status, or subject to discrimination need to be identified and addressed by social workers who work with such clients. Think of these disparities as *human rights*

Table 10.2   Guidelines for Cultural Competence in Practice

Guidelines for Social Workers

Professional Development	Interactions with Clients
Learn the history of diverse groups served by the agency.	Adapt communication styles.
Recognize the limits of cultural competence.	Adapt all phases of the planned change process, including assessment tools, practice theories and models, and definitions of success.
Seek training in cultural competence.	Resist tendency to overgeneralize about and stereotype diverse groups of people.
Utilize supervision for professional growth.	Resist tendency to become defensive if interactions become challenging.
Remember the impossibility of being culturally neutral.	Work to understand how clients view us and our agency, including help-seeking values.
Pursue opportunities to engage with diverse groups.	Utilize strengths perspective with clients.

Guidelines for Organizations

Organizational Development	Interactions with Client Groups
Learn the history of diverse groups served by the agency.	Conduct outreach activities.
Develop inclusive written materials.	Design inviting physical environment.
Train staff in cultural competence.	Develop culturally appropriate agency policies.
Diversify staff.	Develop culturally appropriate practice models.
Develop culturally sensitive agency policies.	Include feedback from diverse groups into program evaluation.
Recognize limitations of a charity orientation to providing services.	Commit to have client base reflect the makeup of the community.
Remember the impossibility of being culturally neutral.	Learn about and develop best practices in cross-cultural social work.
Include commitment to diverse groups and cultural competence in agency mission.	Develop comprehensive and varied referral network.
Maintain compliance with federal laws on antidiscriminatory practices.	Provide accommodations for persons with disabilities.
Maintain compliance with state and local laws on antidiscriminatory practices.	Provide accommodations for persons whose first language is not English or who use sign language.

issues and work hard to understand what societal attitudes, conditions, and policies contribute to them.

In order to understand specifically how cultural competency positively impacts the success of interventions and how *cultural incompetence* negatively impacts the success of interventions, refer to Table 10.3. Consider how your level of cultural competence will influence how successful or unsuccessful interventions might be.

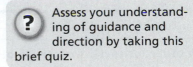
? Assess your understanding of guidance and direction by taking this brief quiz.

Table 10.3   Impact of Cultural Competence and Incompetence on Social Work Practice

Components of Cultural Competency	Impact of Cultural Competence	Impact of Cultural Incompetence
Knowledge Understands meaning of culture and is aware of history of diverse groups and intergroup relations, knowledgeable about social policy impact on diverse groups, and insightful about impact of diversity on social development and functioning	**Understanding** Results in multilevel interventions that consider history and context, incorporate history and diversity, and influence social policies	**Misunderstanding and lack of information** Results in less effective multilevel interventions not based on history and context, ignores history and diversity, and does not challenge social policies
Self-awareness Aware of how personal history and experience influence practice; understands impact of privilege and oppression experiences; works to reduce own biases, stereotypes, and ethnocentricity	**Recognizes biases** Increases accuracy of assessment of clients based on personal experience, aware of own privilege or oppression, and works to address biases and stereotypes	**Operates on biases** Prone to inaccurate assessment of clients based on personal experience, lacks awareness of own privilege or oppression, and unaware of need to address biases and stereotypes that negatively impact clients
Values Focuses on social work values such as social justice and appreciation of diversity, works for equality and empowerment, works to alleviate oppression, and promote human rights	**Incorporates social work values into interventions** Bases multilevel interventions on social justice and human rights, includes cultural differences in intervention, and empowers clients to reduce oppression	**Unaware of relevance of social work values** Does not recognize how social justice and human rights provide foundation for practice, unaware of impact of inequality, and lack of power on client functioning and intervention success
Skills Incorporates culturally competent communication skills in assessment, planning, implementation, and evaluation at micro, mezzo, and macro levels of practice	**Uses culturally competent approaches** Designs and implements culturally appropriate interventions, uses culturally appropriate evaluation techniques and standards, and is more likely to be effective	**Uses culturally inappropriate approaches** Designs and implements culturally inappropriate interventions, uses culturally inappropriate evaluation techniques and standards, and is less likely to be effective

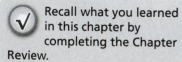 Recall what you learned in this chapter by completing the Chapter Review.

Cultural Competence Audit: A Workbook Activity

In order for social workers to become and remain culturally competent, it is vital to have a concise format to use in completing an audit of their cultural competence as well as that of their agencies. It is also important to utilize the results of such audits to work continuously toward meeting diverse clients' expectations. In consultation with your field instructor, conduct a cultural competence audit of your practicum agency. This will require you to gather information, ask questions sensitively and without judgment, and to process your findings with your supervisor. In the following table, list the areas of strength you identified in your audit, as well as the needs for ongoing development that you see. Suggest strategies that your agency could use to grow in its cultural competence.

Strengths in Cultural Competence	Needs for Development of Cultural Competence	Strategies for Development of Cultural Competence

Cultural Examples to Consider: A Workbook Activity

Many factors influence the behavior and decisions of clients. One important set of factors, but certainly not the only one, is the client's cultural and ethnic background. A list of situations that a social worker might encounter follows. Read each one carefully and answer each of the following questions for all of the situations.

A. What *diverse beliefs, values, minority status, or customs* are operating in this situation that might explain or clarify the client's behavior or choices?

B. What *individual, family, or cultural strengths* might be identified in these situations?

C. How might these *situations be misunderstood* if you are not familiar with the beliefs and customs of the client?

D. What *additional information or skills* would you need to be competent in this situation?

1. A low-income couple with six children lives in a small and crowded house and has great difficulty financially. They choose to have additional children, which will strain the family even more financially.
   A. _____
   B. _____
   C. _____
   D. _____

2. The family of a hospital patient moves into the hospital room and begins using cultural healing practices unknown to the medical staff.
   A. _____
   B. _____
   C. _____
   D. _____

3. A family with a child who is deaf refuses to let him learn sign language.

   A. _____

   B. _____

   C. _____

   D. _____

4. A family with conservative religious views will only accept services from faith-based organizations.

   A. _____

   B. _____

   C. _____

   D. _____

5. A family chooses to home school their children and refuses to cooperate with the governmental guidelines regarding the education of their children.

   A. _____

   B. _____

   C. _____

   D. _____

6. An enrolled member of an American Indian tribe is in need of social services, but is reluctant to accept them from an agency that provides these services to individuals and families from many different backgrounds.

   A. _____

   B. _____

   C. _____

   D. _____

7. A family eligible for needed social services available on proof of citizenship chooses not to use these services.

   A. _____

   B. _____

   C. _____

   D. _____

8. An elderly woman who could benefit from mental health services declines them.

   A. _____

   B. _____

   C. _____

   D. _____

9. A student with a severe learning disability refuses university-provided accommodations and is in danger of being placed on academic probation because her grade-point average is following the university requirement for good academic standing.

A. _____

B. _____

C. _____

D. _____

Organizational Cases to Consider: A Workbook Activity

Respond to the following statements that might be made by leaders and employees of social services agencies in regard to their work with diverse groups. Identify a social work value related to this situation that might guide a response. Refer to the NASW Standards for Cultural Competence in Social Work Practice that describes the ways in which social workers and agencies are to conduct themselves in regard to cultural competence.

Agency Statement	Value-Based Response
"We do not serve many diverse clients."	
"Clients of color tend to go to agencies that focus on their specific needs rather than coming to us."	
"It shouldn't matter if our employees are mostly white."	
"We don't discriminate. We offer the same services to people from all groups."	
"We provide annual training in cultural competence to all our employees."	
"Some groups expect accommodations that are not reasonable and that we cannot provide."	

Suggested Learning Activities

- Attend cultural and religious celebrations and activities that are meaningful to many of the clients or consumers served by your agency (e.g., powwows, religious ceremonies, and gay pride events).

- Invite respected members of various ethnic and religious groups to explain how cultural and religious factors might influence clients' perceptions of the agency's programs and services and whether they would be inclined to use those services.

- Listen to music and read books and poetry by members of cultural or minority groups served by your agency.

- Visit agencies that specifically serve members of minority groups (e.g., refugee programs, women's centers, gay and lesbian community centers, and advocacy groups for persons with disabilities). Ask how their programs differ from yours.

- Seek special training designed to help human services personnel respond more effectively to diverse clients.

- Examine assessment tools used in your agency to determine if they are culture-bound or culturally inappropriate.

- Seek opportunities for cultural immersion experiences.

Suggested Readings

Anderson, Joseph, and Robin Wiggins Carter, eds. *Diversity Perspectives for Social Work Practice*. Boston: Allyn and Bacon, 2003.

Appleby, George A., Edgar Colon, and Julia Hamilton. *Diversity, Oppression, and Social Functioning: Person-in-Environment Assessment and Intervention*. 3rd ed. Boston: Allyn and Bacon, 2011.

Chin, Jean. *Diversity and Leadership*. Thousand Oaks, CA: Sage Publications, 2014.

Dhooper, Sirjit Singh, and Sharon S. Moore. *Social Work Practice with Culturally Diverse People*. Thousand Oaks, CA: Sage Publications, 2000.

Dominelli, Lena. *Anti-Racist Social Work*. 3rd ed. New York: Palgrave MacMillan, 2008.

Gerstein, Lawrence, P. Paul Heppner, Stefania Aegisdottir, Ming A. Leung, and Kathryn Norsworthy. *Essentials of Cross-Cultural Counseling*. Thousand Oaks, CA: Sage Publications, 2011.

Hunt, Matthew. *Race, Racial Attitudes and Stratification Beliefs*. Thousand Oaks, CA: Sage Publications, 2011.

Lee, Courtland. *Multicultural Issues in Counseling: New Approaches to Diversity*. 4th ed. Hoboken, NJ: Wiley and Sons.

Leon-Guerrero, Anna, and Chave Frankfort-Nachmais. *Essentials of Social Statistics for a Diverse Society*. Thousand Oaks, CA: Sage Publications, 2015.

Lum, Doman. *Culturally Competent Practice: A Framework for Understanding Diverse Groups and Justice Issues*. 4th ed. Florence, KY: Brooks/Cole, 2011.

National Association of Social Workers. *NASW Standards for Cultural Competence in Social Work Practice*. Washington, DC: NASW Press, 2007.

Paniagua, Freddy. *Assessing and Treating Culturally Diverse Clients*. New York: Sage, 2013.

Rothman, Juliet. *Cultural Competence in Process and Practice: Building Bridges*. Boston: Allyn and Bacon, 2008.

Shaefer, Richard. *Racial and Ethnic Groups*. 13th ed. Upper Saddle River, NJ: Prentice Hall, 2012.

Sisneros, Jose, Catherine Stakeman, Mildred C. Joyner, and Catheryne L. Schmitz. *Critical Multicultural Social Work*. Chicago: Lyceum, 2008.

Sue, Donald, and David Sue. *Counseling the Culturally Diverse: Theory and Practice*. 6th ed. New York: John Wiley and Sons, Inc., 2013.

Wronka, James. *Human Rights and Social Justice: Social Action and Service for the Helping and Health Professions*. Thousand Oaks, CA: Sage Publications, 2007.

11

Professional Social Work

©GEORGE WADA / FOTOLIA

LEARNING OUTCOMES

- Describe the enhancement of social functioning as the domain of the social work profession.
- Move from the role of practicum student to that of a professional social worker.
- Summarize the knowledge and skills required of social work roles.
- Research the licensing requirements for social workers at all levels of practice.

CHAPTER PREVIEW

This chapter focuses on the profession of social work, including social functioning, which is the unique domain of social work practice. It offers information on *professional social work behavior,* moving from the role of practicum student to the role of professional social worker, and skills expected of the *generalist social worker* at the micro, mezzo, and macro levels. It discusses the variety of *social work roles* required and offers insight into the balance of the *art and science of social work practice.*

Social work is one of many helping professions. Social workers often work closely with other helpers such as physicians, nurses, speech therapists, psychologists, substance abuse counselors, and school counselors. It is important to understand what it is that social workers do that is not done by the members of other helping professions. Each profession, including social work, has characteristics and responsibilities that are unique to them.

BACKGROUND AND CONTEXT

All professions are expected to be unique and all professionals are expected to have special and unique knowledge and skills. They understand certain phenomena better than those who do not have this special training. Because they adhere to a code of ethical conduct, their clients and the public at large can expect ethical conduct and behavior from them. They are accountable for their decisions and actions. Professionals also lay claim to a certain domain of activities, which is the basis for professional licensing and certification. From a legal perspective, professionals are responsible for providing their clients with a certain standard of care, and if they fail to do so, they may be sued for malpractice or professional negligence. Broadly speaking, a *profession* is an occupation that possesses certain characteristics:

- A *sense of "calling"* to the profession by those entering it by virtue of their values, interests, or natural abilities
- Unique *body of knowledge and theories* from which special skills and techniques are derived
- *Unique set of skills and abilities* to perform professional tasks that other professionals or persons cannot perform
- Set of *professional values and a written code of ethics* that guide practice activities
- *Professional, accredited education* for those entering the profession
- Practitioners who share a distinct *culture, specialized language* or *terminology, sense of purpose, identity, history, and set of values*
- *Capacity and authority*, usually by law, *to regulate practice*, admitting new members and ensuring quality of services to clients
- *Sanction by the community or state* to perform certain activities

Social workers see themselves as professionals and they describe their occupation as a profession. As a social work student you are expected to behave in a professional manner during your practicum, so it is important to understand exactly what a profession is and what professional behavior looks like. How does one decide whether clients are treated in a truly professional manner and always receive professional services? Does the presence of professionally trained social workers in an agency have an observable and positive effect on the nature and quality of the services received by clients?

The social work profession uniquely assumes responsibility for promoting the social functioning of individuals, families, and communities at the *micro, mezzo*, and *macro levels*. This means that social workers not only provide services to individuals, families, groups, organizations, and communities, but just as importantly work to implement social policies and promote societal conditions that will also support social functioning. The term *social functioning* refers to the social well-being of people and especially their capacity and opportunity to meet their basic needs such as food, shelter, safety, and self-worth, and to satisfactorily perform their social roles such as spouse, parent, student, employee, and citizen. It is the promotion of social functioning that is the unique focus and domain of the profession.

Intervention

Behavior: Critically choose and implement interventions to achieve practice goals and enhance capacities of clients and constituencies.

In what circumstances might a social worker be expected to simultaneously intervene at the micro and macro levels?

A profession can be viewed as an organized effort to actualize its core values. Social work is often described as a *values-driven profession* because so much of what a social worker does is guided by a particular set of core values. However, all professions are rooted in a particular set of values. The social work profession has a foundation of values that include service, equality, promotion of human rights, and working toward social justice. These social work values are at play in all of the interactions social workers have with clients, and form the basis for their work. You will find it interesting to think about, observe, and participate in interventions that are intentionally based on social work values.

The social work profession holds high standards for its members, including the demonstration of professional behavior. This is vital for you as a new social worker to understand, because adhering to these standards will help to ensure that clients receive the highest quality of services. Engaging in nonprofessional behavior puts clients at risk, reduces the quality of services, undermines the public image of the profession, and may violate the profession's ethical principles. Although social work is a profession, social workers may or may not behave in a professional manner. Nonprofessional behavior leads to diminished quality of services and may also violate the National Association of Social Workers (NASW) *Code of Ethics*.

 ? Assess your understanding of background and context by taking this brief quiz.

GUIDANCE AND DIRECTION

A big challenge you will face in your practicum, but hopefully one you will take on enthusiastically, is making the transition from the status of student to the role and expectations of a professional social worker. As a student in the classroom, you were allowed to listen without responding or to learn about theory without having to apply it. In the practicum, all that changes. Consider how the roles of student and social worker differ, as shown in Table 11.1.

Intervention

Behavior: Select appropriate intervention strategies based on the assessment, research knowledge, and values and preferences of clients and constituencies.

Critical Thinking Question: What is your plan for integrating with you learned in the classroom setting with the real world demands of selecting appropriate interventions with actual clients and client systems?

Table 11.1 Student Versus Social Worker Role

Student Role	Social Worker Role
Learns passively	Learns actively and applies learning
Engages in theoretical discussions and hypothetical decisions	Applies theory to real clients
Has occasional absences from class or practicum without consequence to self or client	Needs to be fully present to ensure quality
Defers to others in decision making and intervention	Takes initiative in developing and implementing interventions
Assumes partial responsibility	Assumes full responsibility
Bases work on theory and academic preparation	Bases work on academic preparation as well as accumulated experience and practice wisdom
May take client feedback personally and react emotionally	Sees client feedback as crucial to professional growth

As you move from the role of **student to professional**, evaluate yourself honestly in terms of where you are on the continuum between the two. Push yourself to leave a passive and partial student role behind, choosing to do whatever you can to assume the roles and responsibilities of a professional. Do not wait until you are in your first social work position to make this transition. Your future clients deserve the highest level of professionalism you can offer when you are a student as much as they will when you have finished your education and training.

A primary purpose of the practicum is to help you develop a **professional identity** as a social worker. To achieve this identity means that you have a clear understanding of the purpose of the profession, your roles and responsibilities as a social worker, the

> This video highlights the variety of professional roles played by social workers. How does it reinforce the need for generalist preparation for social work practice? www.youtube.com /watch?v=M3hzv4z3aHQ

profession's core values and ethical guidelines, and the skills and knowledge needed to perform social work tasks and activities. You can begin developing a professional identity by observing other social workers and reflecting on their behavior, decisions, and attitudes. You will notice all of the professional social work roles that you learned about in the classroom being played out in real-life situations. Tables 11.2, 11.3, and 11.4 illustrate the **social work roles** played at the micro, mezzo, and macro levels of social work practice, accompanied by the major **social work skills** required at each level of practice.

Read the **job or position description** for social workers in your agency and determine if it is consistent with the profession's stated purposes, values, and practice roles. Watch for variation between how social workers define their own roles and responsibilities and how their roles may be defined by administrators or funding sources. Ask your field instructor or other social workers how they attempt to meet the expectations of high-level administrators and fiscal managers while still adhering to the mission and purpose of the profession and fulfilling their obligations to their clients.

You will begin to notice how the values, knowledge base, and approach of the social work professional are different from those of other helping professionals such as clinical

Table 11.2   Micro-Level Practice Roles: Required Social Work Knowledge and Skills

Social Work Role	Knowledge Required	Skills Required
Advocate	Understand social policy, programs, and policies	Identify resources and gaps
Broker	Know resources, service systems, and gaps in services	Match services to clients by through appropriate referrals and linkages
Case manager	Understand how to meet client needs from client perspective	Monitor, manage, and coordinate services
Counselor	Understand orienting theories and practice models	Utilize practice models to address the client's psychosocial needs
Educator	Identify educational needs of clients and others	Provide education to address identified needs
Mediator	Understand dynamics of interpersonal conflict and resolution	Utilize techniques to resolve conflicts that promote social functioning
Networker	Understand dynamics of social systems	Promote linkages between individuals and/or social systems

Table 11.3   Mezzo-Level Practice Roles: Required Social Work Knowledge and Skills

Social Work Role	Knowledge Required	Skills Required
Administrator	Understand organizational structure, dynamics, and development	Utilize techniques of supervision and administration
Facilitator	Understand interactions of social systems and stakeholders in practice situations	Promote communication within social systems and progress toward mutual goals
Mediator	Understand dynamics of conflict between groups and organizations	Utilize conflict resolution techniques that promote the interest of involved parties
Program developer	Know how to assess need for program developer and how to implement vision	Utilize organizational skills to design and develop programs to address identified needs

psychologists, nurses, school counselors, physicians, and vocational counselors. The uniqueness of the social work profession will become apparent if you truly understand the profession's core values and ethical principles, as well as the concept of social functioning. The **uniqueness of the social work profession** lies in its commitment to the overall social functioning of people as well as its commitment to working for social change and social justice. However, contrary to the beliefs of many social work students, social work is not unique because it pays attention to the whole person, the client's environment, and the ecological perspective. These are ideas also commonly discussed in textbooks for nursing, education, counseling, and occupational therapy. The distinctive identity of social work comes from its commitment to both enhancing the social functioning of clients and creating social environments, conditions, and social policies that promote positive social functioning.

Enhancing social functioning occurs at all levels of social work practice. Individuals and families can improve their ability to fulfill their own needs through social work

Table 11.4   Macro-Level Practice Roles: Required Social Work Knowledge and Skills

Social Work Role	Knowledge Required	Skills Required
Community developer	Understand conditions within communities that need to be addressed to build community capacity and strengthen social bonds	Support community goals and address community needs to strengthen community's ability to support residents
Community organizer	Know community needs and community readiness for social change	Promote social change that focuses on an identified social need or problem
Policy analyst/developer	Understand the impact of social policy on clients and the process for forming and influencing social policy	Build coalitions, mobilize resources, and effect social change through policy formation
Researcher	Familiarity with research approaches, methodology, and ethics	Conduct research to build knowledge base about social conditions and problems and evaluate the effectiveness of programs, models, and policies
Social planner	Understand social movements and macro-level planned change	Systematically influence societal attitudes, policies, programs, and institutions

intervention. Groups can be developed and improved as they work to enhance social functioning of groups of people. Organizations who promote social functioning can be established. Community well-being can be promoted, which in turn promotes the social functioning of those who reside within it. Finally, social policy practice can enhance social functioning through social policy development that supports individuals, families, and communities. Tables 11.2, 11.3, and 11.4 illustrate in condensed form how this can happen. Table 11.2 lists the common social work roles at the micro level and describes the *basic or advanced knowledge and skills* required to fulfill these roles. Table 11.3 lists the common social work roles at the mezzo level, and describes the knowledge and skills required to fulfill these mezzo-level roles. Table 11.4 lists the common social work roles at the macro level, and describes the knowledge and skills required to fulfill these macro-level roles. Use these tables to help you understand what exact roles you will be playing in your practicum, and think about what knowledge and skills you will need to fulfill these roles effectively.

Professional licensing and certifications are important facets of the social work profession, and it is vital to research and understand what you will be required to do in order to become licensed in your state. Each state has its own statutes regulating the licensing of social workers, but there are also commonalities between them. The following facets of the licensing process must be understood in order to plan for becoming licensed if you choose to do so, or if you are required to do so by the laws in your state.

- *Educational requirements*

  Some states have only one level of licensure based on the level of education in social work achieved, and some states have multilevel licensure for various levels of education in social work. This includes the BSW, MSW, DSW, and PhD levels of academic preparation.

- *Scope of practice*

  Depending on the scope, focus, and responsibilities of practice, a certain level of licensure will be required in some states. For example, states will give specific descriptive terms to these licenses, such as *clinical social worker* or *independent social worker*.

- *Supervised Experience*

  States require a specified number of hours of professional social work experience, usually post-degree, and these hours must be supervised by those with specific credentials and possibly also by those with training in supervision. These hours, usually from 1,000 to 3,000, must be acquired over a certain period of time, be documented, cover certain areas of professional tasks, and be supervised. Some agencies provide supervision by other licensed social workers employed in the agency, and others may not offer this. They may help you pay for the supervision you need, but require you to obtain this supervision yourself. At times you may have to pay the entire cost of supervision and arrange for it on your own.

- *Licensing Examination*

  A written examination is required and varies based on the level of licensure the candidate seeks. The Association of Social Work Boards (ASWB) provides the examinations used by most states, and offers four levels of examinations.

Each state selects the examinations most closely aligned with their licensing requirements. ASWB offers information about the examinations, a tutorial on how to take examinations, and online practice tests. In addition, a number of private organizations sell licensing examination preparation courses, which guide candidates for licensing through the preparation process, including sample questions and feedback.

Speak to your practicum supervisor and your faculty supervisor about licensing in your state or states in which you may practice. Learn about and try to understand the requirements so that if and when you pursue licensure, you will be ready to begin the process quickly. Make connections with other licensed social workers and ask about their experiences with licensure, including their recommendations and possible pitfalls you can avoid if you have adequate information and preparation.

Following licensure, social workers are required to engage in and document what is called *continuing education*. A certain number of hours will be required each year in order to maintain an active license, and documentation of these hours will be required annually or perhaps when requested by a random audit of licensees. Start now to identify sources of potential continuing education, which can include conferences, in-service education within agencies, academic courses, webinars, and other online training. Some states have required annual hours of continuing education in specific areas of practice, such as social work ethics. They usually only accept continuing education that is preapproved by the state agency that licenses social workers.

Maintaining one's licensure in good standing is very important for social workers and their clients. To maintain good standing, social workers must provide quality services. States have provisions for clients, employers, or members of the public who wish to file complaints about licensed social workers. Complaints may be about ethical violations, breach of contract, practicing outside one's level of training or competence, or inappropriate dual relationships. State licensing boards will investigate any such complaints and issue their findings, which sometimes result in professional sanctions or loss of licensure. It is vital that you understand what constitutes such unprofessional behavior, particularly to the degree that might result in the loss of a license.

The licensing requirements for social work vary from state to state, and a license obtained in one state may or may not be accepted in another state. This is called *reciprocity*, and it is not necessarily available between all states. In addition, the various types and titles of licenses in specific states will also vary. It is important to inform yourself about the licensing requirements of any state in which you intend to practice, and work toward meeting those requirements.

Finally, you will probably find it helpful to remember that for all the emphasis on social work knowledge, theory, and research, you will not be effective if you do not pay close attention to what many consider the *art of social work*. This is actually a combination of empirical knowledge and creativity that makes social work effective in many situations. Although the art of social work is somewhat difficult to describe, it is not hard for social workers to

 Review this video about preparing for social work licensing exams. How can you use the information provided to help guide your practicum learning? www.youtube.com/watch?v=7Lldz8-f0r8&spfreload=1

Evaluation

Behavior: Apply evaluation findings to improve practice effectiveness at the micro, mezzo, and macro levels.

Critical Thinking Question: What responsibility does a social worker have to monitor, evaluate, and improve services to clients?

understand because of the emphasis in the profession on building relationships that will often be at the heart of interactions with clients at all levels of practice.

Often called a personal or professional style of practice, the art of social work is much more than the use and dependence on intuition or a lack of commitment to social work knowledge and professional skills. It may be somewhat hard to define, but it is nonetheless vital to working with individuals, families, groups, organizations, and communities. Social workers who are genuine, compassionate, and caring are likely to possess the ability to communicate this compassion in honest and open ways. The manner in which knowledge and skills are applied is one form of the art of social work, because this approach is tailored to each individual client situation based on the ability to not only understand clients, but identify the unique ways in which a relationship can be built in order to help clients.

Ethical and Professional Behavior

Behavior: Make ethical decisions by applying standards of the National Association of Social Workers Code of Ethics, relevant laws and regulations, models for ethical decision making, ethical conduct of research, and additional codes of ethics as appropriate to context.

Critical Thinking Question: Upon what values and ethics of the profession is the concept of generalist practice based? Why is it important to understand this?

? Assess your understanding of guidance and direction by taking this brief quiz.

V Recall what you learned in this chapter by completing the Chapter Review.

Another way in which the art of social work is expressed is through innovation and creativity, which means that social workers must be able to imagine new ways of doing things. Such innovation requires the ability to do existing tasks in a new way. It also requires the ability to complete different tasks to teach the same goal in a better way. It means that social workers do not let themselves be bound by agency policy, the status quo in service provision, and a stagnant set of practice skills. Social workers who innovate are those who continue to ask questions, seek the input of clients, and engage with others who also value critical and creative thinking.

A final way in which social work practice requires artistic and creative activity is in building on one's unique personal and professional characteristics as they relate to being a social worker. Since social workers often say that they *use themselves as a tool for helping others*, they must know their own strengths and gifts for helping others, building on them through a career. Characteristics of a social worker that can be enhanced to better serve clients include the ability to stay positive in the face of client adversity, a belief in the good in people, a sense of optimism about addressing social problems, and a high level of emotional strength that results in a positive perspective. All of these can be used to maintain oneself as a social worker over the length of a career, to communicate positivity to clients, and to be able to remain in this challenging profession.

Social Work Licensing: A Workbook Activity

In order to learn the requirements of social work licensing in your state, research the licensing statutes governing the profession in your state.

1. What levels of licensing are available in your state?

_____

_____

_____

2. What are the names of the various licenses available?

_____

_____

_____

3. What are the educational requirements of each license?

_____

_____

_____

4. What licensing examinations are required for each license? How often are the examinations given?

_____

_____

_____

5. What licensing preparation materials are available and recommended by other social workers?

_____

_____

_____

6. How much supervision is required annually?

_____

_____

_____

7. What are the requirements of supervisors?

_____

_____

_____

8. What are the continuing education requirements for each license?

_____

_____

_____

9. What guidelines are followed when clients or others make a formal complaint against a licensed social worker?

_____

_____

_____

Moving from Student to Professional: A Workbook Activity

Refer to Table 11.1, Student Versus Social Worker Role, and reflect on the process of moving from a student to a professional. Answering the following questions and discussing them with professional social workers will help you to understand what is expected of you as you make this transition. Ask your field instructor to discuss the following ideas and questions with you.

1. What are the main differences between a student and a social worker?

_____

_____

_____

2. What would you expect of me in order to consider for a professional position at your agency?

_____

_____

_____

3. What problems have you observed in practicum students that limit their professional readiness for a position?

_____

_____

_____

4. What is your definition of professionalism?

_____

_____

_____

5. Where do you see me in terms of my transition to a professional social worker?

_____

_____

_____

6. What can I do to maximize this experience so that I am ready for practice?

_____

_____

_____

Suggested Learning Activities

- Attend local chapter meetings of NASW or the meetings of other social work–related professional organizations and decide what issues are of greatest concern to the social workers in your community.

- Join NASW as a student member and work to understand how local, state, and membership opportunities contribute to the development of social work at these levels.

- Review announcements of social work conferences and workshops to determine what topics are of interest to social workers.

- Watch for media portrayals of social workers in newspapers, magazines, on television, or on the Internet to determine how social work is described and whether it is usually presented in a positive or negative light.

- Join NASW as a student member, which will allow you to keep abreast of professional social work issues and programs and support its work.

- Investigate a variety of social work membership organizations, such as Association for Community Organization and Administration, the National Association of Black Social Workers, the Association of Oncology Social Workers, the National Association of Puerto Rican/Hispanic Social Workers, the Clinical Social Work Federation, the National Indian Child Welfare Association, the Rural Social Work Caucus, the Society for Spirituality in Social Work Practice, the North American Association of Christians in Social Work, International Federation of Social Workers, and the Social Welfare Action Alliance.

Suggested Readings

Barker, Robert L. _The Social Work Dictionary_. 5th ed. Washington, DC: NASW Press, 2003.

Commission on Accreditation. _Educational Policy and Accreditation Standards_. Alexandria, VA: CSWE, 2008.

DuBois, Brenda, and Karla Miley. _Social Work: An Empowering Profession_. 8th ed. Boston: Allyn and Bacon, 2014.

Finn, Janet L., and Maxine Jacobson. _Just Practice: A Social Justice Approach to Social Work_. 2nd ed. Peosta, IA: Eddie Bowers Publishing, 2008.

Gambrill, Eileen. _Social Work Practice. A Critical Thinker's Guide_. 3rd ed. New York: Oxford University Press, 2009.

LeCroy, Craig. _The Call to Social Work: Life Stories_. 2nd ed. Thousand Oaks, CA: Sage Publishing Company, 2012.

National Association of Social Workers. _Code of Ethics_. Washington, DC: NASW Press, 1999.

Payne, Malcolm. _Modern Social Work Theory_. 4th ed. Chicago: Lyceum, 2014.

12

Social Work Ethics

©WEERAPATI003 / FOTOLIA

CHAPTER PREVIEW

This chapter describes *professional values and ethics* and highlights the ways in which professional codes of ethics can guide practice. It describes *ethical competencies, ethical decision making*, and a process for *resolving ethical dilemmas*. Tools are provided that demonstrate how primary social work values can be promoted through the use of specific agency practices and policies. The use of an *ethics audit* is also discussed as an organizational quality improvement technique to monitor and maintain ethical service provision.

Every day, social workers make decisions and take actions based on ethical principles. These principles have a profound and far-reaching impact on practice. They also have a significant impact on a student's practicum. You have studied the *National Association of Social Workers (NASW) Code of Ethics* and devoted classroom time to the discussion of ethical questions and issues. Up to this point, the topic of professional ethics may have seemed rather abstract, but in your practicum you will meet these questions and dilemmas face to face. This will require that you acquire the ability to recognize, understand, and deal with ethical situations and ethical dilemmas. This chapter briefly reviews the nature of professional values and ethics, discusses a number of ethical issues common to social work, and offers guidance on identifying ethical issues and resolving ethical dilemmas. The workbook activity will heighten your awareness of ethical concerns within your practicum setting.

BACKGROUND AND CONTEXT

Each profession has a code of ethics that provides an ethical and value base for practice. These codes usually focus on professional responsibilities to those they serve, to the organizations for which they work, and to society at large. This is true for social work ethics, which you will be asked to apply daily in your practicum. Social work ethics are built upon a set of values central to the profession and that give general guidance to social workers engaged in ethical decision making. *Ethical decision making* is the process of critically and thoughtfully incorporating ethics into the decisions made at all phases of the planned change process, into organizational development, and into larger-scale efforts such as research and social justice efforts.

The term *ethical dilemma* describes a situation in which the social worker has two or more ethical obligations (e.g., to take action to protect the client from imminent harm and also to protect the client's right to privacy) but cannot adhere to one principle without violating another because of their conflicting and sometimes mutually exclusive nature. Rather than providing clear-cut guidance for resolving on each dilemma, the *NASW Code of Ethics* provides general principles that the social worker uses to make ethical decisions. Having a protocol or set of principles to use in this process is both necessary and invaluable.

The standards for ethical conduct by social workers may be described as *ethical competencies*. These competencies require knowledge that goes beyond a rigid and universal interpretation of practice situation. It also requires skills and actions based on the analysis of ethical situations and the consideration of the values of all stakeholders. Following is a list of ethical competencies that your practicum can help you develop. They can be divided into knowledge and skill categories.

Engagement

Behavior: Apply knowledge of human behavior and the social environment, person-in-environment, and other multidisciplinary theoretical frameworks to engage with clients and constituencies.

Critical Thinking Question: In what ways does a sound knowledge of a variety of theoretical frameworks demonstrate a commitment to social work values?

Knowledge for Ethical Competence
- The ethical social worker understands *definitions of ethics and values*, both personal and professional.
- The ethical social worker becomes familiar with the *NASW Code of Ethics*, including its purposes, uses, and limitations.
- The ethical social worker identifies *ethical issues* and situations.
- The ethical social worker understands connections between *ethical and legal issues* in practice.
- The ethical social worker understands *potential ethical violations* and their consequences.

Watch this video that provides a short summary of the four historical periods of social work ethics. How has your own understanding of ethics evolved? www.youtube.com /watch?v=jFvKmog11RU

Professional Identity

Behavior: Use supervision and consultation.

Critical Thinking Question: Who can you ask to help you sort through ethical decisions and dilemmas?

Skills for Ethical Competence

• The ethical social worker develops and uses a *model of ethical decision making*.
• The ethical social worker examines, explores, and resolves *ethical dilemmas*.
• The ethical social worker applies *NASW Code of Ethics* to all levels of practice.
• The ethical social worker applies *critical thinking skills* to ethics in practice.
• The ethical social worker uses *supervision and continuing education*.

Your agency will have a written or informal process for resolving ethical issues and dilemmas. It may use ethics committees, staff discussions, and outside legal and ethics consultations to help make difficult decisions. Hopefully you will be able to participate in such meetings as often as possible, because this will help you develop awareness of and skill in identifying and resolving ethical dilemmas. Ask for opportunities to observe and contribute to sessions such as these. Each situation is unique to some degree, and there is seldom only one right way to deal with it, which is the nature of an ethical dilemma. Over time, you will become more comfortable with this uncertainty and be better able to sort out the competing values and potential consequences of each decision.

When you encounter an ethical dilemma, consider the *ethical decision-making guidelines* offered by Sheafor and Horejsi (2015, 154–5) and begin by seeking answers to questions such as the following:

• Who is your *primary client* (i.e., usually the person, group, or organization that requested the social worker's services and expects to benefit from them)?
• What aspects of the *agency's activity or worker's roles* and duties give rise to the dilemma (e.g., legal mandates, job requirements, agency policy, questions of efficient use of resources, possible harm caused by an intervention)?
• *Who can or should resolve* this dilemma? Is it rightfully a decision to be made by the client? Other family members? The worker? The agency administrator?
• For each decision possible, what are the *short-term and long-term consequences* for the client, family, worker, agency, and community?
• *Who stands to gain and who stands to lose* from each possible choice or action? Are those who stand to gain or lose of equal or unequal power (e.g., child versus adult)? Do those who are most vulnerable or those with little power require special consideration?
• When harm to someone cannot be avoided, what decision will cause the *least harm* or a type of harm with fewest long-term consequences? Of those who might be harmed, who is least able to recover from the harm?
• Will a particular resolution to this dilemma set an *undesirable precedent* for future decision making concerning other clients?
• What *ethical principles and obligations* apply in this situation?

- Which, if any, *ethical principles are in conflict* in this situation and therefore create an ethical dilemma?
- In this situation, are *certain ethical obligations more important than others*?

? Assess your understanding of background and context by taking this brief quiz.

GUIDANCE AND DIRECTION

It is likely that you will encounter some very troublesome situations in which all available choices or options are to some degree harmful and destructive to your client and other people. In such cases, you must decide which option is the *least harmful* and who may be harmed by either decision. Essentially, you are forced to choose the lesser of two or more evils. Although this is hard for even the seasoned social worker, it is a reality you will learn how to address because client situations will require you to do so.

Social work ethics are involved in a number of common circumstances. Having studied these in the classroom, you know what you are required or forbidden to do in theory. Now, in real-life practice situations, you will probably find these guidelines challenging to actually use. An ethical area that may be confusing for you is the question of limits to *client confidentiality*. Clients have a *right to privacy*. However, this right is not absolute. There are limits and exceptions to a client's right to confidentiality, including situations in which social workers are considered to be mandated reporters. You may need to release client information without your client's permission when your client is abusing another person, is planning or has committed a serious and dangerous illegal act that places others in danger, or is threatening harm to himself or herself or to another person. Confidentiality also may not apply when you receive a court order requiring you to release client information or when a contract requires you to share information with a third party or perhaps when your client is a minor.

The perspective of clients on how ethical situations should be handled is important to consider. In order to demonstrate to clients that their concerns will be addressed and their rights will be protected, specific agency procedures and practices should be developed and implemented. Table 12.1 highlights common client concerns that have clear ethical implications and the possible ways in which agencies can address these concerns through policies and procedures.

Before you encounter these issues with your clients, do your best to understand your agency's policies that impact clients personally and intimately. Be certain that you understand the federal and state laws that apply to confidentiality. Make sure that you understand the concept of *privileged communication*. This is the principle that clients can expect that their social worker will not or cannot share information without their consent because information shared with a profession social worker is protected by law. Consult with your practicum supervisor to make certain that you know how and when privileged communication requirements will apply to you and your clients.

Social agencies are guided by professional values and ethics, all of which can be addressed in multiple ways through *agency policies and guidelines*. Table 12.2 lists eight of

Ethical and Professional Behavior

Behavior: Make ethical decisions by applying the standards of the NASW *Code of Ethics*, relevant laws and regulations, models for ethical decision making, ethical conduct of research, and additional codes of ethics as appropriate to context.

Critical Thinking Question: How will you balance the values of client self-determination and the protection of vulnerable populations?

Table 12.1   Client Concerns, and Agency Policies

Client Concerns	Agency Policies to Address Client Concerns
Concern that inferior services have been provided	Grievance policy and feedback on complaint
Embarrassment and guilt at being an involuntary client	Confidentiality statement for staff Release of information policy Privileged communication policy
Difficulty understanding what will be required in treatment or intervention	Informed consent policy
Ambivalence about engaging in intervention	Choice and right to refuse treatment Length of service policy
Desire to review one's records	Documentation policy
Wish to be offered evidence-based practices	Best practices policy Staff credentialing policy Staff development policy Supervision

the primary social work values and shows how agencies can uphold these values through comprehensive and creative agency policies for ethical professional behavior. Review it and ask your field instructor if these agency practices are used in your agency. If some of these agency practices are not used in your agency, consider whether they would be helpful in promoting ethical professional care.

A recommended practice for agencies who wish to monitor their performance in terms of adherence to and use of ethical practices is an *ethics audit*. Such a review of an agency's compliance with its own policies and ethical principles can be done at various time intervals with information gathered from a number of sources. It can then be used to assess the ethical operation of an agency. Following is a glossary of terms that includes all of the items on the ethics audit. Read them in conjunction with the ethics audit (Table 12.3).

- *Advisory Board* (a board that advises the agency on policy, programs, services, and whose members may include clients)
- *Best Practices Policy* (an agency commitment to the use of best practices that are evidence based, superior to other approaches, and in keeping with client need and preference)
- *Bill of Rights* (written document describing client rights, either designed by the agency or required by funding, licensing, or accrediting body)
- *Choice and Right to Refuse* (a policy that guarantees clients the right to choose and decline services)
- *Code of Ethics* (professional codes of ethics related to the professions employed within the agency, which are posted within the agency or implemented informally)
- *Confidentiality Statement* (a signed statement required of agency employees and volunteers that commits them to maintaining client confidentiality)

Table 12.2   Social Work Values and Agency Policies and Procedures to Support Them

Policies and Practices	Dignity and Respect	Safety and Protection	Equality	Autonomy and Self-Determination	Privacy and Confidentiality	Service	Quality and Competency	Cultural Competency
Advisory Board	✓		✓	✓		✓	✓	✓
Best Practices Policy	✓	✓	✓	✓	✓	✓	✓	✓
Bill of Rights	✓	✓	✓	✓	✓	✓	✓	✓
Choice and Right to Refuse	✓			✓		✓		✓
Code of Ethics	✓	✓	✓	✓	✓	✓	✓	✓
Confidentiality Statement	✓	✓		✓	✓	✓		
Conflict of Interest Policy		✓					✓	
Consultation		✓		✓	✓	✓	✓	✓
Credential Verification		✓	✓				✓	✓
Documentation	✓	✓			✓		✓	✓
Ethical Decision Making Process	✓	✓	✓	✓	✓	✓	✓	✓
Ethics Committee	✓	✓	✓	✓	✓	✓	✓	✓
Grievance Policy		✓		✓	✓		✓	✓
Informed Consent Policy	✓	✓		✓	✓	✓	✓	✓
Length of Service Policy		✓	✓		✓	✓	✓	✓
Payment Policy	✓	✓	✓	✓		✓	✓	✓
Privileged Communication Policy		✓		✓	✓			✓
Release of Information	✓	✓			✓			
Staff Development	✓	✓	✓	✓	✓	✓	✓	✓
Supervision		✓	✓	✓	✓	✓	✓	✓

Source: Based on "List of Ethical Competencies" from BSW Competency Catalogue. University of Montana, 2008.

Table12.3   Ethics Audit

Agency Policies and Procedures	In Compliance *(minimal risk to client, social worker, and agency)*	Minor Noncompliance *(low risk to client, social worker, and agency)*	Major Noncompliance *(high risk to client, social worker, and agency)*	Source of Data 1. *Records review* 2. *Staff interviews* 3. *Advisory board* 4. *Client input* 5. *Outside party input* 6. *Other*
Advisory Board				
Best Practices Policy				
Bill of Rights				
Choice and Right to Refuse				
Confidentiality Statement				
Conflict of Interest Policy				
Consultation				
Credential Verification				
Documentation of Services				
Ethical Decision Making Process				
Ethics Committee				
Ethical Violation Policy				
Grievance Policy				
Informed Consent Policy				
Length of Service Policy				
Payment Policy				
Privileged Communication Policy				
Release of Information				
Staff Development and Training				
Supervision				

Instructions: This instrument will assist an agency to assess its own level of compliance with self-designed agency policies and procedures that ensure ethical professional behavior. **Low levels of agency compliance are related to high levels of risk to clients. High levels of agency compliance are related to low levels of risk to clients.** Check the agency's level of compliance with each of its own internal policies and procedures governing ethical practice. In the right-hand column, indicate what source of agency-related data was used to determine level of compliance with ethical agency policies and procedures. Use this tool to identify agency strengths and weaknesses in ethical agency operations, both of which can be incorporated into organizational development efforts.

- *Consultation* (advice, feedback, and recommendations from professionals outside the agency that provide varied perspectives and guidance on agency programs and services)
- *Credential Verification* (process of requiring and verifying professional credentials, degrees, and experience of employees)
- *Documentation* (written description of services provided for the purposes of continuity of care, verification of services, monitoring of client progress, and meeting evaluation requirements)
- *Ethical Decision-Making Process* (a process by which ethical decisions can be approached and made, including ethical dilemmas)
- *Ethics Committee* (an interdisciplinary committee whose members have expertise in their respective fields, are schooled in the ethics of care, and make ethical decisions or make recommendations on ethical issues)
- *Grievance Policy* (a policy that outlines clients' rights to make complaints, file grievances, and receive satisfactory responses from the agency)
- *Informed Consent Policy* (a policy that requires staff members to inform clients of all aspects of the agency's services, including effectiveness, length, cost, and potential positive and negative outcomes)
- *Length of Service Policy* (a policy clarifying the expected length of service, including client and agency rights to change the length of service)
- *Payment Policy* (a clear policy on payment for services, including costs, insurance coverage, sliding fee scales, payment plans, and termination of services for nonpayment)
- *Privileged Communication Policy* (a policy describing the laws governing the protection of and limits to shared information between client and professional)
- *Release of Information* (process by which agency releases client information based on written approval)
- *Staff Development* (provision of or support of professional development of staff members through in-service training and continuing education of licensed professionals)
- *Supervision* (structured supervision of employees to monitor effectiveness, increase knowledge and skills, and provide consultation as needed)

Table 12.3 can be completed by those wishing to evaluate the ethical dimension of their organization. Using the list of social work values and the agency policies and procedures provided earlier, the ethics audit table is a tool to determine if an agency is actually implementing policies that will ensure that the values are guarded on behalf of clients.

The ethics audit can be a very effective learning tool for you. It will help you see how values can be turned into actual practices and procedures that truly promote the welfare of real clients. Imagine yourself as a client in your agency, and ask yourself how important it would be to have policies and procedures in place for specific problems and experiences you may have.

Unfortunately, there are times when social work values and ethics are not protected or when *ethical violations* occur through

Human Rights and Justice

Behavior: Engage in practices that advance social, economic, and environmental justice.

Critical Thinking Question: In what specific ways do human rights and social justice practices intersect with the use of the NASW *Code of Ethics*?

social work action or inaction or through agency problems. It is important to know how violations of ethical codes sometimes result in client complaints and lawsuits so that you can avoid such unprofessional behavior while in practicum. Alleged violations of ethics may include the following:

- Breach of confidentiality
- Lack of informed consent
- Dual relationships
- Incompetence
- Defamation of character
- Termination of services
- Lack of cultural competence
- Inequitable access or service
- Violation of client self-determination

Not only do these behaviors on the part of a social worker or agency raise the risk of malpractice claims, but they can undermine services and potentially bring harm to clients, some of whom may be in vulnerable situations. There may be times when you conclude that your agency violates certain ethical principles or the rights of certain clients. If this occurs, discuss your concerns with your field instructor or faculty supervisor in order to sort out the issues and determine whether an ethical principle is being violated and what choices you have.

In order to function effectively as a social worker, you must be able to distinguish between your *personal values and morals* and those of the client. As a general principle, you should not impose your values and beliefs on the client. However, this is a challenging principle of practice because the social work profession and social agencies are built on and represent a set of values and beliefs about what is good for people and desirable in human relationships. Moreover, some clients engage in behaviors that are clearly wrong and a danger to themselves and others (e.g., assault, rape, robbery, child neglect). In such situations, attempting to be value-free or value-neutral can be extremely dangerous, irresponsible, and possibly unethical.

You may find that your personal moral code conflicts with the values of your clients, your field instructor, your agency, or even the NASW *Code of Ethics*. When you encounter such conflicts, do not ignore them. They are important questions and dilemmas that must be faced honestly and squarely. You will need to decide when you can and cannot suspend your personal moral code. Remember that it is your clients' values that are primary in your interactions with them, not yours. Ask other social workers how they have dealt with such values conflicts with their clients. You can learn from their experiences.

Finally, think about the NASW *Code of Ethics* as a *minimum requirement for ethical conduct* and professional behavior. Find ways to do more than the minimum required, as that will help to prevent complaints or allegations of negligence or misconduct. If the welfare of clients is always the primary focus of your work, it will be easy to provide ethical and competent services, document their provision, and give clients and client systems the services they deserve.

? Assess your understanding of guidance and direction by taking this brief quiz.

V Recall what you learned in this chapter by completing the Chapter Review.

Values and Ethics in Your Practicum: A Workbook Activity

1. What ethical concerns or dilemmas are most frequently encountered in your practicum setting, according to your field instructor?

    _____

    _____

2. How do the social workers in your agency deal with ethical questions and resolve ethical dilemmas (e.g., discussions at a staff meeting, presentations to an ethics committee, consultation with experts)?

    _____

    _____

    _____

3. To what degree and in what way does the NASW *Code of Ethics* influence the decisions and behavior of the social workers employed by your agency (e.g., referred to during case conferences and staff meetings and available to social workers)?

    _____

    _____

4. Does your agency have its own code of ethics or a code of conduct for its employees? If yes, how is it similar to and different from the NASW *Code of Ethics*?

    _____

    _____

5. Does your agency have policies that, in your opinion, are in violation of the NASW *Code of Ethics*? If yes, describe how these policies are in conflict with specific provisions of the NASW *Code of Ethics*.

    _____

    _____

6. How does your agency handle reports of ethics violations on the part of its staff (e.g., written incident reports, temporary suspensions of staff, formal investigations, grievance policies, reports to state licensing bodies)?

    _____

    _____

7. Have any agency social workers or other agency personnel been dismissed or reprimanded for ethics violations? If so, what was the nature and type of misconduct?

    _____

    _____

8. What ethical principles in the NASW *Code of Ethics* do you feel most strongly about? Why?

    _____

    _____

9. Does your agency have policies that are in conflict with your personal moral code? If yes, how will you handle or resolve these conflicts?

    _____

    _____

10. Are there statements or sections in the NASW *Code of Ethics* that are in conflict with your personal moral and ethical standards? If yes, how will you attempt to resolve these conflicts?

    _____

    _____

11. What is the name of the agency in your state responsible for handling formal complaints about ethics violations by licensed social workers? What process is used to investigate possible ethics violations?

    _____

    _____

12. What are the possible sanctions in your state for social workers who commit ethics violations (e.g., loss of license, civil action for monetary damages, criminal prosecution, sanctions by NASW)?

    _____

    _____

Suggested Learning Activities

- Read and study the NASW *Code of Ethics*. It can be downloaded from NASW's website (http://www.naswdc.org).

- If members of other professions (e.g., psychologists, nurses, or teachers) work in your practicum setting, secure a copy of their profession's code of ethics and compare it to the NASW *Code of Ethics*.

- Interview experienced social workers and ask them to describe the ethical issues they most often encounter and the issues that are especially difficult for them to resolve.

- Review your agency's policy manual and identify policy principles that are very similar to the NASW *Code of Ethics*. Identify policies that appear to be in opposition to the NASW *Code of Ethics*.

Suggested Readings

Baird, Brian N. *The Internship, Practicum, and Field Placement Handbook: A Guide for the Helping Professions.* 5th ed. Upper Saddle River, NJ: Prentice Hall, 2011.

Banks, Sarah. *Ethics and Values in Social Work.* 3rd ed. New York: Palgrave Macmillan, 2008.

Barnard, Adam, Nigel Horner, and Jim Wild, eds. *The Value Base of Social Work and Social Care.* New York: Open University Press, 2008.

Corey, Gerald, Marianne Schneider, and Patrick Callahan. *Issues and Ethics in the Helping Professions.* 6th ed. Florence, KY: Brooks/Cole, 2003.

Hartsell, Thomas L., and Barton E. Bernstein. *The Portable Ethicist for Mental Health Professionals: An A-Z Guide to Responsible Practice.* New York: John Wiley and Sons, 2000.

Houser, Rick, and Stephen Thoma. *Ethics in Counseling and Therapy: Developing an Ethical Identity.* Thousand Oaks, CA: Sage Publications, 2012.

National Association of Social Workers. *Code of Ethics.* Washington, DC: NASW Press, 1999.

Payne, Malcolm. *What Is Professional Social Work?* 2nd ed. Chicago: Lyceum Books, 2007.

Reamer, Frederick. *Ethical Standards in Social Work: A Review of the NASW Code of Ethics.* 2nd ed. Washington DC: NASW Press, 2006.

Sheafor, Bradford, and Charles Horejsi. *Techniques and Guidelines for Social Work Practice.* 10th ed. Boston: Allyn and Bacon, 2015.

Somers Flanagan, Rita, and John Somers Flanagan. *Becoming an Ethical Helping Professional: Cultural and Philosophical Foundations.* Hoboken, NJ: John Wiley and Sons, 2007.

Strom-Gottfried, Kim. *Straight Talk About Professional Ethics.* 2nd ed. Chicago: Lyceum Books, 2014.

Thomlison, Barbara, and Kevin Corcoran, eds. *The Evidence-Based Internship: A Field Manual.* New York: Oxford University Press, 2007.

Legal Issues

CHAPTER PREVIEW

This chapter provides an overview of the *legal context of the practicum and social work practice*. This includes basic *legal terminology*, examples of laws that impact clients and social workers, guidelines for *functioning within the laws impacting social work practice*, and suggestions for *avoiding malpractice situations*. It also offers guidelines for social workers when preparing and giving *court testimony* in legal practice situations.

Social work, like all professions, is guided and impacted greatly by the law. Every social services agency is shaped and guided by specific codes or legal considerations. Some agencies were formed in response to a law requiring states or the federal government to provide specific programs and services. In some agencies, a client's eligibility for services is defined by law. In many instances, a social worker's actions are dictated by law, as in the case of mandated reporting of child abuse. Many social workers are licensed by state law and must practice in keeping with the provisions of that law and its provisions.

As a practicum student, you must understand the legal context of your professional practice. You must be alert to potential actions of yours and your agency that may violate the law and to the types of situations that might give rise to a lawsuit against an agency, a social worker, and even a social work student. You also need to understand which laws require you to take a specific action or which preclude you from certain actions. Because the legal context directly impacts social workers and clients, social workers must acquire a basic understanding of the laws and legal procedures that most directly impact their practice setting and clients served. They must become familiar with specific laws related to their practice roles, duties, and job description.

BACKGROUND AND CONTEXT

Social workers are often involved in helping their clients, groups, or organizations negotiate or utilize the legal system. This may involve the following *professional tasks:*

- Advocating for and supporting individual clients and families
- Securing protection for clients
- Obtaining reparations for clients
- Securing various legal services for clients in need

Social workers may also become involved in *macro-level legal proceedings* and *legislative efforts* such as

- Promoting new laws
- Providing testimony on the impact of social policies on clients
- Assisting groups involved in class action suits.

In these cases of *macro practice*, the social worker must be skilled in the following:

- Preparing clients or groups to provide legislative testimony
- Drafting legislation to establish or amend current social policies
- Providing expert testimony at legislative hearings
- Encouraging client involvement in social policies that impact their lives
- Promoting voter registration efforts
- Engaging in efforts that will empower clients and groups to advocate for themselves

Because practicum students are acting in the capacity of social workers, they are held to the same *standards of practice* and ethical behavior that social workers are, and therefore it is vital to understand as much of the legal context of your agency as possible. It is also important to act in accordance with agency policy, professional standards, university policy, and the National Association of Social Workers (NASW) *Code of Ethics* in order to provide the highest quality services to clients while also avoiding the possibility of malpractice allegations or lawsuits. It is recommended that you secure student *professional liability and malpractice insurance* through your university, the agency, NASW, or independently.

Laws impacting both social work and clients are based on specific professional and societal values. They may have been enacted to promote social justice or to protect and

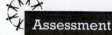

Assessment

Behavior: Select appropriate intervention strategies based on the assessment, research knowledge, and values and preferences of clients and constituencies.

Critical Thinking Question: In what ways can the likelihood of malpractice allegations be reduced if the selection of interventions meets this standard?

ensure human rights. Such values include those outlined in Table 13.1. Think about the relationship between social work values and laws that are in place. Consider whether the laws you are familiar with actually support social workers, to what degree, and if not, why not. A social worker engaged in policy practice will need to clarify the values underlying laws that they propose and support as well as those they oppose. As you learn about the laws specific to your agency and your clients, consider which of these social values underlie the laws you will be following or working to change.

Issues related to the **written documentation** of social work practice are important for practicum students to understand. From a legal perspective, social workers and practicum students must operate on the assumption that any of their professional records, case notes, reports, and correspondence may eventually become the target of a **subpoena**, gathered and reviewed by attorneys, and read in court. They need to be thoughtful and cautious about what they put into a written record and how they write it, for at some point they may be asked to explain and defend their statements. Chapter 5 focuses on communication in social work practice and provides a wealth of suggestions and guidelines for how to develop documentation skills that will protect clients, social workers, and agencies alike.

Because a growing number of social workers are being sued for malpractice, this possibility must be considered daily, even as a practicum student. Although it is not common for social work students to be sued for **negligence** or **malpractice**, it is possible.

Table 13.1   Social Work Values and Laws That Support Them

Social Work Values	Laws Supporting Social Work Values
Protection and safety	• Orders of protection • Duty to warn
Equality and access to services	• Equal opportunity and nondiscrimination laws • Accessibility laws
Least harm	• Just cause • Client consent to treatment
Quality of life	• Environmental protections • Landlord/tenant laws
Privacy and confidentiality	• Privacy laws • Release of information
Full disclosure	• Informed consent • Privacy laws
Empowerment of vulnerable populations	• Child and adult protection laws • Parental notification laws
Right to direct one's own care	• Advance directives • Right to refuse treatment
Right to quality and competent services	• Social work licensing • Consumer protection laws

Malpractice and professional negligence fall under a category of law known as tort law. A *tort* is a private or civil wrong or injury that results from actions other than the breach of a formal legal contract and the commission of a crime. In order for the plaintiff (e.g., a social worker's client or former client) to be successful in this type of lawsuit alleging malpractice against a defendant (e.g., the social worker or practicum student), the plaintiff's attorney must prove four points:

1. The social worker had a *professional obligation* or duty to provide the plaintiff with a certain level of service, a certain standard of care, or a certain manner of professional conduct.
2. The social worker was *negligent or derelict* in his or her professional role because he or she did not live up to this recognized obligation or duty, standard of care, or expected professional conduct.
3. The plaintiff suffered *injury or harm* (e.g., physical, mental, emotional, or financial) as a result of what the social worker did (act) or did not do (omission) and this act or omission had a foreseeable harmful consequence for the plaintiff.
4. The social worker's act or omission was a direct or *proximate cause* of the harm experienced by the plaintiff.

A wide variety of *acts or omissions* can place social workers or the agencies for which they work at risk of being sued and held liable for causing harm to their clients or to individuals harmed by their clients. Such acts or omissions on the part of the social work might include the following:

Watch this video by NASW Assurance Services describing the areas in which social work malpractice claims are made by category, as well as the steps toward ethical self-protection. What situations in your practicum setting need to be considered when working toward ethical self-protection? www.youtube.com /watch?v=sYeXgPk6cUQ

Acts that may place social workers at risk

- Dual relationships between social worker and client
- Sexual or romantic involvement with a current or former client
- Misrepresentation of professional training, experience, and credentials
- Breach of client civil rights
- Violation of privacy or confidentiality
- Misdiagnosis or use of harmful, inappropriate, or ineffective interventions
- Treating clients without consent

Omissions that may place social workers at risk

- Failure to clearly outline duties of social worker and client
- Failure to warn others when a client discloses clear intent to inflict serious physical harm on someone
- Failure to alert others when a client discloses intent to harm self
- Failure to attempt to prevent a client's suicide
- Failure to provide needed treatment and services to a client or premature release, termination, or abandonment of a client
- Failure to maintain and protect confidentiality
- Failure to maintain accurate professional records and a proper accounting of client fees, payments, and reimbursements

Human Rights and Justice

Behavior: Apply their understanding of social, economic, and environmental justice to advocate for human rights at the individual and system levels.

Critical Thinking Question: How do the concepts of social work effectiveness and negligence relate to the concepts of human rights and social justice?

 Assess your understanding of background and context by taking this brief quiz.

- Failure to refer clients to other services or professionals when indicated
- Failure to protect a client from harm caused by other clients in a group, program, or facility
- Failure to report suspected child or elder abuse, neglect, or exploitation

Certain clients and practice situations place social workers and agencies at a higher risk of being sued than others. These clients and situations may include the following:

- Clients who are a real physical danger to others
- Clients who have been separated from their children because of actions taken by the social worker or agency (e.g., foster care placement and custody evaluations)
- Clients with complex and intense needs requiring social workers to provide highly technical and competent services
- Clients at risk to commit suicide
- Clients who are very suspicious of others and quick to blame and accuse others of some wrongdoing
- Clients with a history of alleging malpractice and negligence and bringing suits against various professionals
- Clients who are very manipulative and deceptive

GUIDANCE AND DIRECTION

Make a special effort to become familiar with the *laws relevant to your practicum setting*, including the *laws that regulate services* your agency provides and the *laws that regulate professional social work practice*. Depending on the nature and purpose of your agency, you will need to become familiar with federal and state codes, and sometimes local ordinances, that apply to your clients and the services your agency provides. Your clients' lives are affected directly and indirectly by such laws. For example, you may need to understand laws pertaining to the following areas when you engage in *micro-level practice with individuals and families*.

- Marriage, parenthood, divorce, and child custody
- Child or elder abuse and neglect
- Partner violence and abuse
- Termination of parental rights, foster care, and adoption
- Guardianship, conservatorship, power of attorney, durable power of attorney for health care
- Involuntary hospitalization of persons with mental illness
- Involuntary placement of persons who are suicidal or a threat to others
- Parental notification regarding services provided to minors
- Adult and juvenile adjudication, probation, and parole
- Crime victim assistance

- Immigration and refugee status
- Buying and selling of illegal drugs
- Family planning, reproductive rights, and abortion
- Education of children with disabilities
- Discrimination in employment and housing
- Confidentiality in health and mental health settings
- Reporting of contagious diseases and public health hazards
- Personal debt and bankruptcy
- Disability accommodation
- Restorative justice

Social work supervisors and administrators working at the *mezzo or macro level of practice with organizations and communities* will need a basic understanding of laws related to such issues as employee matters and financial management. Although as a practicum student, it is likely that you will only be able to observe the administrative function of social work, laws that impact your agency are an important part of the context of providing quality services and of maintaining good employees and employee relations. Watch for opportunities to learn about laws pertaining to the following:

- Contracts, leases, and rental agreements
- Property and liability insurance
- Employee compensation and benefits
- Workers compensation and unemployment insurance
- Hiring and dismissal of employees
- Employee unions
- Financial recordkeeping
- Accessibility for persons with disabilities
- Restrictions on political action and lobbying by public employees
- Sexual harassment
- Drug-free workplaces
- Affirmative action
- Whistle-blowing in cases of alleged ethics violations or mistreatment of clients
- Mediation processes for individuals, groups, and organizations

In some settings, social workers are commonly required to appear in court. If social workers in your agency commonly appear in court, request the opportunity to observe their *court testimony*. Determine their role and function in court, how they prepare for a court appearance, what types of questions they are asked by attorneys and how they respond, what written documents they provide the court, and if their recommendations tend to be followed by judges. Give special thought to legal and ethical issues that may arise when social workers advocate for their clients, when they are asked to participate in involuntary treatment of clients, or when they must testify on behalf of one client and against another. Identify the social work interventions that follow those documents and orders.

Diversity and Difference in Practice

Behavior: Apply and communicate understanding of the importance of diversity and difference in shaping life experiences in practice at the micro, mezzo, and macro levels.

Critical Thinking Question: In what ways might the experiences of diverse clients lead them to view the legal aspects of intervention differently?

Watch this attorney provide guidance for child welfare social workers about effective testimony in court. What roles, responsibilities, and suggestions given can guide your thinking about possible future court testimony you may be required to give? www.youtube.com /watch?v=kCkVArsby5g

Learn about social workers who testify as expert witnesses and what is required of them. If social workers in your agency are not routinely involved in court proceedings, seek the opportunity to observe this activity within another agency setting. Although students will not usually testify in court, observing and learning from the experiences of those who do will be invaluable to them.

If possible, read the case records of clients whose cases are heard in court. Read the petitions and other legal documents filed on behalf of or against your agency's clients. Read the court orders found in client records. If you have questions about what these records mean, ask your field instructor to explain their significance and what is expected of social workers in these situations. Becoming skilled in providing court testimony can be enhanced by separating the stages of court testimony into those described in Table 13.2.

An agency policy and procedures manual generally describes a standard of care and service owed to, and expected by, the client. Thus, in a malpractice lawsuit, a social worker's failure to follow agency policy may be used as evidence of *professional negligence*. An agency places itself at higher legal risk when it has an official policy that is not or cannot be regularly followed by its employees. Agencies and malpractice insurance will not protect social workers who do not abide by the policies of their agency, especially if this results in harm to clients. The best way to avoid becoming involved in a *malpractice lawsuit* is to be proactive in learning about and acting on the following guidelines:

- Read the *NASW Code of Ethics* regularly and abide by its guidelines.
- Adhere to *agency policy*, procedure, and protocol.

Table 13.2   Guidelines for Testifying in Court

Stages of Providing Court Testimony	Guidelines
Preparation for Court Testimony	• Understand laws impacting intervention. • Read client files and understand history and prior legal proceedings. • Anticipate questions from attorneys and presiding judges. • Rehearse testimony, including providing your credentials, describing your intervention, answering questions, and making recommendations. • Be ready to provide professional and objective rationale for recommendations. • Request supervisor observation of court testimony.
Providing Court Testimony	• Dress professionally and in accordance with court requirements. • Demonstrate a calm, professional, and respectful demeanor. • Answer what is being asked. • Use professional terminology. • Present your professional training and credentials clearly. • Provide factual, objective, and documented information.
Post-court testimony Review	• Solicit feedback and constructive instruction on professional testimony. • Learn from preparing testimony. • Learn from questions resulting from testimony or mistakes made. • Incorporate the experience into preparation for subsequent testimony.

- Make every effort to **practice competently** and avoid situations beyond your level of competence.

- Utilize **supervision** regularly to ensure that your techniques are legal, ethical, and therapeutically sound.

- Recognize situations of **high legal risk**.

- Consult with your agency's **legal counsel** whenever confronted with troublesome or confusing legal issues or questions.

- Obtain **malpractice insurance** if your agency does not provide it for you.

- Avoid **dual relationships** with clients.

- Protect **client confidentiality** and inform clients about the limits of confidentiality.

- Maintain up-to-date, accurate, and complete **client records** that are free of hearsay and judgmental language.

- Obtain written permission from clients to **release information** about them to others.

- Document any **client complaints or grievances**, and the steps you took to resolve them.

- Understand and abide by laws pertaining to **privileged communication** for social workers in your state.

- Abide by all **mandatory reporting laws** requiring you to report suspected abuse or neglect.

- Abide by **duty to warn** principles when third parties are threatened.

- **Refer** clients to other professionals and programs when you are unable to provide the services they require and document your efforts to make a referral.

> ### Ethical and Professional Behavior
>
> **Behavior: Use supervision and consultation to guide professional judgment and behavior.**
>
> **Critical Thinking Question**: How will you use supervision by social workers and consultation with other professionals to help you maintain ethical standards of practice? How do legal and ethical issues overlap, inform, and sometimes differ?

You are not likely to become entangled in a malpractice lawsuit if you follow the guidelines just described, so do not let concerns over legal risk and malpractice keep you from learning or acting in the best interests of your clients. However, it is important to be careful to avoid legal consequences. Adhere to what would be considered **reasonable, customary, and prudent practice** by an average citizen, a jury, or a judge. The actions you take on behalf of clients must be fair, in good faith, and in keeping with how other professionals would tend to act. If you need clarification in any particular area, seek guidance and consultation from your social work supervisor and/or agency legal counsel.

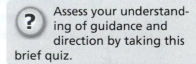 Assess your understanding of guidance and direction by taking this brief quiz.

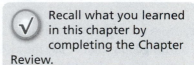 Recall what you learned in this chapter by completing the Chapter Review.

Legal Issues and Concerns: A Workbook Activity

The following questions are designed to heighten your awareness of the legal context of social work practice and the legal considerations that are relevant to your practicum agency. Discuss these questions and issues with your field instructor and with experienced social workers in your agency. Your agency may also have a legal department and staff attorneys who can respond to your questions and explain legal principles.

1. Is eligibility for your agency's services in any way defined by law? If so, what statutes, legal rules, and regulations are used to determine who is eligible and who is not?

_____

_____

2. Are certain individuals legally required or mandated to obtain services from your agency (e.g., those on probation and subject to court-ordered treatment or those whose children are in foster care)? If so, what specific statutes apply to these individuals and situations?

_____

_____

3. Do those individuals who are pressured to make use of your agency have a right to refuse to participate? If so, do they face any consequences for that action?

_____

_____

4. Is your agency licensed by the state (e.g., a child-placing agency and residential center for youth)? If yes, identify the specific license(s) and the laws and regulations that apply to these licensures.

_____

_____

5. What outside agencies or organizations (e.g., governmental agencies, accrediting bodies, and citizen review boards) are authorized to interview staff about their practices and review the records kept by your agency (e.g., client records, client services, and financial records)?

_____

_____

6. Does your agency have malpractice insurance that provides employees with legal defense against allegations of wrongdoing and/or pay the assessed damages if found guilty? If so, what limitations and restrictions apply (e.g., must the employee be following agency policy and behave in an ethical manner before he or she be covered the insurance policy)?

_____

_____

7. What are the possible legal consequences for a social worker who takes action that conflicts with or violates the agency's written policy?

_____

_____

8. Has the agency or any staff member been sued for negligence or malpractice? If yes, what was the nature of the allegation(s) and the outcome of the lawsuit(s)?

_____

_____

9. What agency policies apply in the following client situations that may have legal ramifications?

Practice Situations	Agency Policy
A client who may not be mentally competent to make legal, medical, or financial decisions	
A client who is a minor in need of services and whose parents may or may not be informed	
A client who puts himself or herself at risk by refusing or withdrawing from treatment	
A client known to have or suspected of having committed a serious crime	
A client who has been ordered to receive services from your agency	
A client who has lied, withheld information, or falsified an application in order to become eligible for benefits or services	
A client who states that he or she intends to bring a lawsuit against a social worker or agency	
How to proceed when a client asks to read or copy the records in his or her case file	
How to obtain a client's permission to release records to your agency or another one	
When and how to report suspected child or elder abuse or neglect	
How to obtain a client's informed consent to participate in programs and receive services	
How to handle and record the receipt of gifts from a client	
How to respond to a subpoena for client records or to be a witness in a trial or court action	

Suggested Learning Activities

- Examine your agency's policy manual and identify policies that refer to the need for staff to conform to specific legal codes or requirements.
- Identify situations in which there might be a conflict between what is required by the NASW *Code of Ethics* and the requirements of a specific state or federal law.
- Observe court proceedings, especially ones in which your agency is involved.
- Determine whether your agency has a staff attorney. If so, familiarize yourself with the legal services provided by the attorney to staff social workers.

Suggested Readings

Albert, Raymond. *Law and Social Work Practice: A Legal Systems Approach*. 2nd ed. New York: Springer Publishing Company, 2000.

Baird, Brian N. *The Internship, Practicum, and Field Placement Handbook: A Guide for the Helping Professions*. 5th ed. Upper Saddle River, NJ: Prentice Hall, 2011.

Bernstein, Barton E., and Thomas L. Hartsell, Jr. *The Portable Guide to Testifying in Court for Mental Health Professionals: An A–Z Guide to Being an Effective Witness*. Hoboken, NJ: John Wiley and Sons, 2005.

Birkenmaier, Julie, and Marla Berg-Weger. *The Practicum Companion for Social Work: Integrating Class and Field Work*. 3rd ed. Boston: Allyn and Bacon, 2011.

Houston-Vega, Mary K., Elane M. Nuehring, and Elizabeth R. Daguio. *Prudent Practice: A Guide for Managing Malpractice Risk*. Washington, DC: NASW Press, 1997.

Israel, Andrew. *Using the Law: Practical Decision Making in Mental Health*. Chicago: Lyceum Books, 2011.

National Association of Social Workers. *Code of Ethics*. Washington, DC: NASW Press, 1997.

Reamer, Frederic. *Social Work Malpractice and Liability*. 3rd ed. New York: Columbia University Press, 2006.

Sheafor, Bradford, and Charles Horejsi. *Techniques and Guidelines for Social Work Practice*. 10th ed. Boston: Allyn and Bacon, 2015.

Slater, Lyn, and Kara Finck. *Social Work Practice and the Law*. New York: Springer Publishing Company, 2011.

14

Planned Change Process

©ROMOLO TAVANI / FOTOLIA

CHAPTER PREVIEW

This chapter presents the *planned change process*, which is the central approach of social work at the micro, mezzo, and macro levels of practice. *Guidelines and considerations* for engaging in planned change are offered. The *phases of the planned change process* are described. Conceptual frameworks guiding social work practice are defined and described, including *professional perspectives, explanatory/orienting theories, and practice theories/models*. The *context* of the planned change process is also described, including the agency, community, and social policy context.

Fundamentally, the practice of social work is about the process of planned change. In the practice of social work, the worker takes deliberate and specific steps to encourage and facilitate movement toward a certain goal. Your practicum offers an excellent opportunity to observe and critically examine the values, beliefs, ethical principles, theories, and knowledge base that guide social workers' efforts to bring about a desired change.

All social agencies are committed to and structured around deep-seated beliefs about how clients, families, organizations, communities, or broad social conditions change. Identify the assumptions about change that are embedded in your agency's programs and policies as well as in its various approaches to practice. Identify your own beliefs about how, why, and under what circumstances desirable change by individuals, families, small groups, organizations, and communities is possible and probable. In addition, work to integrate the theories and models you learned in the classroom into your practicum experiences, guided by the content of this chapter.

BACKGROUND AND CONTEXT

As explained in Chapter 11, Professional Social Work, social work is often seen as the profession that supports and promotes the social functioning of individuals, groups, and communities and also works to establish societal structures and policies that support that social functioning. *Planned change* at all levels, including the micro, mezzo, and macro levels, is the central focus of social work. Social workers assist clients, families, and communities to make changes that will improve their lives or change the conditions and social policies that impact their lives. Planned change is intentional, structured through the four phases of the planned change process (i.e., engagement, assessment, intervention, and evaluation), and based on orienting theories and practice models. Potential issues and changes are anticipated, and specific approaches and techniques are used at each stage.

Using the term *planned* does not mean to suggest that planned interventions always result in desired outcomes. Many *positive and negative factors and variables* influence the process itself and the outcomes. Because clients and communities are in constant interaction with wider social environments, and because these clients and social environments are in a state of constant change, social work interventions are more dynamic than the term *planned* might suggest.

Practice-informed Research

Behavior: Use and translate research findings to inform and improve practice, policy, and service delivery.

Critical Thinking Question: What practice models are most commonly used with the clients of your agency, and how are they rooted in research?

Social workers engaged in planned change see the *connections and mutual interactions* between people and the social environments of which they are a part. They also know that in order to be truly effective, they need to be skilled in and committed to interventions that reflect the ways in which people's lives are influenced by societal conditions and social policies. They must believe in clients' and communities' abilities not only to address their own needs and goals but also to empower themselves as they change and enhance their social environment. They must fully understand exactly how and why planned change efforts are effective or not. The following *principles of planned change* can be used by beginning social workers, but also by those experienced in the profession.

- Planned change is built on *hypotheses* that certain interventions will produce specific outcomes.
- Planned change is built on *professional perspectives, orienting theories*, and *practice models*.
- Planned change is effective when built upon *good assessments*.
- Planned change is effective when *assessment is ongoing* and continuous throughout interventions.

- Planned change is always based on *incomplete information*, but interventions must begin with what is known.
- Planned change is most effective when based on *client input and goals*.
- Planned change is impacted by *client/client system characteristics*.
- Planned change is effective when *goals and objectives are amended* as needed.
- Planned change may lead to *partial success*.
- Planned change may be impacted by *unexpected and unforeseen factors*.
- Planned change efforts are likely to be met with *barriers and resistance*.
- Planned change is guided and limited by *agency programs, protocol, and gaps* in services.
- Planned change is guided and limited by *social policies*.

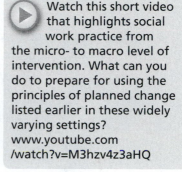 Watch this short video that highlights social work practice from the micro- to macro level of intervention. What can you do to prepare for using the principles of planned change listed earlier in these widely varying settings? www.youtube.com/watch?v=M3hzv4z3aHQ

Planned change efforts do not take place in a social vacuum. In fact, such efforts are greatly impacted by a wide variety of external factors and characteristics of the various contexts influencing interventions. These external factors may help support interventions or undermine efforts. They may be resources that can be incorporated into the plan. For interventions to be effective, these contextual considerations must be taken into account, integrated into the plans, and factored into the overall success of the intervention (Table 14.1).

Although these three levels of intervention may have different targets for change, they are all built on the same *process of planned change*. In addition, social workers often practice at multiple levels simultaneously, recognizing the connections between them and moving between levels as the situation requires. Social work at all of these levels, whether the client is an individual or a community, typically moves through the *phases of planned change*, which are listed and described here.

1. *Engagement Phase of Planned Change*

   Social workers at all levels of practice engage with clients and client systems in order to establish effective working relationships that form the basis for effective assessment, intervention, and evaluation of planned change.

2. *Assessment Phase of Planned Change*

   Social workers gather, sort, and interpret information related to the client or client system functioning (including strengths and needs), identify goals and objectives, and develop intervention plans based on client input and an understanding of orienting/explanatory theories prior to and during intervention.

3. *Intervention Phase of Planned Change*

   Social workers implement intervention plans, monitor progress of planned change efforts, and adapt intervention plans as necessary to achieve desired change.

4. *Evaluation Phase of Planned Change*

   Social workers evaluate the effectiveness of intervention plans toward desired change using a variety of measures, terminate planned change process when appropriate, and incorporate results into future planned change processes.

Human Rights and Justice

Behavior: Apply their understanding of social, economic, and environmental justice to advocate for human rights at the individual and system levels.

Critical Thinking Question: How can an in-depth understanding of the context of social work practice as presented in Table 14.1 lead to social and economic justice?

Table 14.1   Characteristics and Contexts Impacting Planned Change

Client Characteristics

Definition of and meaning assigned to situation

Goals and desires

Personal values

Self-awareness and insight

Level of motivation and engagement

Voluntary or involuntary status

Social support available

Issues of diversity

Social Worker Characteristics

Skill level

Knowledge base

Training and preparation

Personal values

Professional values

Level of rapport and engagement

Quality of assessment completed

Agency context

Agency mission

Available programs and services

Agency priorities

Agency resources

Level of cultural competence

Timeliness of services

Use of evidence-based practices

Community context

Community assets

Community needs and problems

Attitudes toward and support of clients

Attitudes toward and support of agency

Informal resources available to supplement agency services

Social Policy context

Existing laws regulating practice

Existing laws mandating services

Laws limiting or prohibiting services

Political context

Value base of social policies

Effectiveness of social policies in meeting client needs

This list of phases gives the impression that the change process is quite orderly and linear, but that is seldom the case. Typically, the client and worker move back and forth between these phases several times during the intervention process. In addition, others involved in the intervention, such as extended family members, may not move through the intervention process at the same pace or with the same goals in mind. This can make the change process more complex and unpredictable and needs to be taken into account.

Social workers use what are called *conceptual frameworks* to guide practice. A *conceptual framework* is a way of organizing ideas about social work practice and includes practice perspectives, orienting theories, and practice models. It is a very broad term that is an umbrella term for all of the foundations for practice. A *professional perspective* is an intentional viewing of a practice situation using a certain professional lens, which helps to clarify and magnify a particular facet of the person-in-environment. Using these professional lenses helps us to examine, draw attention to, and shine a light on what needs attention in any given situation.

Intervention

Behavior: Use inter-professional collaboration as appropriate to achieve beneficial practice outcomes.

Critical Thinking Question: When collaborating with other professionals, especially those from other disciplines, what professional perspectives might they be using that you would need to understand?

All practice situations require a *strengths perspective* in order to highlight strengths and resources upon which to build an intervention. An *ecosystems perspective* prompts us to consider the impact of the social environment on our clients, as well as the interaction between our clients and their social environments. A *diversity perspective* ensures that we consider the ways in which diversity of all kinds impacts a client's experience and view of that experience. Depending on the situation, a social worker may use one perspective more than another to understand the unique features of that situation. A *generalist perspective* helps a social worker determine at which level of practice to engage and which of a variety of models should be used.

Orienting/explanatory theories are those that contribute to a social worker's body of knowledge about how individuals, families, groups, communities, and societies develop and change over time. They often build on and synthesize the social and behavioral sciences such as psychology, sociology, economics, and political science. Such theories attempt to explain human behavior, human development, social forces that shape human experiences, political contexts, and economic systems that impact individuals, families, and communities. Although necessary to good practice because they help us understand what might be happening and why, these theories do not provide guidance on how to facilitate planned change. Examples of orienting theories include social systems theory, human development theory, group dynamics theory, organizational theory, and community development theory.

Practice theories/models are those that offer specific guidelines about how to intervene at various levels of practice. They build on orienting/explanatory theories and suggest that certain situations call for specific practice theories. They are the actual approaches and techniques chosen to use in real interventions. They build on the information obtained in the assessment stage, addressing the problems and issues identified in that stage. They are hopefully chosen based on client preference. They should be based on evidence and research in order to be recommended and chosen in specific practice situations.

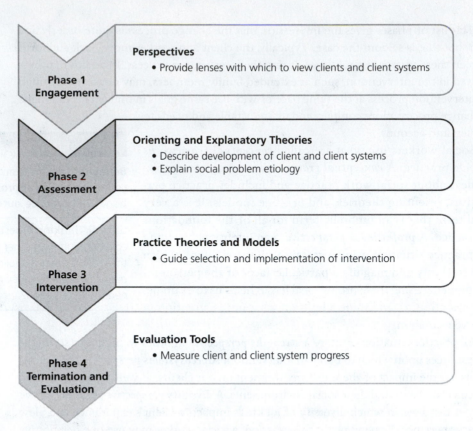

Figure 14.1
Planned Change Process

Figure 14.1 shows the ***relationship between the conceptual frameworks*** defined previously, including professional perspectives, orienting/explanatory theories, practice theories/models, and actual interventions. The blending of these conceptual frameworks and others is done in any effective planned change process that is based on social work knowledge, theory, evidence-based practice, best practices, and social work values.

Based on this diagrammatic representation of how conceptual frameworks are used to design effective, theory-based, and individualized intervention plans, a number of practice examples are included in the Appendix. Review these examples that range from micro to macro practice. Compare them to the list of various professional perspectives, orienting theories, and practice models presented in Table 14.2 so that you can learn to identify and use specific practice models for specific needs. The following examples are included in the Appendix:

- **Micro-Level Practice Examples**
  - Intervention with an individual
  - Intervention with a family
- **Mezzo-Level Practice Examples**
  - Intervention with a group
  - Intervention with an organization

- **Macro-Level Practice Examples**
  - Intervention with a community
  - Intervention with a social policy

Refer to the examples in the Appendix so that you can *see in a visual way how conceptual frameworks are linked in the planned change process* to elicit positive outcomes. Use the template provided in the Appendix to guide your thinking and actions related to the planned change process. It will help you not only understand the stages of the planned change process, but also what conceptual frameworks and strategies are used at each stage.

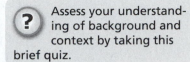

? Assess your understanding of background and context by taking this brief quiz.

GUIDANCE AND DIRECTION

It is important to identify the practice frameworks (perspectives, explanatory/orienting theories, and practice theories/and models) used in your agency. Whether *implicit or explicit*, these frameworks influence how your agency designs its programs and services and how it works with clients. Once you identify them, ask yourself a number of probing questions to develop a deeper understanding of the planned change process and its theoretical foundation.

Determine why these particular practice frameworks are appropriate and most effective for the clients served by your agency. Consider what your agency's choice of practice frameworks reveals about the agency's beliefs and assumptions concerning the causes of personal and social problems, how and why clients and client systems change, and what actions are most likely to facilitate change. Learn about how success is measured and ask about the importance placed on identifying and using client strengths.

Your practicum agency will expect you to use the *regularly utilized forms of intervention* engaged in by other social workers and will train you in these approaches. Do your best to learn the skills required to implement these interventions, remembering that many of these skills can be generalized and transferred to another setting even if that organization takes a different approach to intervention. Over time you will see how interventions, even though they may seem similar for several clients, are customized based on different needs and goals. You will begin to see how your own interventions will be tailored for those reasons as well. As you grow in experience and confidence, your ability to craft appropriate interventions will increase.

Recognize that your practicum experience is limited to one setting and that other agencies and programs may be quite different from the one you know best. There are significant differences between programs, even when they have similar goals and serve the same types of clients. Try to learn how and why other agencies have adopted forms of intervention, practice perspectives, and theories and models that are different from the ones used in your practicum setting.

Each practice model requires you to engage in specific social *work roles*. Do your best to clarify if a practice model requires a social worker to be a counselor, educator, mediator, or case manager, for example. During your practicum, try to gain experience in as many social work roles as possible in order to understand the nature of these roles and better understand your own abilities. Do not limit yourself to the performance of only a few practice roles. Most likely your career in social work will require that you assume many different practice roles and perform a wide range of tasks and activities. This variety of roles is also one of the most attractive aspects of the social work profession because social workers can move between roles, creatively addressing needs in a variety of ways and at a variety of levels.

Refer again to the four phases of the planned change process, and carefully consider in more depth your role in each phase. As you become involved in the *engagement* phase of planned change, it is incumbent on you to use a variety of perspectives. Make sure that you use the skills of rapport building, active listening, and partnering to build a strong initial professional relationship. This phase requires that you and the client or client system understand the problem or need, task at hand, and perspectives of all those involved. This first phase of planned change will require you to learn how to use yourself as the tool for change, since the next three stages of planned change hinge on your ability to connect in a meaningful way with your client.

In the *assessment* phase of planned change, whether you are assessing a client, a community's capacity to serve its citizens, an organization's ability to provide services, or a social policy's ability to address the needs of a group of people, there are general guidelines that can help you do a thorough and effective assessment. When assessing client situations, make sure to assess for strengths as well as problems and use assessment tools that are effective and appropriate. Include the client in the assessment process. Prioritize the identified needs in order to maximize your effectiveness. Consider the impact of diversity on your interventions. Pay attention to any ethical and legal issues related to assessment. Ask yourself what value judgments you might be making. Consider the socio-historical context of your client or client system. Continually ask yourself what else you might need to know in order to have a comprehensive assessment upon which an effective intervention can be built.

Becoming skilled in the assessment phase of planned change will require that you think about the following considerations important to intervention at all levels. As you design *interventions* from the micro level to the macro level, certain guidelines for effective interventions will be of help to you and your clients. The intervention plan must address both strengths and needs, be built on as comprehensive an assessment as possible, and be feasible and reasonable for both the client and social worker. The plan should be mutually developed by the client and social worker, based on a theory of change that matches the client's needs, and within your knowledge base and skill level. Remember that your intervention may need to be modified at some point. Make sure that the plan has incremental steps and reasonable goals. Make plans for how you will terminate the helping relationship and evaluate the outcomes. Do what you can to minimize negative effects on clients, avoid being overly intrusive into your clients' lives, address important issues of diversity, and include a timeline and termination plan.

Diversity and Difference in Practice

Behavior: Present themselves as learners and engage clients and constituencies as experts of their own experiences.

Critical Thinking Question: What NASW cultural competence standards are necessary at each phase of the planned change process? Do they vary depending on whether you are engaged in micro, mezzo or macro practice?

As you enter the *termination and evaluation* phase of the planned change process, you may be terminating the process for a number of reasons. There may have been a predetermined length of service. The client may have wished to terminate early, or needed to do so for various reasons. Ideally, termination will have been anticipated and structured in a positive way. No matter how an intervention ends, it needs to be evaluated for effectiveness. Consider how to design evaluations for your interventions. This is the time to measure the outcomes of the intervention in relation to the goals and objectives that were identified in the assessment and intervention phases. The profession of social work is rightfully asked to hold itself accountable and to demonstrate its ability to address social issues in effective and efficient ways.

Social workers are asked to use what is commonly called *evidence-based practice*, which means that they need to base their interventions on some form of empirical evidence whenever possible and engage in proactive program evaluation to determine the effectiveness of services provided. Such research on practice often leads to what is termed *best practices*. This refers to what the profession considers to be ideal approaches for specific clients based on its values and its research on what is effective, what is in the best interests of clients, and what clients wish for themselves. Learn to research evidence-based and best practices in your field so that you can pattern your work after them, knowing that as your career proceeds, you may be involved in the development of best practices.

> ▶ Watch this video about David, a man whose social functioning is significantly impacted by his diagnosis of Asperger's. What would you need to know in order to design an intervention plan for David as he works to gain skills in managing his diagnoses, which also include depression and panic disorder?

Having considered the four distinct but overlapping phases of the planned change process, now *think about them as a whole*. Think about how they relate to each other and build upon the work done at each previous stage. Think about how, when, and why particular theories are used at specific phases of the planned change process. Consider the ways in which particular helping skills are used at specific stages and why they are effective when used at the right time. Recall what you learned earlier about following and furthering techniques that are applied intentionally at certain points in the intervention. As beginning social workers may not always see how the phases inform each other, it is helpful to reflect on the following guidelines:

- The four phases of the planned change process are separate but connected.
- Following techniques are used most effectively in the engagement and assessment phases.
- Furthering techniques are used most effectively in the assessment and evaluation phases.
- Assessment is ongoing throughout the phases of planned change.
- Orienting theories help to inform and guide the assessment process, providing an understanding of clients and client systems.
- Practice models help to inform and guide the intervention process, providing specific approaches to address needs and problems.
- Potential changes to the planned change process are anticipated and incorporated as needed.
- The evaluation of the intervention is based on whether or not, and to what degree the goals and objectives were achieved.

Drawing upon your classroom learning about the theories that guide social work practice, and combining those with the sample orienting/explanatory theories and practice models, consider how your practicum learning experiences at the micro, mezzo, and macro levels will help you design interventions with a solid theoretical base. Figures 14.2 through 14.4 illustrate a number of the commonly used theories at all three levels.

Orienting/Explanatory Theories		
Behavioral	Biopsychosocial	Crisis
Cognitive	Cycle of Change	Hierarchy of Needs
Medical Model	Moral Development	Object Relations
Psychodynamic	Psychological Learning	Social Behavioral
Social Exchange	Social Systems	
Practice Theories and Models		
Behavioral	Client Centered	Cognitive Behavioral
Crisis Intervention	Empowerment	Family Preservation
Family Reunification	Harm Reduction	Motivational Interviewing
Solution Focused	Strategic Family Therapy	Structural Family Therapy
Task Centered		

Figure 14.2
Micro-Level Theories

Orienting/Explanatory Theories		
Chaos	Family Life Cycle	Family Systems
Group Development	Group Dynamics	Multicausal
Organizational Development	Role	Social Exchange
Social Learning	Social Systems	Subculture
Practice Theories and Models		
Empowerment	Harm Reduction	Mutual Aid Group
Organizational Development	Program Development	Psychoeducational Group
Self-Help Group		

Figure 14.3
Mezzo-Level Theories

Orienting/Explanatory Theories		
Conflict	Multicausal	Political Economy
Social Exchange	Social Learning	Social Movement
Social Systems	Strain	Structural
Subculture		
Practice Theories and Models		
Community Development	Community Organization	Harm Reduction
Policy Practice	Research Practice	Social Change
Social Development	Social Planning	Structural Change

Figure 14.4
Macro-Level Theories

Becoming skilled in micro-level social work will necessitate your consideration of the following questions. Think about them as they might relate to the clients you are serving if your practice is at the *micro level with individuals and families*. Base your answers on what you have learned in the classroom about individuals and families.

- Why do clients change?
- What is the role of internal and external motivation?
- What is the importance of readiness and capacity to change?
- What is the impact of the larger social environment on clients' opportunity to change?
- How much impact does voluntary versus involuntary involvement have on change?

> Watch this video as you consider how understanding the ways in which trauma impacts young children is an example of an orienting theory. How does knowledge about trauma help social workers design interventions based on trauma-informed practice? www.youtube.com/watch?v=Xg2RWFgBj8U&index=5&list=PL71574161D61A7B53

Becoming skilled in mezzo-level social work will necessitate your consideration of the following questions. Think about them as they might relate to the clients you are serving if your practice is at the *mezzo level with groups and organizations*. Base your answers on what you have learned in the classroom about individuals and families.

- In what ways can groups be effective in ways that individual interventions cannot?
- What types of groups are suitable for particular client needs and problems?
- How does an understanding of group dynamics help guide planned change?
- What is the role of capacity building in organizational change?
- What types of organizational structures lend themselves to ongoing change?
- How does an understanding of organizational structure help guide planned change?

Becoming skilled in macro-level social work will necessitate your consideration of the following questions. Think about them as they might relate to the clients you are serving if your practice is at the *macro level with community and policy practice*. Base your answers on what you have learned in the classroom about individuals and families.

> Assess your understanding of guidance and direction by taking this brief quiz.

- What role do community problems and assets play in planned change?
- What social conditions tend to provide the impetus for community change?
- What is the role of social capital in achieving positive community change?
- How does an understanding of social problems lead to sound social policy?
- In what ways does policy practice impact individuals and families?

> Recall what you learned in this chapter by completing the Chapter Review.

Evidence-Based Practice: A Workbook Activity

In order to integrate perspectives, theories, and models into your practicum, respond to the following critical thinking questions.

1. What social problems, diagnoses, or conditions are commonly present among your clients?

_____

_____

2. What orienting theories help to explain these social problems, diagnoses, or conditions?

_____

_____

3. What practice theories have evidence to show that they are effective for clients facing these social problems, diagnoses, or conditions?

_____

_____

_____

_____

4. Conduct research on additional practice models used for clients such as yours. Record them here.

_____

_____

_____

Planned Change Process Example: A Workbook Activity

This activity will help demonstrate that you understand the phases of the planned change process. Select a client or client system in your agency with which you are familiar. This example can be at the micro-, mezzo-, or macro level of intervention. Write a short case study describing the client or client systems (i.e., individual, family, group, organization, community, and social policy). Complete a flow chart resembling those in the Appendix describing which perspectives, orienting theories, practice models, and evaluation tools should be used for this planned change process. Use the lists of theories presented in this chapter, and refer to the examples in the Appendix. The intervention can be at any level of practice. Share and discuss this product with your field instructor and faculty supervisor.

Suggested Learning Activities

- Examine the data-gathering and assessment tools and instruments used in your agency.

- Ask social workers or other professionals in your agency to identify the perspectives and theories that guide their practice. Ask why those frameworks are preferred over other possibilities.

- Identify the beliefs, values, and assumptions implicit in the perspectives, theories, and models used in your agency.

- Ask social workers or other professionals in your agency to describe how they and the agency determine whether they are being effective in their work with clients.
- In the *Encyclopedia of Social Work* (Mizrahi, 2010), read chapters on the various practice frameworks used in your agency and by social work professionals.
- Refer to the *Social Work Desk Reference* to see what interventions are recommended in certain situations.

Suggested Readings

Coady, Nick, and Peter Lehmann, eds. *Theoretical Perspectives for Direct Social Work Practice.* 2nd ed. New York: Springer Publishing Company, 2008.

Corcoran, Jacqueline, and Joseph Walsh. *Clinical Assessment and Diagnosis in Social Work Practice.* 2nd ed. New York: Oxford University Press, 2010.

Cournoyer, Barry R. *The Evidence-Based Social Work Skills Book.* Boston: Pearson Education, 2004.

Finn, Janet L., and Maxine Jacobson. *Just Practice: A Social Justice Approach to Social Work.* 2nd ed. Peosta, IA: Eddie Bowers Publishing, 2007.

Gambrill, Eileen. *Social Work Practice: A Critical Thinker's Guide.* 3rd ed. Cary, NC: Oxford University Press, 2012.

Hohman, Melinda. *Motivational Interviewing in Social Work Practice.* New York: Guilford Press, 2011.

Hull, Grafton, and Karen Kirst-Ashman. *Understanding Generalist Practice with Families.* 7th ed. Pacific Grove, CA: Brooks/Cole, 2015.

Jordan, Catheleen, and Cynthia Franklin. *Clinical Assessment for Social Workers: Qualitative and Quantitative Methods.* 3rd ed. Chicago: Lyceum Books, 2011.

Karls, James M., and Maura O'Keefe. *Person-in-Environment System Manual.* 2nd ed. Washington, DC: NASW Press, 2008.

Lister, Pam. *Integrating Social Work Theory and Practice: A Practical Skills Guide.* Florence, KY: Routledge, 2012.

McKenzie, Fred. *Understanding and Managing the Therapeutic Relationships.* Chicago: Lyceum, 2011.

Mizrahi, Terry, and Larry E. Davis. *Encyclopedia of Social Work.* 20th ed. Washington, DC: NASW Press and Oxford University Press, 2008.

Netting, F. Ellen, Peter McKettner, Steven L. McMurty, and M. Lori Thomas. *Social Work Macro Practice.* 5th ed. Boston, MA: Pearson Education, 2012.

O'Hare, Thomas. *Evidence-Based Practices for Social Workers: An Interdisciplinary Approach.* 2nd ed. Chicago: Lyceum Books, 2015.

Payne, Malcolm. *Modern Social Work Theory.* 4th ed. Chicago: Lyceum Press, 2015.

Roberts, Albert R. *Social Workers' Desk Reference.* 2nd ed. New York: Oxford University Press, 2009.

Saleeby, Dennis, ed. *The Strengths Perspective in Social Work Practice.* 6th ed. Boston: Allyn and Bacon, 2013.

Sheafor, Bradford, and Charles Horejsi. *Techniques and Guidelines for Social Work Practice.* 10th ed. Boston: Allyn and Bacon, 2015.

Turner, Francis. *Social Work Treatment: Interlocking Theoretical Approaches.* 5th ed. New York: Oxford University Press, 2011.

Evaluating Your Practice

©AURIS / FOTOLIA

CHAPTER PREVIEW

The evaluation of social work practice is a vital component of both ethical and professional standards. This includes the evaluation of practicum, ongoing evaluation of practice, evaluation of client outcomes, and program evaluation. This chapter will provide basic information on the *process of student evaluation* used by programs of social work education and encourage you to examine and evaluate your own performance so you can make the best possible use of the practicum as a learning opportunity. It will also describe the *purposes and types of evaluation commonly used in social work practice* and the *concepts of best practices and culture of evaluation*. Also contained in this chapter is a *framework for analyzing ineffective interventions* and learning from them.

   The evaluation component of social work practice, both in the practicum setting and in the subsequent practice, is a vital phase of intervention, both for the client and the practitioner. Clients expect and deserve competent social workers, and ethical social work practice requires that the best interests of vulnerable clients take center stage. A successful practicum prepares you for competent and responsible practice. Your competence as a practicum student is developed over time when classroom knowledge and practicum experiences are integrated through real social work experiences. ***Ongoing monitoring and frequent evaluations of your performance*** as a social worker are necessary to determine whether you are making progress, identify strengths, and focus on areas of performance that may need special attention and remediation. It is important to understand the role of ***evaluation as a tool for professional growth*** and to think ahead about how evaluation, including self-evaluation, can be incorporated into your professional practice.

BACKGROUND AND CONTEXT

Because your university requires that your practicum experience be evaluated, the tools and processes involved in that evaluation will be covered first in this chapter. Schools of social work education use some type of rating scale or evaluation tool to monitor and evaluate student progress, with the ultimate question being asked as to whether a student's performance meets the ***standards expected of the entry-level social work practitioner***. The evaluation process compares the student's performance to standards and criteria established by schools and required by the ***Educational Policy and Accreditation Standards of the Council on Social Work Education***, and also to the learning goals, objectives, and activities outlined in the student's learning agreement.

Evaluations of student performance are of two types: formal and informal. An ***informal evaluation*** consists of the ongoing verbal feedback and suggestions offered by the field instructor. This type of evaluation takes place on a weekly or even a daily basis and is provided both in scheduled meetings and as needed in practice situations. A ***formal evaluation*** is a detailed review, rating, and comparison of the student's performance with agreed-upon evaluation criteria, standards, and learning objectives for the practicum. It occurs at the end of each academic term or more often, depending on school policy or special circumstances.

Formal evaluations are based on a school's specific evaluation criteria and placed in a written report. This report typically consists of the ratings assigned to the various items on the school's evaluation tool and a few paragraphs of narrative that describe special strengths and abilities and/or special problems and deficiencies in performance. The report may also describe how needed learning experiences will be secured or deficiencies corrected prior to the next formal evaluation.

The areas addressed in the practicum evaluation are usually very similar to those addressed in the ***performance evaluation of social workers employed by an agency***. In order to ensure high-quality performance and reduce their exposure to lawsuits and employee grievances, agencies strive to make their expectations of both employees and students as clear as possible and to use personnel evaluation tools and rating scales that are as objective as possible. These same forces have prompted programs of social work education to develop evaluation tools that are as valid and reliable as possible.

A practicum evaluation tool should be both clear and specific in its descriptions of standards and criteria and also flexible enough to accurately and fairly evaluate the practice of social work, which is complex and difficult to observe directly. An evaluation should be objective to the degree possible, but even a well-designed procedure will require judgments by the field instructor. For example, ratings of a student's level of cooperation, motivation, adaptability, and use of supervision are difficult to assess except when in an extreme form (i.e., very high or very low motivation). Consequently, there will be times when the field instructor and practicum student disagree on the actual ratings given on a formal evaluation.

An evaluation can be considered fair, accurate, and relevant when it meets the following standards. These standards are related to the ***tools of evaluation*** and also the ***process of evaluation***.

Tools of evaluation

- The evaluation tools address the ***areas of performance or competency*** that are truly important to professional social work and to the agency's mission and goals.
- The criteria used to evaluate the student are ***clear and objective***.
- The performance ***criteria and standards are realistic*** given the student's level (e.g., first semester versus second semester, BSW versus MSW).
- The evaluation tools give ***consideration to extenuating circumstances*** that may influence the evaluation (e.g., the student had limited opportunity to learn or demonstrate certain skills and the supervisor had limited time to observe the student's performance).
- The evaluation tools ***recognize student growth*** and good performance as well as ***student problems*** or need for continued learning.

Process of evaluation

- The ***evaluation criteria, standards***, and the agency's preferred practices and outcomes are ***made known to the student*** at the beginning of the practicum or at the beginning of the time period to be evaluated.
- The student's performance is compared to ***written standards*** rather than to unstated or implied standards.
- The student has been given ***adequate orientation and training***.
- The student has been given ***ongoing feedback on professional growth***.
- The student has been given ongoing feedback and ***warnings of unsatisfactory performance*** prior to the formal evaluation.
- The evaluation can cite ***examples of performance*** that form the basis of the ratings.
- The evaluation takes into consideration the ***nature and complexity*** of the assignments given to the student.

In some instances, the field instructor or the practicum coordinator may conclude that the practicum arrangement is unworkable and unsatisfactory for the student, the field instructor, or both. This may happen when it becomes apparent that the agency cannot meet the student's learning needs or because the student's performance is irresponsible, unethical, or far short of expectations. Examples of performance problems that may prompt the field instructor or the school to consider terminating the practicum include the following:

- ***Harmful behavior*** toward clients, agency staff, or the agency's reputation
- ***Irresponsible and unprofessional behavior*** (e.g., late for work, missing scheduled appointments, unable to spend the required hours in the practicum setting)

- *Inadequate communication skills*, either verbally or in writing
- *Defensive or hostile attitude toward supervision* and resistance to learning
- *Inappropriate behavior* toward clients or colleagues
- *Inability to manage emotions* in a manner that interferes with work (e.g., bizarre behavior, inability to concentrate, aggressiveness, withdrawal, inappropriate emotional expression)
- *Inappropriate sharing of personal views*, experiences, and problems with clients
- *Dual relationships* with a client (e.g., dates a client, sells a product to a client)

Some behaviors by the student are considered so serious that they may result in the student's immediate dismissal from the practicum. These include the following:

- Clear and serious *violations of the NASW Code of Ethics*
- Clear and repeated *insubordination*
- *Theft or the clear misuse* of agency money, equipment, or property
- *Concealing, consuming, or selling drugs* on agency premises
- *Intoxication or being under the influence of drugs or alcohol* when at work
- *Reckless or threatening actions* that place clients and staff at risk of serious harm
- Deliberately *withholding information* from a supervisor or from agency personnel that they need to know in order to properly serve clients and maintain the integrity and reputation of the agency and its programs
- *Falsifying agency records* and reports
- *Soliciting or accepting gifts* or favors from clients in exchange for preferential treatment
- *Sexual or romantic relationships* with clients
- Clear *violations of strict agency* policy
- *Failure to correct or improve* inadequate performance
- *Inability to deal with the emotional and stressful aspects* of practice

As mentioned earlier, evaluation of practice is an essential component not only of practicum learning but of social work practice in all arenas and at all levels. It is important to understand the purposes, types, processes, and uses of evaluation in social work practice. Evaluation is done to protect clients, ensure that quality services are provided, measure the impact of services and programs on client functioning, demonstrate effectiveness to funding sources, and contribute to the professional body of knowledge of the social work profession.

The profession has committed to *evidence-based practice* that is measured through the use of a variety of evaluation tools and approaches that measure both *client progress* and *social work effectiveness*. Each of these approaches is done to meet a certain evaluative goal, and each one results in information that can be used to continually inform the profession and improve practices. Table 15.1 illustrates *three categories of social work evaluation* commonly used in social agencies and includes both definitions of terms and examples of these categories of evaluation approaches. Consider how these approaches are used in both practicum evaluations and evaluations of social workers in your agency. Pay attention to the ways in which these categories could help you organize your thinking about what needs to be evaluated, why it should be measured, and how such measurements are made.

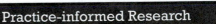
Practice-informed Research

Behavior: Use practice experience and theory to inform scientific inquiry and research.

Critical Thinking Question: Based on your practicum experiences, what research project would answer the questions you have about practice? What research design would you propose to study these questions?

Table 15.1   Categories of Social Work Evaluation: What We Are Measuring and Why

Quantitative Evaluation	Qualitative Evaluation
Purpose: To measure intervention outcomes in a numeric manner that allows for quantification of results, analysis of success, and demonstrated level of change	*Purpose:* To measure intervention outcomes using a non-numeric approach that allows for the description of outcomes in subjective, individual, narrative, and nonquantifiable ways
Examples: Pre- and post-tests, standardized instruments, surveys, questionnaires, external review	*Examples:* Interviews, client satisfaction instruments, narrative evaluation tools, self-evaluation, and report by client/client system
Process Evaluation	**Outcome Evaluation**
Purpose: To measure the intervention process in terms of fidelity, the stages of planned change, monitoring and adapting of objectives, and completion of intervention effort	*Purpose:* To measure the results of the intervention process in terms of level of success, achievement of goals and objectives, and changes over time
Examples: Completion rates, assessment of fidelity to intervention model, process recordings	*Examples:* Pre- and post-tests, standardized instruments, surveys, questionnaires, goal attainment scaling, logic model, and longitudinal studies
Evaluation of Social Work Performance	**Evaluation of Client/Client System Progress**
Purpose: To measure the quality and level of performance of a social worker, organization, or social program in achieving intervention goals and objectives	*Purpose:* To measure the quality and level of progress of a client/client system, which is the target of change in terms of the achievement of intervention goals and objectives
Examples: Supervisory feedback, self-assessment, quality assurance, peer review, external review, agency compliance with standards, program evaluation, client satisfaction instruments, advisory board input	*Examples:* Pre- and post-tests, standardized instruments, achievement of goals and objectives, goal attainment scaling, self-evaluation and report of client/client system, observation, level of functioning scales

Think about how practice evaluations are actually one way of *testing hypotheses*, as described in Chapter 6, The Organizational Context of Practice. Even if based on empirical evidence of previous effectiveness, interventions can be seen in every client case as a hypothesis that a particular intervention will be effective with a specific client or client system. Refer to Table 6.1, which provides samples of practice hypotheses at the micro, mezzo, and macro levels and apply them to your agency. Your agency no doubt makes hypotheses about its services and programs and must find ways to test these hypotheses in meaningful and effective ways. Consider what hypotheses you have proposed in your interventions, reflecting on how your evaluation approaches support these hypotheses or do not.

There are some limitations to evaluation in social work. The following list illustrates these limitations. This list does not suggest that evaluation is not essential or should not be emphasized. Rather, it shows what we as social workers need to do better.

- Not everything social workers do is measurable.
- Not everything about clients' social functioning is measurable.
- Not everything is quantifiable.
- There are time and money constraints in agency settings.
- There can be a lack of commitment to evaluating practice.
- There can be a limited knowledge of program evaluation techniques.
- Some evaluations lack rigor in design of tools and use of inappropriate evaluation tools.
- There can be a lack of connection between those doing practice research and those engaged in practice.
- Agency or intervention goals and objectives may lack clarity, which makes it difficult to measure their achievement.
- Unclear definitions of what exactly is being measured result in inadequate information.
- A misunderstanding about whether success or failure is related to the characteristics of the social worker or the client results in insufficient information to draw conclusions.

Ethical and Professional Behavior

Behavior: Make ethical decisions by applying the standards of the NASW Code of Ethics, relevant laws and regulations, models for ethical decision making, ethical conduct of research, and additional codes of ethics as appropriate to context.

Critical Thinking Question: Upon what research-related ethical conduct is your agency's evaluation process based?

Agencies wishing to provide services that are demonstrated as effective must develop a *culture of evaluation*. This means that the agency considers evaluation of its services to be as important as the provision of its services. Such a culture would encourage the following characteristics. Watch for and ask about whether and to what degree your agency has developed such a culture of evaluation.

- Commitment to achieving *mission* of agency
- Commitment to *measuring effectiveness*
- Allocation of *time and resources* to evaluation
- *Training of staff* in evaluation philosophy, processes, and uses of evaluation to improve practice
- Commitment to *developing empirical knowledge* upon which to base services
- Commitment to *innovation* in addressing current and emerging social issues
- Creative combination of evaluation techniques to *measure in multiple ways*
- Using *culturally relevant measures* of outcomes
- Protocol for *sharing results* of evaluation, dissemination of knowledge gained, and utilizing results for program improvement and growth

After viewing a portion of this video that describes the importance of culturally resonant research and program evaluation, how can this learning be applied to the research and program evaluation done by your agency?
www.youtube.com
/watch?v=GEubejt8oUg
[0:00–3:17]

Effective social work organizations are also committed to measure their work against a set of evaluation concepts. Table 15.2 lists and defines a number of evaluation concepts commonly used in social work agencies. They range from what is acceptable to what is considered the best in practice approaches. Discuss these concepts with your field instructor and try to determine at which level on the following practice quality continuum your agency currently operates.

Table 15.2   Practice Quality Continuum

Evaluation Concept	Definition	Uses
Standard of care	Generally agreed-upon minimum standard for provision and quality of services	Provides basic level of expectation for services as understood by practitioners, agencies, and professional organizations
Accepted practice	Generally agreed-upon approach to the provision of services to clients with specific needs and resources	Provides common, standardized approach for services to clients with similar needs and resources
Emerging practice	Innovative and promising approaches based on advances in orienting/explanatory theories and the practice models associated with them, but that are not yet fully evaluated empirically	Promotes the development of improved services and outcomes for specific populations, allows for adaptations of accepted practice, and incorporates emerging knowledge into existing practice
Evidence-based practice	Empirically tested and affirmed approaches that are based on accepted orienting/explanatory theories and that have demonstrated effectiveness over time	Provides standardized and effective services based on empirical testing and allows for ongoing testing of innovative approaches
Best practice	Recommended practice approaches found to be most effective and of highest quality, combined with guidelines for incorporation into practice at the individual, agency, social policy, or research level, and selected because they are best practices for a given situation based on client preference and suitability	Promotes highest standards for service provision, provides criteria upon which to build intervention, and ensures quality of practice at all levels

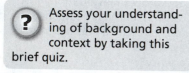

? Assess your understanding of background and context by taking this brief quiz.

GUIDANCE AND DIRECTION

In all phases of your practicum and your subsequent practice, you will be observed, guided, encouraged, assigned tasks, given feedback, and evaluated. In your practicum, your field instructor should provide an *informal and ongoing critique* so that you know how you are doing from week to week. You will be evaluated in a more *formal and systematic manner* at the end of each academic term, using the evaluation tool required by your agency. This tool will rate you on the specific values, attitudes, knowledge, and skills that your school defines as important to your professional development. Obtain a copy of this evaluation tool early in your practicum so that you will have opportunities to learn and grow in each of the areas of performance to be evaluated. You may also be evaluated on the completion of the tasks, projects, and activities you planned at the beginning of your practicum. Review your learning goals for the practicum regularly to determine if you are making satisfactory progress.

Your field instructor and faculty supervisor will ask for your opinion on how the practicum is proceeding, and they may ask for any suggestions or questions you might have. You may be asked the following questions as they evaluate you and continue to structure your learning:

- Are the *tasks and activities* that you are performing different from what you expected?
- What aspects of your practicum do you consider to be of *highest priority*? *Lowest priority*?
- Are the *demands on your time* reasonable?
- What do you *hope to learn and accomplish* in the next month? By the time you complete your practicum?
- Do you get *enough supervision*?
- Is this the *right type of social work practice* and practicum setting for you?
- What aspects of practice in this agency are *most and least appealing*?
- What new or *additional learning experiences* do you want or need?
- How well do you *get along with agency staff*?
- Which practicum tasks have you *completed most and least successfully*?
- Have you been able to strike a *workable balance* between the demands of the practicum, your other academic work, and your personal life and responsibilities?
- Do you have other *comments, complaints, observations, or questions*?
- What can be done to *improve the learning experience* for the next practicum student?

When reviewing and thinking about your performance in the practicum, your field instructor may also ask himself or herself questions such as these:

- Has this student demonstrated *dependability and professionally responsible* behavior?
- Can this individual be *counted on* in a stressful and demanding situation?
- Would this student be able to *handle a social work position* in this agency?
- Would I want this person to be a *social worker for my mother*? For my child? For a good friend of mine?
- Would I be willing to write a strong *letter of recommendation* for this student?
- Would I *hire this person* for a social work job?

Behaviors and personal qualities that impress a field instructor include the following: initiative, dependability, honesty, punctuality, capacity to meet deadlines, perseverance, ability to handle conflict in interpersonal relations, sensitivity to others, ability to achieve goals and objectives, ability to plan and organize work, clear writing, motivation and willingness to work hard, receptivity to new learning, self-awareness and openness to examining personal values and attitudes, capacity to work under pressure, personal maturity, emotional stability, respect for clients and other students, fairness in decision making, and professionalism.

Behaviors and qualities that cause a field instructor to doubt a student's ability to perform as a social worker include the opposite of the previously listed behaviors, especially dishonesty, missing deadlines, disrespect for others, manipulation and efforts to bend rules and requirements, attempts to secure special concessions or privileges, not informing supervisors of problems, and inability to keep personal problems from interfering with professional tasks and activities.

Think of the *evaluation as a learning experience* that can help you become more self-aware, insightful, and skilled. Become aware of any feelings of inadequacy or any emotional triggers that might be activated during the process of evaluation. If you know what they are, you are more likely to benefit from supervision and suggestions for improvement than if you lack this level of self-awareness.

Prepare yourself intellectually and emotionally for the formal evaluation session so that you will be open to hearing feedback about your performance. When receiving feedback on your performance, strive to maintain openness toward what you are hearing. Refer to the parallel processes of the student and client in regard to intervention and evaluation described in Chapter 3, Learning from Supervision, which highlights the similarities between students and clients in terms of ambivalent feelings toward being observed and evaluated. Understanding these parallels will help you become more empathetic with your clients. Although it may be difficult to hear a frank appraisal of your work, avoid being defensive. Consider this feedback carefully and work to improve in the areas noted, knowing that feedback is actually a gift to you that will make you a better practitioner.

Human Rights and Justice

Behavior: Engage in practices that advance social, economic, and environmental justice.

Critical Thinking Question: What is the relationship between the evaluation of social work practice and social justice?

In addition to constructive criticism, you will receive positive feedback related to areas in which you are doing well. Take note of what your field instructor sees as your skills and gifts. If you want more specific feedback about what you have done well so that you know what your skills or abilities are, ask for it. Review the Student Self-Assessment of Practicum Strengths in Chapter 1, and complete the assessment again as a post-test. Compare your self-assessment with the one you did at the outset of your practicum to determine if the strengths you identified there have been demonstrated in your performance and if the ones you did not identify earlier have been demonstrated over time. It will be helpful to see your professional growth to this point in practicum. This will underscore the fact that throughout your career you will continue to develop the strengths needed for professional practice. Build on your strengths because they will form the basis of your professional knowledge and abilities.

Strive to understand what your field instructor observed in your performance that led them to a particular conclusion concerning your work. Seek descriptions and examples of any poor performance and ask for specific suggestions on how it can be improved. Request descriptions of your performance in specific areas that were rated higher than others. Reflect on these descriptions and determine why you perform some tasks and activities better than others. If you and your field instructor disagree on the adequacy of your performance, prepare factual documentation supporting your point of view. However, if you agree that your performance is deficient, it is best to acknowledge the problem rather than entering into a pointless argument that can only leave you looking dishonest or lacking in self-awareness.

Evaluation

Behavior: Apply evaluation findings to improve practice effectiveness at the micro, mezzo, and macro levels.

Critical Thinking Question: How can you use the experience of being evaluated as a student to improve your effectiveness as a social worker?

Remember that although you are just beginning your practice as a social worker, you have much to offer. Build on those gifts, attributes, values, and skills over time, knowing that professional growth is your responsibility. Continue to evaluate your own growth, expecting yourself to continuously acquire new learning, exhibit new skills, and advance practice.

Finally, reflect on the ways in which your performance in practicum needs improvement in order for future interventions to be successful. Consider the connection between your competence, the effectiveness of your interventions, and the level of successful outcomes. There are many explanations for the level of success in interventions. Learning from interventions that would not be considered effective can teach us a great deal. Lack of desired success or disappointment in the outcomes of an intervention can be traced to a variety of factors, including those described in Table 15.3.

Use the information in this table to help you reflect upon and discuss with your field instructor or faculty supervisor the ways in which your success or the success of your clients could be explained through a combination of these factors. Consider in

Table 15.3   Understanding Ineffective Interventions

Level of Practice	Client Contributors to Ineffective Interventions	Social Worker Contributors to Ineffective Interventions
Individual client	• Lack of ability and capacity • Lack of motivation • Little social support • Lack of self-efficacy • Multiproblem situation	• Lack of skill • Lack of knowledge • Lack of rapport • Insufficient assessment • Inappropriate intervention
Family	• Lack of ability • Lack of motivation and capacity • Lack of unity • Dysfunction • Multiproblem situation	• Lack of skill • Lack of knowledge • Lack of rapport • Insufficient assessment • Inappropriate intervention
Group	• Lack of cohesion • Lack of participation • Disruptive members • Lack of motivation • Involuntary membership	• Lack of skill • Lack of knowledge • Lack of rapport • Insufficient assessment • Inappropriate intervention
Organization	• Lack of mission • Insufficient funding • Political factors • Inaccessibility • Culturally insensitive	• Lack of skill • Lack of knowledge • Lack of rapport • Insufficient assessment • Inappropriate intervention
Community	• Factions • Negative social indicators • Lack of resources • Political factors • Varying priorities	• Lack of skill • Lack of knowledge • Lack of rapport • Insufficient assessment • Inappropriate intervention

retrospect how your work could have been better with this knowledge, as well as how future interventions could be enhanced as you learn about what contributes to and detracts from successful interventions.

In addition to client and social worker contributors to less than effective interventions, it is also important to consider the context in which interventions are undertaken with clients who may be individuals, families, groups, organizations, or communities. Examples of the context in which practice is done and that influence the effectiveness of interventions include:

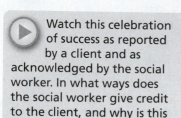
Watch this celebration of success as reported by a client and as acknowledged by the social worker. In what ways does the social worker give credit to the client, and why is this important to do?

- Timing of the intervention, including potential waiting lists
- Nonsupportive social environments for clients
- Funding limitations that influence service provision
- Agency reputation or inaccessibility
- Social policies that negatively impact service provision
- Complexity of the problems being addressed
- Potential variables that impact outcomes but not taken into consideration

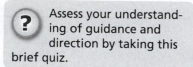
Assess your understanding of guidance and direction by taking this brief quiz.

Finally, think about the importance of celebrating successful outcomes, especially of clients and client systems. Remember that even though you worked hard to help clients, in the end, it is their success to be celebrated. Although you can take gratification from such good outcomes, refrain from taking all the credit for success. In addition, your definition of and expectations for success may not be the same as your clients. In most situations, except perhaps at times in involuntary situations, clients are the ones who define what success it and to what degree it has been achieved.

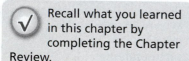
Recall what you learned in this chapter by completing the Chapter Review.

Self-Assessment of Practicum Strengths Post-Test: A Workbook Activity

Refer to the Self-Assessment of Practicum Strengths assessment in Chapter 1, Purpose and Expectations for Practicum. You completed this at the outset of your practicum as a pretest measure of your strengths for practicum. Complete it again now that your practicum is completed, and analyze the areas in which you have shown significant professional growth as well as the areas in which you still need development.

Analyzing Ineffectiveness: A Workbook Activity

Using the information in this chapter and that contained in Table 15.3, Understanding Ineffective Interventions, discuss the concept of ineffective interventions with your field instructor by identifying an intervention that they considered ineffective and that taught them significant lessons in some way. Use the following critical thinking questions together to structure your analysis of this ineffective intervention.

1. What intervention at any level of practice can you share that taught you something important about practice, and from which you can learn?

_____

_____

_____

2. What client contributors might have been partially responsible for the ineffective outcomes?

_____

_____

_____

3. What social work contributors might have been partially responsible for the ineffective outcomes?

_____

_____

_____

4. How did this experience improve your ability to design and implement effective interventions?

_____

_____

_____

5. How can this experience and others like it help you as a student?

_____

_____

_____

Suggested Learning Activities

- Compare the practicum evaluation instrument used by your school with the evaluation tool used to evaluate the performance of social workers in your agency. This will help you identify what is expected of social workers that is not expected of practicum students.

- Evaluate yourself using both your school's evaluation instrument and the sample tool in the learning agreement/evaluation tool for generalist social work in Chapter 3 Developing a Learning Plan.

- Identify fears you may have about being evaluated and discuss them with your supervisor.

- Talk with other practicum students about their experiences with the evaluation process.

Suggested Readings

Brun, Carl F. *A Practical Guide to Social Service Evaluation.* Chicago: Lyceum Books, 2005.

Courneyer, Barry R., and Mary J. Stanley. *The Social Work Portfolio: Planning, Assessing, and Documenting Lifelong Learning in a Dynamic Profession.* Pacific Grove, CA: Brooks/Cole, 2002.

Ellis, Rodney A., Kimberly Crane, Misty Y. Gould, and Suzanne Shatila. *The Macro Practitioner's Workbook: A Step-by-Step Guide to Effectiveness of Organizations and Communities.* Florence, KY: Brooks Cole, 2008.

Grinnel, Richard, and Yvonne Unrau. *Social Work Research and Evaluation.* 10th ed. New York: Oxford University Press, 2013.

Kapp, Stephen, and Gary Anderson. *Agency-Based Program Evaluation: Lessons from Practice.* Los Angeles: Sage Publications, 2010.

Magnabosco, Jennifer, and Ronald Manderscheid. *Outcomes Measurement in the Human Services: Cross-Cultural Issues of Methods in the Era of Health Reform.* 2nd ed. Washington, DC: NASW Press, 2011.

National Association of Social Workers. *Code of Ethics.* Washington, DC: NASW Press, 1999.

Roberts-DeGennaro, Maria, and Sondra Fogel. *Using Evidence to Inform Practice for Community and Organizational Change.* Chicago: Lyceum Books, 2010.

Rzepnicki, Tina, Stanley McCracken, and Harold Briggs. *From Task-Centered Social Work to Evidence-Based and Integrative Practice: Reflections on History and Implementation.* Chicago: Lyceum Books, 2012.

Shaw, Ian. *Practice and Research: Contemporary Social Work Studies.* Williston, VT: Ashgate, 2012.

Sheafor, Bradford, and Charles Horejsi. *Techniques and Guidelines for Social Work Practice.* 10th ed. Boston: Pearson Education, 2015.

Smith, Michael. *Handbook of Program Evaluation for Social Work and Health Professionals.* New York, NY: Oxford University Press, 2010.

Thayer, Bruce, and Monica Pignotti. *Science and Pseudoscience in Social Work Practice.* New York: Springer Publishing, 2015.

Unray, Yvonne, Peter Gabor, and Richard Grinnell. *Evaluation in Social Work: The Art and Science of Practice.* 4th ed. New York: Oxford University Press, 2007.

Westerfelt, Alex, and Tracy Dietz. *Planning and Conducting Agency-Based Research.* 4th ed. Boston: Pearson Education, 2010.

16

Merging Self and Profession

©MD3D / FOTOLIA

LEARNING OUTCOMES

- Integrate personal and professional perspectives on social work practice.
- Develop self-care plan.
- Identify the need for ongoing professional development.
- Summarize the dynamics of a satisfying professional career.

CHAPTER PREVIEW

This chapter provides content on the *integration of the personal and professional aspects of social work as a profession*, including effective ways to engage in a personally meaningful profession while also promoting balance through *effective self-care strategies*. Information on burnout, compassion fatigue, and vicarious trauma is offered, as are reflective questions designed to stimulate critical thinking about the personal *challenges of social work as a profession*.

Your choice of social work as a profession was very likely an outgrowth of your commitment to helping others, facilitating social change, and contributing to social justice. Hopefully your practicum experience has reaffirmed your commitment to the profession and enhanced your knowledge and skills as well. Your commitment to ensuring the welfare of others, making a significant difference in the world, and promoting social justice has hopefully been reinforced up to this point in time, and reflecting on the integration of you as a person with you as a professional will help you consider the relationship between the two.

185

BACKGROUND AND CONTEXT

Each of us is an individual with a unique personality and set of abilities and interests that are brought to the choice of a profession. In addition, each profession has a discreet set of demands and required skills. For you to be satisfied and effective as a social worker, there must be a good *match between you and the profession* as well as a good *balance between your personal and professional selves*. Selecting a career or occupation is one of the most important decisions you will ever make. That decision will have far-reaching implications for your basic contentment in life as well as the level of satisfaction you find in your work. Your clients will be best served if you understand how to *use yourself as a professional tool* that is built upon *self-awareness*, commitment to professional values, and ongoing professional growth.

Ethical and Professional Behavior

Behavior: Use reflection and self-regulation to manage personal values and maintain professionalism in practice situations.

Critical Thinking Question: In what ways can reflection and self-regulation be used to maintain a healthy balance between your personal and professional lives? How will this help both you and your clients?

Watch this video about committing ourselves to impossible tasks, holding ourselves to unreasonable standards, and letting audacity be our hallmark. What messages resonate with you as a social worker? www.youtube.com /watch?v=iTFq9p6WWpk

Many social workers describe themselves as *called to the profession of social work* because they are committed to and passionate about helping others and they find the profession's values compatible with their own. They want to make a positive contribution to their community and world, and they see that the practice of social work is a way of doing that. Some also feel drawn to the profession because events and experiences in their lives have opened their eyes to certain problems and to the needs of other people. Others are attracted to social work because they have the natural skills and abilities necessary to the profession and see social work education as a formal way of acquiring the ability to make even more impact in terms of social justice. Most are drawn to social work by virtue of the way they think the world should be, the responsibility they feel to act on behalf of others, and the belief that they are compelled to become involved in social justice efforts.

It is important for those preparing for such a rewarding and challenging career to become skilled in *merging the personal and professional aspects of practice*. They must have a *high level of self-awareness* so they can make good choices in relation to the type of job they seek, practice self-care and stress management, and balance personal and professional responsibilities. Social workers must be aware of their unique gifts, their values, and their biases. Such self-awareness is critical to becoming a professional who is effective in his or her use of self in engaging with clients. Social workers must understand how their particular style and manner of interacting is perceived by others, especially by clients. Those planning to enter social work must be emotionally healthy, skilled in communication, able to build and maintain relationships, able to manage stress, and willing to continually learn and grow, both personally and professionally. It is a career-long challenge to maintain a balanced perspective on both personal and professional lives and commitments, and to maintain them in such a manner that they both flourish.

Choosing a helping profession as one's life's work means that you care deeply about those you serve. This commitment to others may take a toll on your personal life unless you learn to find a healthy balance between work and personal life. It is not possible to make a complete separation between our personal and professional lives. Our work affects our personal lives and our personal lives affect our work. Our personal experiences and life circumstances have the potential to impact our work both positively and negatively, and we must learn to manage the impact of our personal life for the benefit of our clients. We also must take care to protect the quality of our personal lives in light of the demands of the profession in terms of time, emotional energy, and the potential personal toll of dealing with the painful experiences of clients and injustices in society. Of course, this is no easy task, but it is necessary if we are to be effective as professionals and healthy as individuals.

It is important to find this balance because it is easy to allow your concern for clients to overcome you and your personal life. You may worry about them or take more responsibility for them than is healthy for you. It is important to set clear *professional boundaries* between your personal life and your work early in your career because this will help you retain your energy, enthusiasm, and optimism while also preventing discouragement and burnout. Ask your field instructor for suggestions on how to do this.

> **Ethical and Professional Behavior**
>
> **Behavior: Engage in practices that advance social, economic, and environmental justice.**
>
> Critical Thinking Question: How might the ability to maintain a balance between personal and professional lives be considered a practice that advances social justice?

The relationship between *career satisfaction* and one's overall satisfaction with oneself and life is a close and intertwined one. Those who are satisfied with their careers and who maintain their overall well-being in a challenging profession tend to exhibit a variety of individual characteristics, abilities, and attitudes. These are the professionals who maintain perspective on themselves and their work, continue to learn and grow, remain optimistic, and continuously grow in their skills. Contextual and organizational factors also contribute to career satisfaction and longevity among social workers committed to the profession. Finally, societal factors also contribute in very important ways to the context that either supports or undermines professional satisfaction and success. Those three categories of contributing factors are highlighted in Table 16.1, which lists specific contributions in each area.

Keep these factors in mind as you begin the search for a professional position in the field of social work. The work itself will be both challenging and rewarding, so the work environment should also contribute to your overall well-being as a professional. This is an example of the ways in which the social work profession and the social systems surrounding it interact over time, ultimately impacting both clients and the professionals serving them.

> **?** Assess your understanding of background and context by taking this brief quiz.

GUIDANCE AND DIRECTION

Social work requires an *integration of professional knowledge, ethics, and self-awareness*. It is not enough to know about people, to have skills, to know theories, or to understand models and techniques. You as a person must merge with you as a professional. Remember that all the skills and knowledge in the world are not enough to make you an effective social worker. You also need to bring your personal gifts, strengths, creativity, passion, and commitment to the social work profession. It is in the unique blending of your personal qualities and your professional education that you will become a truly skilled and qualified social worker.

Table 16.1   Contributing Factors to Professional Satisfaction

Individual Factors

- Knowledge and skill necessary for effective practice
- Values consistent with professional goals
- Balance of collaborative and autonomous approach to work
- Optimism, enthusiasm, self-efficacy, and belief in possibilities
- Ability to manage stress
- Flexibility, openness, and commitment to professional growth

Organizational Factors

- Reasonable workload and adequate funding
- Agency support and training
- Opportunity for professional growth and creativity
- Inclusion in agency mission and program development
- Collegiality, sharing of responsibility, and empowerment
- Invited participation in agency visioning

Societal Factors

- Political economy supportive of social justice efforts
- Positive societal attitudes toward clients and profession
- Social policy effectiveness that supports social work efforts
- Societal commitment to prevention of social problems
- Societal commitment to promotion of social justice
- Societal support of social work mission

Who you are as a person is just as important as what you know or what you can do. View your practicum as an opportunity to grow both personally and professionally, and to blend your unique personality and professional style with the requirements of your chosen profession. Over time the two parts of you will blend so that you will bring everything that is unique about you to your personal way of being a social worker.

Seek opportunities to continuously enhance your professional growth. For example, read professional books and journals, attend workshops and in-service training, try out new skills and techniques, think critically about intervention strategies, carefully observe the behavior and practice of social workers in your agency, and spend time talking with knowledgeable and skilled practitioners. Engage in critical self-reflection, asking yourself and trusted colleagues what you can do to continue growing. Open yourself to feedback so that you see yourself as others do. You will certainly see your own growth over time, and this will not only reinforce your choice of social work as a profession but also remind you of the importance of self-awareness as a tool for helping others.

Ask for feedback from coworkers, your field instructor, and clients. Use this information to better understand who you are, what you have to offer, and what you may need to change in

Practice-informed Research

Behavior: Use practice experience and theory to inform scientific inquiry and research.

Critical Thinking Question: How can your questions about what you learn in practicum translate into actual research? How is practice wisdom related to research?

order to become a skilled and effective social worker. You are certain to see that you have grown over time, your questions have become more probing, and your reflections are more sophisticated. This will reinforce the fact that *you are growing as a professional*. Your practicum is truly a job-related experience. It is relevant preparation for practice and the job market. Do your best and remember that the skills you develop now, combined with favorable evaluations and recommendations from your field instructor, can help you obtain employment in the profession.

Observe *how social workers in your agency deal with challenges* such as high caseloads, potentially modest salaries, unmotivated and difficult clients, seemingly intractable social problems, funding cuts, and the stress of dealing with deeply emotional and painful situations on a daily basis. Begin now to develop stress management skills and habits that will help you avoid excessive job-related stress or burnout. Learn how to set limits; define and keep *personal and professional boundaries*, which will maintain your level of well-being; make time for your family and yourself; and maintain a positive outlook on clients and the work you do. Refer to Table 16.1, which highlights individual, organizational, and societal factors that contribute to professional satisfaction in social work.

Think about how you will deal with the *stresses and challenges of professional social work*. Learn how to avoid negative consequences for yourself and continue to maintain optimism and belief in possibility. You will need to find ways to avoid *burnout*, which is the result of overworking, lack of support, and the inability to balance the demands of work with one's personal life. You also need to be aware of and avoid *compassion fatigue*, to which social workers who care deeply about the welfare of others may fall prey if they are not able to manage the impact of extending oneself to benefit clients over time. Finally, make certain you understand the possibility of *secondary or vicarious traumatic stress*, which is the negative impact on social workers of bearing witness to the pain and suffering of others and taking on the pain and trauma themselves. All of these are possible, and you must find a way to prevent this from happening, deal with it productively should it occur, and help others in the social work profession stay healthy as well.

To manage these challenges and maintain the quality of both your personal and professional life, refer to Table 16.2, Matching Self-Care Strategies with Areas of Stress for Social Workers. It highlights the challenges of social work as holistic, including stressors in the physical, intellectual, psychological, social, cultural, and spiritual realms of life and practice. It suggests that social workers who experience stress in these areas of their professional life design a holistic self-care strategy that employs approaches in a variety of areas. Social workers, like you, who are committed to their profession over time, will develop their own individual approach to self-care that maintains both personal and professional well-being.

Begin developing the habit of monitoring your own professional growth. Ask yourself these questions regularly, knowing that your responses will help you to design a professional development plan and adjust it over time.

- What is my *vision* for myself as a social worker?
- Do I feel a *calling* to the profession of social work?

Engagement

Behavior: Use empathy, reflection, and interpersonal skills to effectively engage diverse clients and constituencies.

Critical Thinking Question: In what ways is the use of empathy with clients a potential risk factor for the personal and professional well-being of clients?

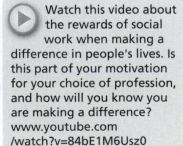

Watch this video about the rewards of social work when making a difference in people's lives. Is this part of your motivation for your choice of profession, and how will you know you are making a difference? www.youtube.com /watch?v=84bE1M6Usz0

Table 16.2 Matching Self-Care Strategies with Areas of Stress for Social Workers

This tool is designed to encourage you to thoughtfully identify the realms of your life in which you might potentially experience stress as a social worker. It also provides a way to identify individualized strategies to manage the stresses in these areas by engaging in self-care activities in these same realms of your life. Apply this tool to yourself by identifying the stressors you have experienced during your practicum and designing and committing to self-care strategies that will help you manage this stress and keep you fresh, optimistic, and healthy.

Areas of Stress	Strategies					
	Physical Self-care	Intellectual Self-care	Psychological Self-care	Social Self-care	Cultural Self-care	Spiritual Self-care
Physical Stressors Fatigue, overwork, neglected health and fitness						
Intellectual Stressors Continual need to learn new techniques and expand knowledge						
Psychological Stressors Worry, anxiety, stress, guilt, counter-transference, inadequate coping skills						
Social Stressors Impact of work on relationships, dealing with colleagues and supervisors						
Cultural Stressors Cross-cultural work, discomfort with diversity						
Spiritual Stressors Impact of work on values and belief system						

- How can I maintain my **commitment** in the face of the challenges and stresses of the profession?
- What **social work values** are most important to me as I embark on this career?
- Am I **growing** as a person and a professional?
- Do I **know myself** better than I did last month? Last year?
- Am I **satisfied** with who I am and what I am doing?
- How can I **continue to grow** and change in a positive way?
- Do I continue to see the **potential, possibility, and strengths** of clients?
- Am I **optimistic** about social change?
- What **self-care activities** can I engage in to maintain energy and optimism?

- After *5, 10, or 15 years in the profession*, in what type of social work do I expect to be engaged?
- What *advice* would I give to social work students who are just starting practicum?
- What *impact* do I hope to make as a social worker?

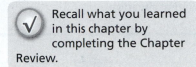

? Assess your understanding of guidance and direction by taking this brief quiz.

√ Recall what you learned in this chapter by completing the Chapter Review.

Professional Development Plan: A Workbook Activity

Using the following format, begin the process of developing a professional development plan. Consult with your field instructor and faculty supervisor, incorporating their guidance into your plan. You may add additional areas for professional growth upon which to focus your time and energy.

Areas for Professional Growth	Plan	Timeline
Knowledge Attainment		
Understanding of … Evidence regarding …		
Skills Acquisition		
Development of … Mastery of …		
Social Work Role Mastery		
Clinical role Supervisory role		
Degrees, Certifications, Licenses, Specialties, and Credentials to Earn		
Licensure Advanced credentials		
Professional Experiences to Secure		
Generalist practice Specialty practice		
Career Goals		
Short-term goals Long-term goals		
Professional Collaboration		
Social work community of practice Interdisciplinary community of practice		

Suggested Learning Activities

- Interview experienced social workers in your agency and in other agencies. Ask about their level of job satisfaction, as well as their strategies for self-care.
- Speak with social workers who have obtained advanced degrees (MSW, PhD, or DSW) and ask them to help you consider the possibility of further education.

- Observe the self-care practices of those around you and adopt those that match your needs.
- Determine the ways in which your agency supports its workers in terms of self-care, stress management, and critical incident debriefing in the face of very challenging situations.

- Examine the social work job openings advertised in local and regional newspapers, public agency bulletins, and NASW news. (The NASW website is www.socialworkers.org.)

Suggested Readings

Birkenmaier, Julie, and Marla Berg-Weger. *The Practicum Companion for Social Work: Integrating Class and Field Work*. 3rd ed. Boston: Allyn and Bacon, 2011.

Rothman, Juliet Cassuto. *The Self-Awareness Workbook for Social Workers*. Boston: Allyn and Bacon, 2000.

Schon, Donald A., and Aleksandr Romanovich Luria. *The Reflective Practitioner: How Professionals Think in Action*. New York: Basic Books, 1990.

Seden, Janet, Sarah Matthews, Mick McCormick, and Alun Morgan. *Professional Development in Social Work: Complex Issues in Practice*. Clifton, NJ: Routledge, 2010.

Skovholt, Thomas, and Michelle Trotter-Mathison. *The Resilient Practitioner: Burnout Prevention and Self-Care Strategies for Counselors, Therapist, Teachers, and Health Professionals*. 2nd ed. Clifton, NJ: Routledge, 2010.

17

Leadership for Social Justice

©EVERYTHINGPOSSIBLE / FOTOLIA

LEARNING OUTCOMES

- Summarize the role and characteristics of leaders.
- Identify offensive and defensive leadership tasks.
- Summarize emerging issues requiring effective social work leadership.
- Commit to development of leadership traits for social justice.

CHAPTER PREVIEW

Now that your practicum is nearing its completion, you have nearly fulfilled all of the requirements necessary to obtain your degree. No doubt you are excited about job possibilities and thinking seriously about the personal satisfaction with and ramifications entering the world of social work. This is a *time of transition*. What lies ahead for you? Where will you work? What will be expected of you? What kind of social worker do you hope to become? What contributions can you make to the welfare of others and to the profession of social work? What will you learn? What contributions will you make? Perhaps even more important, what kind of person do you want to become? This chapter invites you to *reflect on these questions*.

BACKGROUND AND CONTEXT

The *mission of social work* is rooted in social change and *social justice*, and hopefully your practicum has reinforced the importance and centrality of that emphasis to your work. Whether your professional work finds you working at the micro, mezzo, or macro level, social justice is at the forefront. Because of the ongoing and challenging nature of the fight for social justice, social workers must embrace the role of leader in order to achieve the goals of social justice. Because of the personal and professional commitment to the welfare of others through the promotion of social justice, the practice of social work usually brings both challenges and rewards. Hopefully your journey as a social worker will involve a professional life filled with meaning and purpose, and you will emerge as a leader within your community and the profession you have chosen based on a commitment to social justice.

It is both exciting and perhaps daunting to think about being a social worker in light of the numerous social problems facing people and society in general. There are many problems to be addressed and numerous clients to be served. Injustices must be challenged and many programs need to be envisioned, designed, or improved. There is so much to be done and not enough resources devoted to the challenge. There is also much more to learn as you move from the academic world of a practicum student to the real world of the professional social worker. Finally, a great deal is expected of social workers, and much responsibility is given to them.

Because you have completed the requirements for a social work degree in a program accredited by the Council on Social Work Education, your professors and field instructor have concluded that you are ready to begin the practice of social work. Although you may still feel anxious and not quite prepared to assume the full responsibilities of a social worker, your professors and supervisors believe that you possess the knowledge and basic skills needed to move into a social agency and apply what you have learned. You have been educated in an academic setting, trained in a social agency, and exposed to many social problems and various ways of addressing them. Do not underestimate what you have learned and what you are capable of doing. You are now becoming a professional social worker by virtue of all you have learned and the ways in which you have demonstrated your competence and commitment to ethical practice.

Even though you are moving into the role of a professional, it is important to reflect often on what you have learned academically about the unique mission of social work and its commitment to those in society considered most vulnerable and oppressed. Social work is a profession deeply committed, by both its history and current practice, to creating communities and a society that will nurture the well-being of individuals and families and to making sure that all people have access to the basic resources and opportunities necessary to live with dignity. You have entered a profession that is committed to challenging systems and institutional structures that do not treat people in a fair and humane manner.

Good social work practitioners view the practice of social work as much more than the tasks and activities listed in their job description or suggested in their agency's mission statement. They work hard at whatever they are hired to do, but also assume additional responsibilities that they identify and care about because of their commitment to the welfare of others. Social work, at its unique best, is *going beyond one's job description* and acting on a commitment to social justice. It means weaving together the networks of people and resources that can bring about needed changes at the community, state, and national levels. A true social work leader sees what is possible and is not constrained by a job description or by limited resources. A leader develops a vision, knows what needs to be done, and makes things happen. A social work leader builds on acquired knowledge and skills and generates synergy by bringing committed people together.

You have no doubt been schooled in the *person-in-environment perspective* that is fundamental to the way social workers view people, assess human problems and concerns, and design interventions. Social workers, whether employed to work at the micro or macro level, must be cognizant of the wider societal context of the lives and problems of their clients and the context of the agencies, programs, and interventions that address these client concerns. For example, a social worker employed at the micro level as an advocate for those in poverty should question why poverty exists and take a macro-level leadership role in addressing the myriad of macro-level contributors to poverty. Conversely, social workers working on the macro level to change social policies must never forget the very serious impact of any social policy changes on the lives of individual people struggling with poverty.

This is a very broad and demanding mission, but a crucial one that a leader will embrace. Whatever your job description will say, the *entire spectrum of social functioning* is germane to your work. If you do micro-level social work, many larger social systems will be the context for your work. If you engage in macro-level social work, it is on behalf of many individuals and families. Commit now to always looking for the connections between social systems in order to enhance social functioning at all levels.

The realities and time pressures associated with employment in an agency that has a particular mission and program tend to set in motion a number of forces that might narrow the range of your concerns, interests, and vision. You will feel very busy with all of the demands of your job, but it will be important that you find ways to *remain involved in social issues beyond the scope of your work responsibilities*. Doing so will help remind you that others care about their work as much as you and can serve as a source of inspiration for you. Strive to maintain a wide range of interests, involvements, and professional activities. Seek out new ideas, even when they are not immediately applicable in your everyday work.

As you enter into the work of a particular agency, you may discover that the agency uses an *unfamiliar conceptual framework or rationale* to guide its practice activities. As you are exposed to new practice theories, remember that each one needs to be examined in terms of its potential to enhance practice effectiveness, its appropriateness for use with particular types of clients in particular settings, evidence of its effectiveness, its stated or implied assumptions about clients and the process of change, and its compatibility with social work values. If you become competent in a number of approaches, you will *prepare yourself for leadership* by virtue of your knowledge and ability to bring various strategies to your work.

To know whether you are being effective over time, and to develop expertise in your work efforts, you will need to document your work and study the outcomes of your practice, both individually and in concert with other professionals and agencies. Be ready to change your approach if you are not being as effective as you had hoped or think is possible. Needless to say, much of what social workers do and much of what clients experience is difficult to measure, but resist the temptation to use this as an excuse for not making a genuine effort to evaluate your practice. You cannot improve your practice unless you are willing to look at it critically and allow others to offer constructive criticisms.

To the extent possible, build your knowledge base upon empirical and scientific studies, but remember that there are many other sources of useful knowledge. Some are empirical and some are not. It is important to balance the *positivist view of knowledge building*, which rests primarily on the scientific method of understanding, with contributions from *practice wisdom*, which refers to the collective professional experiences and observations of practitioners and the *postmodern view of knowledge*, which values the contributions of alternative theories, qualitative research, and deconstruction of assumptions. Add to that the additional insights derived from study of politics, humanities, religion, and classic and modern literature. Finally, *learn from your clients* as you listen to their stories and experiences, and add their wisdom to yours. These widely varying sources of knowledge will be exactly what you need for practice. Consider Table 17.1 that describes the contributions and limitations to understanding a variety of sources of knowledge. Commit yourself to learning from these sources over time.

Table 17.1   Sources of Knowledge: Contributions and Limitations

Source of Knowledge	Contribution to Understanding	Limitation to Understanding
Theory	Orienting theories provide guide for describing and understanding. Practice theories provide models and techniques for intervention.	Orienting theories are guides only, and do not always consider individuality and diversity. Practice theories must be tested and used with intention.
Empirical Evidence	Research tests effectiveness. Research leads to evidence-based and best practices.	Research can lead to tendency toward reductionistic and deterministic view of clients. Interventions are only considered best practices when they are best for individual clients and client systems.
Postmodern Thought	Postmodern thought suggests that not all knowledge for practice is empirical. Postmodern thought avoids conclusions based on empiricism alone.	Postmodern thought must be accompanied by empiricism to be complete. Postmodern thought is broad and can be hard to test or apply.
Practice Wisdom	Practice wisdom promotes self-reflection and professional growth. Practice wisdom provides opportunity for refinement of knowledge.	Practice wisdom alone is not complete enough for practice. Knowledge gained in practice may be biased and untested.
Client Accounts	Client accounts are reminders that clients are the experts on their lives. Client accounts are reminders of whose values are central.	Client accounts may be incomplete and lack insight. Client accounts may not take into account other perspectives.
Interdisciplinary Knowledge	Knowledge outside social work provides broad scope of information. Knowledge outside social work provides the basis for intervention.	Knowledge outside social work is not based on the same values as social work. Knowledge outside social work must be synthesized into coherent whole and applied.

As you use new research findings and theories drawn from the social and behavioral sciences, consider the observation by social scientists that such knowledge is *socially constructed*. Our knowledge of a social or psychological phenomenon or a particular human problem is shaped and limited by the context in which it was studied by our individual assumptions and values, by our position in relation to the problem, and by the language used to describe it. It is very much tied to culture, history, economics, and politics. Our knowledge is, at best, incomplete and only temporarily true. The awareness that knowledge is a social construction helps us put data and conclusions in perspective and realize that the concepts and theories used in practice, no matter how well conceived and impressive, are purely human inventions. It is your prerogative and responsibility to thoughtfully question all findings and claims, regardless of their source.

It is the job of critically reflective social workers to analyze and be willing to deconstruct their knowledge and what is being told to them. This means that you must examine what you know, question how you came to know it, ask yourself how this view might be inaccurate or limited, and become comfortable at times with not knowing everything you need to know. Social work leaders do this because they want and need to, not because they are students and are being asked to for an assignment or learning experience. In a similar vein, recognize that the *concept of client* is a human invention or *social construction* that has arisen out of our cultural views and presumptions about who is in need of help, who is powerless to help himself or herself, and who is qualified to help another person. Always be sensitive to the possibility that agencies, social workers, and other professionals can misuse their power and authority to label a person, family, or group as troubled and in need of certain services or interventions. Remember also that the designation of one person as a client and another as a social worker does not mean that the social worker is more knowledgeable or more insightful than the client. Rather, the opposite could be true. The lines between social worker and client, although useful, are arbitrary and can limit our ability to relate to each other in significant ways.

Becoming involved in *professional organizations* can support your work, challenge you intellectually, and also can remind you to engage with others who are involved in the struggle to create a just society. Remember that you are expected to contribute to the ongoing development and shaping of the profession, and that social work educators need to hear your observations and suggestions as much as clients need your skills. You will be expected to voice your opinions about directions you believe the profession should take based on your observations and your projections of future needs. For example, you will need to speak up when you see your profession becoming focused too heavily on one aspect of social work to the detriment of its overall mission.

> ▶ After viewing this video on social transformation, compare the content with the way in which the profession of social work and schools of social work view their mission. How are they consistent with each other, and how will this guide your practice? www.youtube.com /watch?v=PfTe4j1Zc9g

Deciding to live and work in the *world of ideas and questions* and committing to lifelong learning are important for social workers to remain effective over time. There are numerous approaches you can take to continue learning and growing, which will not only make you more effective but will also make you a better, more informed, and capable practitioner. The following professional growth responsibilities are often expected of social workers:

- Read *professional literature* for professional development and to remain current in the field

- Attend *advanced training* to enhance knowledge and skills
- Join or form a group of professionals that takes seriously its commitment to *continuing education and peer supervision*
- *Look globally and internationally* for possible solutions to nagging and serious social problems
- *Learn from your clients* who experience on a daily basis what you may only observe, read about, or imagine
- *Identify the connections* between social conditions and social problems resulting from them
- Stay *connected to schools of social work* through training and conferences, and offering guest lectures
- Talk on a regular basis to *those with whom you fundamentally disagree* in order to retain an open mind and clarify your own beliefs and values
- Find ways to come to know and *understand yourself* better over time
- *Supervise practicum students*, recalling what it was like to be a student

Recognizing your ability to be a *catalyst for change* will be important, which means that you can bring individuals and groups together, contribute your skills and knowledge, and stimulate positive movement or changes that would not have occurred without your intervention. Remember that you are not alone in your efforts to help others. There are many social workers who will support and encourage you in your efforts. Seek them out, offer your support in return, and find avenues of renewal for yourself, both personally and professionally.

You already know how important it will be to take care of yourself, recognize the good in the world as well as the problems, celebrate large and small successes, learn to laugh, and cultivate the sources of your passion and strength. It will be vital to use your family, friends, spiritual beliefs, and core values to guide you, and take pride in your chosen profession.

? Assess your understanding of background and context by taking this brief quiz.

GUIDANCE AND DIRECTION

As a social worker you will encounter many situations of *oppression and social and economic injustice.* You will also encounter situations in which agency policies, programs, and practices are in need of revision to make them fairer and more effective. You will want to change these situations but may quickly discover that bringing about needed and meaningful change can be a difficult and slow process. In order to bring about change you must be willing and able to assume the *role, tasks, and responsibilities of leadership*. Desirable changes do not happen by accident. Rather, they are set in motion by individuals who assert themselves, articulate their beliefs, and step forward to take on the hard work of leading.

Although it may be true that a few leaders are the so-called born leaders, most had to learn the skills of leadership much like they learned any other skill. Aspiring leaders must consciously and continually cultivate the development of those qualities, ways of thinking, attitudes, and interpersonal skills that are associated with effective leadership. Leadership is much more than having good ideas. It is not enough to know what needs to be done. Leadership is the ability to make things happen and to inspire others to join in the effort. Leaders must have a clear vision of what they want to accomplish. It is the leader's vision that gives him or her the critically important sense of purpose, direction, and self-confidence to make difficult decisions. Equally important, they must be able to articulate this vision and explain it in words that others understand. The vision must be one that can be translated into action steps and programs that are inspiring but also feasible and realistic.

This **sense of purpose** must be evident in all that the leader does. Indecisiveness and the unwillingness to take action when action is clearly necessary can deeply undermine confidence in a leader's ability. It is better for a leader to occasionally make a bad decision than to avoid making a critically important decision, so learn to be decisive and bold when necessary as well as thoughtful and well prepared.

Effective leaders **lead by example**. Followers are inspired and motivated by the passion, resolve, courage, hard work, and sacrifices of their leaders. Leaders must model the behaviors they want to see in others. They should not ask others to do what they are unwilling to do themselves. Leaders must demonstrate respect and genuine concern for the wishes, values, and abilities of those they lead. They must be willing to curtail some of their own preferences and plans in order to avoid moving too far ahead of those they lead. Leaders cannot lead unless there are people who choose to follow them.

> ### Human Rights and Justice
>
> **Behavior: Apply their understanding of social, economic, and environmental justice to advocate for human rights at the individual and system levels.**
>
> **Critical Thinking Question**: How do effective communication skills help leaders advocate for human rights?

Effective leaders must maintain open and honest communication with those they lead. This communication must keep everyone focused on the goal while attending to the concerns, fears, and ambivalence they may have about investing their time, energy, and money in working toward this goal. Good leaders anticipate possible conflicts and disagreements among those they lead. They are proactive in taking steps to prevent or resolve these conflicts before they can distract from goal achievement and splinter the followers into competing factions.

Leaders must be skilled in the **art of collaboration and building bridges** between individuals and organizations. They must reward others for their cooperation and share the credit for success with others, even those with whom they may disagree. Leaders must be willing to compromise when this is a necessary step toward reaching the sought-after goal.

The exercise of leadership always occurs within a **context of competing and conflicting forces**. Leaders work to shape, guide, and redirect those forces, so they move in directions that produce the desired effect and move people toward the desired goal. Because leaders must function within environments and situations that are unpredictable and always changing, they must be willing to take necessary risks and cope with ever-present ambiguity and uncertainty.

Effective leaders possess a **high level of self-awareness**. They understand their own strengths and limitations and constantly examine their own motives and behavior. They understand themselves well enough to see when their leadership style is effective and how they are perceived by others. Some leaders destroy their capacity to lead by allowing feelings of self-importance and a need for recognition to dominate their decisions or by becoming arrogant and overly confident because of past successes. Decide now that you will never let that happen to you.

> Watch this video about the necessity of combining an inward and outward perspective to create social change. How can these ideas be integrated into the social work concepts of self-awareness and commitment to social justice? www.youtube.com /watch?v=U0YbXHMANCI

In addition to the factors mentioned previously, the following personal qualities and abilities are important to the exercise of effective leadership. Identify which of these characteristics describe you right now and which might describe you in the near future as you head into leadership positions in the profession.

- Capacity to *think critically* and examine personal decisions and actions
- Capacity to *articulate a vision* and purpose in ways people can understand
- *Perseverance* when faced with difficulties and disappointments
- Ability to *delegate responsibility* and teach or *empower others* to perform as well as they can
- Ability to *make difficult decisions* in complex and fluid situations
- Willingness to *assume personal responsibility* for one's decisions and the outcomes resulting from actions taken
- Personal flexibility, *openness to new ideas*, and the capacity to work with people with various abilities and from diverse backgrounds
- Ability to *create a sense of belonging and community* among those working toward the same goals
- Ability to *make effective use of available time* and get things done
- Willingness to *assess one's own effectiveness* in a nondefensive manner and to adopt approaches that will be more effective
- Ability to take *proactive* rather than reactive approach to work

Ethical and Professional Behavior

Behavior: Make ethical decisions by applying the standards of the National Association of Social Workers (NASW) Code of Ethics, relevant laws and regulations, models for ethical decision making, ethical conduct of research, and additional codes of ethics as appropriate to context.

Critical Thinking Question: Which ethical competencies in Chapter 12 are most closely related to the characteristics of an effective leader committed to social justice?

Leaders in the social work profession find themselves in the midst of public debates, tensions, competing points of view, and value systems which are on the far ends of the spectrum. Each of these contemporary discussions highlights the challenges of leadership in bringing together varying opinions, values, and preferred approaches to preventing or dealing with social problems and issues. For example, social work leaders must lead their organizations through discussions such as the following ones. Think about how you as a leader will negotiate these conversations in a way that fulfills the social work mission.

- Are social services a *human right or a privilege*?
- What is the most effective combination of *private and public responses* to social problems?
- What is the best balance between *universal entitlement and eligibility* criteria?
- At what *level(s) of practice* are social problems best addressed, from *micro to macro*?
- Should a *scarcity of resources* guide and control what a leader attempts to accomplish?
- How should *personal responsibility* be balanced with the *availability of social safety nets*?

Work hard to become what is commonly referred to as a *transformational leader*—someone who understands and embodies the interpersonal and moral aspects of leadership. Using their passion, vision, deeply held beliefs, and strong moral values, transformational leaders inspire others. They are able to get others to join with them because they are enthusiastic and energetic. Their integrity leads others to trust them. Their genuine desire to see others succeed makes others more motivated and enthusiastic. This form of leadership, which is motivated by the welfare of everyone involved in a common effort, is markedly different from the form of leadership that pays attention only to the tasks at hand. Try to become the sort of leader who balances the work to be done with the professional and personal support of those working together.

Clearly, it is a challenge to be an effective leader in one's agency or profession. It is an even more difficult undertaking when the leader's goal is to *promote social and economic justice*. However, this is at the heart of social work. At a fundamental level, justice can be defined as fairness in social interactions. Although there are several categories or types of justice, social and economic justice are of special concern to social workers. *Social justice* refers to the basic fairness and moral rightness of the social arrangements and institutional structures that impact the people of a community or society. *Economic justice* (also called *distributive justice*) can be defined as that dimension of justice having to do with the material or the economic aspects of a community or society.

Because social and economic injustices are, by definition, embedded in existing *institutional arrangements and social policies*, many political, economic, and cultural forces are at work maintaining the unjust conditions. Those who seek change will encounter many powerful individuals and groups who will want to maintain the status quo. In order to secure real change, a leader working for social justice must be willing to take substantial risks and make significant personal sacrifices when engaging in social justice work.

In order to accomplish social change and promote the welfare of all, leaders must both make positive things happen and prevent or block negative things from happening. This can be referred to as *offensive and defensive approaches to social justice work*. *Offensive approaches to social justice* are those proactive, positive, and affirmative practices that promote planned social justice work. They build on and capitalize on existing forces for change, resources, and values. They require specific knowledge and skills related to making things happen. *Defensive approaches to social justice* are those resistance, critiquing, and reframing practices that fight the status quo and block forces opposing social justice. Table 17.2 highlights the defensive approaches involved in social justice work, and Table 17.3 illustrates the defensive approaches involved in social justice work. Keep these lists as a resource to guide your thinking as you move into professional practice.

Throughout your career, social issues, societal conditions, and projects for the future will require that you understand and adapt to these shifts. Keep informed of the *emerging issues in social work leadership* that will require vision, innovation, critical thinking, and a willingness to improve practice over time. Because of societal and global changes in the social environment, social work itself must change in order to address and embrace those changes. The use of technology in practice presents many advanced methods for providing services, but also involves a number of clinical and ethical issues such as quality of services, confidentiality, and adaptations to practice approaches. The

Diversity and Difference in Practice

Behavior: Apply and communicate understanding of the importance of diversity and difference in shaping life experiences in practice at the micro, mezzo, and macro levels.

Critical Thinking Question: What are some important connections between diversity and social justice that you have observed in practicum? What do they tell you about the role of social work?

Table 17.2   Social Justice Efforts and Offensive Leadership Approaches

Phase of Social Justice Effort	Offensive Leadership Approaches
Consciousness-Raising and Assessment	Learn
	Anticipate forces for and against change
	Recognize problems and resources
	Clarify values
	Promote use of ecosystems perspective
	Scan social environment
	Promote social justice
Building Coalitions	Identify stakeholders
	Inspire participation
	Identify common concerns
	Collaborate
	Mentor other stakeholders
	Empower constituencies
	Focus on solidarity
	Model
Planning and Organizing	Envision
	Engage stakeholders
	Set goals and objectives
	Develop resources
	Build capacity for change
	Encourage innovation
	Acquire political power
Implementation	Put plan into action
	Influence target system
	Supervise
	Monitor and adjust plan as needed
	Maintain focus
	Deal with opposing forces
Evaluation	Evaluate effectiveness
	Transfer power to those impacted
	Share lessons learned
	Disseminate findings
	Contribute to body of knowledge
	Leverage success
	Sustain social change
	Develop best practices
	Evaluate effectiveness

Table 17.3   Social Justice Efforts and Defensive Leadership Approaches

Phase of Social Justice Effort	Defensive Leadership Approaches
Consciousness-Raising and Assessment	Challenge easy and surface-level answers
	Deconstruct myths
	Ask critical questions
	Resist status quo
	Critique forces against change
	Challenge injustice
Building Coalitions	Avoid silo approach to change
	Resist efforts to separate stakeholders
	Challenge special interests
	Recognize resistance
	Block fragmentation of efforts
Planning and Organizing	Avoid surface-level goals and objectives
	Reframe single-level change to multilevel change
	Counter scarcity paradigm of resources
	Block efforts to exclude stakeholders
	Block counterorganizing and splitting efforts
Implementation	Challenge pessimism
	Resist consolidation of power
	Block cuts to funding
	Neutralize resistance
	Address efforts to undermine progress
Evaluation	Block efforts to return to status quo
	Address critiques of efforts
	Address efforts to discredit intervention

limits of funding for social services demands that organizations commit to true interdisciplinary approaches that recognize the mutual interactions between professional perspectives, the contributions of a variety of professions to the solving of social problems, and the approaches to practice that are truly broad and comprehensive.

Additional *emerging issues* include the need to *create knowledge* through program evaluation and the *development of best practices* designated as such by empirical evidence and solicited client input. Future social work practice depends on the ability of leaders to create and build theories, both those that explain social phenomena (orienting and explanatory theories) and those that guide intervention plans at all levels (practice theories and models). This requires leaders and administrators who support social work professionals in their professional development. They must help social workers develop the ability to rely on practice wisdom, empirical evidence, and what is commonly referred to as a *learning edge* that encourages professionals to lean into innovation and develop a *learning culture* within their organizations. Finally, social work leaders must recognize and incorporate an understanding of the impact of global conditions and cultural diversity into their work in creative and effective ways.

As you identify your leadership abilities and skills, and as you work to incorporate the characteristics listed earlier into your practice over time, also consider some very specific ways in which you can acquire the leadership abilities that will be required of you. Commit to *lifelong professional learning* that will keep you abreast of the social work world. Identify mentors for yourself who will help you develop needed skills, networking opportunities, and supervision. Engage in *interdisciplinary work* whenever possible to maintain a broad and inclusive view of social problems and solutions. Become a part of a *community of practice*, which includes mentors, colleagues, confidantes, and support persons from both social work and other professions. This community of practice will help you learn, grow, prioritize, focus, and maintain commitment in the midst of challenging practice situations.

A good leader remembers the *history of the social movement* in which he or she is involved as well as the lessons of the past. Reflect in a critical and appreciative manner on the evolution of the social work profession and the many significant contributions of social workers to social justice and the building of a social welfare system. Educate yourself about the contributions of the social work profession in such areas as Social Security, civil rights, child labor laws, Medicaid, unemployment insurance, minimum wage, the peace movement, and many others. Consider the contributions made by those who developed theories of practice, those who assumed leadership in the academic preparation of professional social workers, and the countless clients whose lives and stories have provided the motivation and inspiration for such service. This will motivate you as you make your own history as a social worker.

Many social workers say that social work is not what they do, but it is who they are. Their professional lives are guided by their personal beliefs, values, and spirituality, and they believe that being a social worker allows them to live out the beliefs and values they hold dear and about which they feel passionate. That notion indicates a compatible merger between person and the profession, as discussed in Chapter 16. However, always remember that you are now and will always be more than your profession and your job. If your whole identity is tied up in being a social worker, broaden your horizons and life experiences. You need to be healthy for your clients, but also for yourself, friends, and family.

Your practicum will soon come to an end, and your professors and field instructors will tell you that you are ready for professional social work practice. You will have earned the designation of a professional social worker by virtue of your academic preparation, your practicum experience, your commitment to the NASW *Code of Ethics*, and your sense of calling to promote social justice. You have all of the tools needed to be a social worker, whether you are working with individual clients or whether your efforts are focused on large-scale social change. Those tools, including your knowledge, your commitment to helping others, and your helping skills, will all come together in

Evaluation

Behavior: Apply evaluation findings to improve practice effectiveness at the micro, mezzo, and macro levels.

Critical Thinking Question: What vision of the world do you have, that if achieved by you and others during your professional careers, would allow you to consider yourself effective in enhancing the social functioning of your clients and enhancing social justice?

? Assess your understanding of guidance and direction by taking this brief quiz.

? Recall what you learned in this chapter by completing the Chapter Review.

a unique way as you become a professional social worker. In fact, you yourself are the tool by which clients will be served and social justice will be furthered. Welcome to the proactive, progressive, and visionary profession of social work.

Metaphors for Social Justice Practice: A Workbook Activity

Consider the idea of describing your practice through the use of metaphors. These are visual and personal ways of thinking about what social work is, especially in regard to the overall social justice mission of social work. Using a metaphor for your work can help you personalize your commitment and continue to view it as a creative endeavor. Table 17.4 lists several common metaphors for social work practice, with an accompanying description of how these metaphors for social justice work. Think about which of these metaphors, or another one that is not included here, can be useful to you as you enter the world of social work.

Table 17.4   Metaphors for Social Justice Practice

Metaphors for Practice	Correlation with Social Justice
Practice as Journey	Achieving social justice is a journey with road maps, detours, mergers, one way roads, traveling companions, and destinations.
Practice as Tapestry	Achieving social justice is a tapestry woven of variegated elements, combined colors and textures, creative images, and opposing threads.
Practice as Story	Achieving social justice is a story including plot, surprises, an interesting cast of characters, a moral, and an ending.
Practice as Art	Achieving social justice is art combining color, perspective, interpretation, creativity, and mixed methods.
Practice as Vision	Achieving social justice is a vision based on values, possibilities, purpose, forward thinking, and commitment to change.
Practice as Dance	Achieving social justice is a dance involving background music, training, communication with an audience, and interpretation.
Practice as Battle	Achieving social justice is a battle including commitment, enemies and allies, strategy, skirmishes, victory, and defeat.
Practice as Evolution	Achieving social justice is evolution including gradual changes, mutations, progress, ongoing development, and shifts.
Practice as Invention	Achieving social justice is invention based on creativity, recognition of an unmet need, trial and error, and innovation.

Suggested Learning Activities

- Subscribe to electronic listserves offered by professional organizations and advocacy groups to stay abreast of issues of importance to you, as well as legislative and social justice implications of their work.

- Search out websites that will expand your understanding of social work's responsibility to maintain global standards of practice. For example, read the United Nations Universal Declaration of Human Rights.

- Read Pablo Freire's works, which describe the relationship between education and political struggles.

Suggested Readings

Bertolino, Bob. *Advocacy Practice for Social Justice*. Boston: Pearson, 2010.

Bondi, Liz, David Carr, Chris Clark, and Cecelia Clegg, eds. *Towards Professional Wisdom: Political Deliberation in the People Professions*. Williston, VT: Ashgate, 2011.

Chung, Rita Chi-Ying, and Frederic Bemak. *Social Justice Counseling: The Next Steps beyond Multiculturalism*. Thousand Oaks, CA: Sage Publications Company, 2011.

Dolgoff, Ralph, and Donald Feldstein. *Understanding Social Welfare: A Search for Social Justice*. 9th ed. Boston: Allyn and Bacon, 2013.

Figueira-McConough, Josefina. *The Welfare State and Social Work: Pursuing Social Justice*. Thousand Oaks, CA: Sage Publications, 2007.

Finn, Janet, and Maxine Jacobson. *Just Practice: A Social Justice Approach to Social Work*. 2nd ed. Peosta, IA: Eddie Bowers Publishing, 2008.

Freire, Pablo. *Pedagogy of the Oppressed*. New York: Seabury, 1973.

Freire, Pablo. *Pedagogy of the Heart*. New York: Continuum, 1997.

Haynes, Karen S., and James S. Mickelson. *Affecting Change: Social Workers in the Political Arena*. 6th ed. Boston: Allyn and Bacon, 2006.

Hoefer, Richard. *Advocacy Practice for Social Justice*. 2nd ed. Chicago: Lyceum Books, 2012.

LaFosto, Frank, and Carl Larson. *The Humanitarian Leader in Each of Us: 7 Choices That Shape a Socially Responsible Life*. Thousand Oaks, CA: Sage Publications, 2011.

Lieberman, Alice A., and Cheryl B. Lester. *Social Work Practice with a Difference: Stories, Essays, Cases, and Commentaries*. Boston: McGraw-Hill, 2004.

Lum, Doman. *Culturally Competent Practice: A Framework for Understanding Diverse Groups and Justice Issues*. 3rd ed. Florence, KY: Wadsworth Publishing, 2006.

Schillmeier, Michael. *New Technologies and Emerging Spaces of Care*. Williston, VT: Ashgate, 2010.

Thomlison, Barbara, and Kevin Corcoran, eds. *The Evidence-Based Internship: A Field Manual*. New York: Oxford University Press, 2008.

Wronka, Joseph. *Human Rights and Social Justice: Social Action and Service for the Helping and Health Professions*. Thousand Oaks, CA: Sage Publications, 2008.

Appendix
Planned Change Process

(MICRO-LEVEL PRACTICE EXAMPLE
WITH INDIVIDUAL)

A 16-year-old pregnant female was kicked out of her family's home, and the father of her child rejected her after learning of her pregnancy. An outreach team for homeless teens contacted the teen and is developing a stabilization plan that could lead to ongoing intervention.

Engage

Perspectives
- Strengths perspective (survival skills and motivation to parent)
- Diversity perspective (gender issues related to pregnancy and child support)
- Eco-systems perspective (social environment non-supportive)

Assess

Orienting Theories
- Crisis theory (overwhelmed by pregnancy and homelessness)
- Family life cycle theory (early pregnancy and rejection by family)
- Psycho-social development theory (pregnancy precedes identity development)

Intervene

Practice Models
- Crisis intervention (secure emergency housing, crisis counseling)
- Empowerment model (refer to teen pregnancy program)
- Medical model (arrange for medical care)

Evaluate

Evaluation
- Crisis services provided (goal attainment)
- Ongoing services in place (goal attainment, client satisfaction)

Planned Change Process

(MICRO-LEVEL PRACTICE EXAMPLE WITH FAMILY)

A family with limited financial needs has been caring for its 85-year-old widowed father and grandfather, but cannot continue to care for him due to his mild dementia and physical limitations following a series of strokes. They are considering placement options in an assisted living facility or nursing home and are working with a medical social worker in the hospital where he is receiving care.

Engage

Perspectives
- Strengths perspective (strong family commitment)
- Diversity perspective (generational differences in values)
- Eco-systems perspective (current placement untenable for family)

Assess

Orienting Theories
- Crisis theory (urgent need for placement decision)
- Psycho-social development theory (grandfather engaging in life review)
- Family systems theory (caregiving responsibilities impact family)

Intervene

Practice Models
- Crisis intervention (current situation overwhelms coping skills)
- Client-centered casework (grandfather chooses placement)
- Medical model (apply for Medicaid for medical coverage)

Evaluate

Evaluation
- Satisfactory placement made (goal attainment, family satisfaction)
- Medicaid coverage secured (goal attainment, coverage begins)

Planned Change Process

(MEZZO-LEVEL PRACTICE EXAMPLE WITH GROUP)

The YWCA Sexual Assault Program is responding to a community need for a group for survivors of intimate partner violence. No other agency in the community offers this service. The YWCA operates a hotline, an emergency shelter, and a crime victim advocacy program. It plans to design and implement an effective group to enhance current services.

Engage

Perspectives
- Strengths perspective (agency readiness, capacity, and mission)
- Feminist perspective (gender issues central to intimate partner violence)

Assess

Orienting Theories
- Group development theory (stages of group development)
- Group dynamics theory (interactions, leadership, cohesion)
- Socialization theory (impact of gender socialization on survivors)

Intervene

Practice Models
- Empowerment model (support for members' choice and self-efficacy)
- Mutual aid group model (members give and receive support)

Evaluate

Evaluation
- Group effectiveness (completion rates, group cohesion)
- Individual member progress (pre-post test, goal attainment)

Planned Change Process

(MEZZO-LEVEL PRACTICE EXAMPLE WITH ORGANIZATION)

Two family services organizations with similar missions are considering a merger in light of declining resources and increasing community need. They wish to retain their respective signature programs and have committed to assessing the advantages and disadvantages of collaboration versus a full merger. They are designing a strategic planning and implementation process.

Engage

Perspectives
- Diversity perspective (agency missions different)
- Strengths perspective (combined resources needed)
- Ecosystems perspective (agencies vulnerable separately)

Assess

Orienting Theories
- Organizational development theory (identify need for reorganization)
- Social systems theory (interactional dynamics of merging agencies)
- Political economy theory (financial resources necessitate collaboration)

Intervene

Practice Models
- Organizational development model (strategic planning for merger)
- Social planning model (needs assessment, capacity building, merger phases)

Evaluate

Evaluation
- Needs identified (goal attainment)
- Capacity building plan developed (staff evaluation of resources and readiness)
- Merger implemented (client base notified, staff development, funds combined)

Planned Change Process

(MACRO-LEVEL PRACTICE EXAMPLE WITH COMMUNITY)

A manufacturing plant that has employed approximately 1,200 citizens of a small town for over 40 years is planning to close, citing increased labor costs and global competition as the reasons for the closure. An agency known for its advocacy efforts on behalf of displaced workers has partnered with local labor unions and a community economic development organization to mediate between employees and owners in hopes of retaining the plant in the community.

Engage

Perspectives
- Strengths perspective (resources of labor, community, and business)
- Ecosystems perspective (mutual influence of labor, community, and business)

Assess

Orienting Theories
- Conflict theory (labor and management differences)
- Political economy theory (impact of global forces on business)
- Structural theory (business practices and tax incentives)

Intervene

Practice Models
- Community development model (seek economic development funds)
- Community organization model (identify options and incentives, build coalition)
- Empowerment model (engage and mobilize those impacted by closure)

Evaluate

Evaluation
- Funding achieved (goal attainment)
- Citizen involvement (engagement, offer tax incentives)
- Temporary plan to maintain plant in community (contract signed)

Planned Change Process

(MACRO-LEVEL PRACTICE EXAMPLE WITH SOCIAL POLICY)

A statewide coalition of mental health providers, advocacy groups, criminal justice representatives, and law enforcement groups has identified the need for legislative action to change the laws impacting individuals with mental illness who are involved in the legal system for crimes they have committed. The laws under consideration for amendment regulate treatment within the prison system, transport of clients, court policies, and alternatives to incarceration.

Engage

Perspectives
- Strengths perspective (focus on effective and humane policies)
- Ecosystems perspective (highlight challenges faced by individuals with mental illness)
- Diversity perspective (consider societal attitudes toward mental illness)

Assess

Orienting Theories
- Social development theory (support social functioning through social development)
- Empowerment theory (need to involve those with mental illness)
- Social systems theory (interactions between social agencies and social policies)

Intervene

Practice Models
- Social justice model (protect rights of those with mental illness)
- Social change model (work toward humane treatment, research best practices)
- Structural model (draft inter-agency agreements, build capacity)
- Policy practice (draft and lobby for legislation)

Evaluate

Evaluation
- Rights clarified and presented (goal attainment)
- Advocacy groups involvement (engagement and ownership)
- Policies implemented (goal attainment)
- Legislation passed (goal attainment)

Glossary

Administrative function of supervision The facet of supervision that focuses on assigning, monitoring, and evaluation of services, including hiring, assigning, and supervising work; facilitating communication and monitoring effectiveness; and representing the agency to the public.

Agency An organization authorized or sanctioned to act in the place of someone, on behalf of others, or in response to a particular social problem.

Agency policy The processes, guidelines, rules, and procedures put into place in agency settings to provide structure, equal treatment, and clarity of operations within the agency.

Anticipatory empathy Advance understanding and response to the potential range of emotions and reactions clients may have in regard to interactions with social workers, including those specific to involuntary involvement with social service organizations.

Assessment The second phase of the planned change process during which information related to the client or client system social functioning is gathered, sorted, and interpreted, and when goals and objectives for an intervention plan are identified.

Asset mapping A process of measuring the resources available to a community that could either be enhanced because they promote positive communities or used to address negative aspects of communities.

Best practices The practice models and techniques that have been empirically shown to be the most effective for particular practice situations, and that are matched to client need and resources.

Blocking approach The approach to community practice that identifies and strengthens community assets based on the belief that building strong communities will result in the enhancement of social functioning.

Building approach The approach to community practice that identifies and addresses community problems and gaps based on the belief that reducing such community problems will also result in the enhancement of social functioning.

Bureaucracy An organizational structure characterized by a chain of command, hierarchical structure, clear policies, eligibility guidelines, standardized policies and programs, division of labor, centralization of power and communication, and supervision and formal communication patterns.

Burnout Negative thoughts and behaviors that are the result of overwork, lack of support, and the inability to balance the demands of work with one's personal life.

Catalyst for change Bringing individuals and groups together, contributing skills and knowledge, and stimulating positive movement or changes that would not have occurred without this effort.

Community A group of people brought together by physical proximity or by a common identity based on shared experiences, interests, or culture.

Community needs assessment An assessment of a community's needs undertaken by networks of individuals and groups interested in knowing what problems need to be addressed, whether those problems are getting better or worse, the consequences of these problems, and what the community wants to be done about them, all accomplished through surveys, interviews, focus groups, data sources, and participatory action research.

Community of interest and identification A group of individuals who share a sense of identity and belonging because they share a characteristic, interest, or life experience such as ethnicity, language, religion, sexual orientation, or occupation.

Community of place A group defined mostly by geography and specified boundaries (e.g., neighborhoods, suburbs, towns, and cities).

Community of practice A group of like-minded professionals who mutually interact as mentors, colleagues, confidantes, and support persons that helps them learn, grow, prioritize, focus, and maintain commitment in the midst of challenging practice situations.

Compassion fatigue Emotional and physical fatigue that is a result of a caring and committed professional's tendency to extend oneself to clients beyond what is required while not managing the impact of such behavior on one's own well-being.

Conceptual framework An organized way of thinking about practice that provides a broad foundation for all interventions and that includes professional perspectives, orienting/explanatory theories, and practice theories/models.

Continuing education A prescribed number of hours per year of ongoing professional education required by states to maintain one's social work license in good standing.

Cultural competence The ability to effectively partner with diverse clients in the planned change process with diverse clients, utilizing culturally appropriate ways of engagement, assessment, intervention, termination and evaluation.

Cultural sensitivity The understanding of how diverse clients and client groups have been influenced by their culture and how cultural considerations must be a part of effective working relationships.

Culturally appropriate methods   A social work approach that is acceptable, relevant to, and appropriate for a specific cultural group that necessitates involving them in the selection of the intervention.

Culture   The learned patterns of thought and behavior that are passed from generation to generation, including the unspoken and unquestioned assumptions and ideas about the nature of reality, the human condition, and how life should be lived.

Culture of evaluation   An organizational commitment to and practice of program evaluation and the use of evidence-based practice models and techniques.

Cyber liability   Legal liability for breach of client confidentiality or privacy in the use of electronic means of communication.

Decentralization   The process of shifting responsibility for programs from one central location to various regional, state, or local locations.

De-escalation   The process of reducing the threat of client violence toward social workers by employing techniques specific to the situation and level of client threat and protecting the social worker through targeted approaches, which reduce the intensity of client emotion and behavior.

Defensive approach to social justice   Resisting, critiquing, and reframing practices that fight the status quo and blocking forces opposing social justice.

Devolution   The granting of power and responsibility from one level of government to a lower level, granting the lower level of government choice regarding what is provided and how it is provided.

Diversity perspective   The professional lens that helps social workers view and focus on the impact of diversity on a client's social functioning.

Dual perspective   The ability to focus simultaneously on the attitudes, values, and customs of the larger society and the attitudes, values, and customs of the individual client or family.

Dual relationship   A relationship between social worker and supervisor or between social worker and client that mixes and blurs personal and professional roles and that is inadvisable in order to maintain appropriate professional boundaries.

Duty to warn   Legal obligation of professionals to report threats of harm to an individual by one's client to the proper authorities.

Economic justice   That dimension of justice having to do with the material or the economic aspects of a community or society.

Ecosystems perspective   The professional lens that helps social workers view and focus on the mutual interaction between clients and their social environments, including the ways in which the social environment impacts clients both positively and negatively.

Educational function of supervision   The facet of supervision that provides formal and informal training and orientation and arranges for formal in-service staff training required for staff to perform well and enhance their professional development.

Electronic communication   Forms of communication used within and between organizations in regard to agency operation and client records, which include e-mail, faxes, computerized databases, and voice mail, and which must all protect client confidentiality and privacy.

Engagement   The first phase of the planned change process during which the client and social worker establish effective working relationships that form the basis for effective assessment, intervention, and evaluation of planned change.

Environmental scanning   Ongoing process of assessing the multiple contexts of agency practice in order to coordinate with other entities, remain aware of trends and projections related to the work of the agency, and provide data for the purposes of strategic planning efforts.

Epidemiology   The incidence, prevalence, and impact of social problems.

Ethical competencies   The possession of and ability to use knowledge, skills, and values of professional ethics to effectively engage in ethical decision making, resolve ethical dilemmas, and increase the ability of agencies and social policies to embed ethical principles into their mission and services.

Ethical decision making   The process of critically and thoughtfully incorporating ethics into the decisions made at all phases of the planned change process, into organizational development, and into larger-scale efforts such as research and social justice efforts.

Ethical dilemma   A situation in which the social worker has two or more ethical obligations, but cannot adhere to one principle without violating another because of their conflicting and sometimes mutually exclusive nature.

Ethical violations   The intentional or unintentional failure to abide by professional codes of ethics or to engage in unethical behavior.

Ethics audit   A review of an agency's compliance with its own policies and ethical principles can be done at various time intervals with information gathered from a number of sources. It can then be used to assess the ethical operation of an agency.

Ethnocentrism   The tendency to assume that one's own culture is normal and even superior, and that it is an appropriate standard for judging the beliefs and behaviors of others.

Etiology   The causes or group of causes that explain the development of a social problem.

Evaluation   The fourth phase of the planned change process during which intervention outcomes are evaluated against goals and objectives, and the professional relationship is terminated.

Evidence-based practice   Practice methods, theories, and models that are supported by research demonstrating their effectiveness.

Faith-based agency   An organization that provides social services based on a commitment to particular faith, religious tradition, or spiritual belief and that may or may not develop programs in keeping with the tenets of that faith or tradition.

Following techniques   Techniques used to engage clients in the initial phases of the helping relationship, and which can be used to involve clients enough that they will begin to trust the social worker and participate somewhat openly in the planned change process, including assessment, intervention, and evaluation.

Formal evaluation A detailed review, rating, and comparison of performance with agreed-upon evaluation criteria and standards that occurs at regularly scheduled intervals and that becomes part of an employee's work record.

Formal structure The actual structure of an organization that is implemented in its organizational charts, policy and procedure manuals, official chain of command, and documents that explain the structure and function of various organizational units.

For-profit agency A business corporation that sells a set of services and is designed and operated to yield a profit for investors and stockholders.

Furthering techniques Techniques used to move the professional relationship and clients forward toward meeting their goals in the actual intervention and evaluation phases of the planned change process, and which build on the following techniques used to build effective working relationships with clients.

Generalist perspective A way of viewing and thinking about the process and activities of social work practice at all levels, using a variety of orienting theories and practice models, engaging in a variety of social work roles, and adapting one's approach to the needs and circumstances of the client.

Generalist social work competencies The knowledge, skills, and values acquired over time that provide a social worker with sufficient breadth and depth of professional competencies for use in generalist practice.

Help-seeking behavior The ways in which individuals and groups think about, approach, and utilize professional or informal helpers for their problems in social functioning, at times influenced by cultural beliefs, customs, and practices.

High-risk settings Social work settings that potentially produce high risk for threats or actual client violence toward social workers by the nature of clients served and services provided.

Influence The capacity to increase the chances that a desired change may occur.

Informal evaluation The ongoing verbal feedback and suggestions offered by a supervisor that takes place on a weekly or even a daily basis, and is provided both in scheduled meetings and as needed in practice situations.

Informal structure Various networks of employees and unofficial channels of communication that operate through unwritten but universally understood rules.

Institutional discrimination Beliefs and practices that are embedded in laws, social structures, economic systems, and governmental or organizational policy.

Interpersonal communication The verbal and nonverbal interactions between social workers and colleagues, or between social workers and clients throughout the planned change process to facilitate positive professional relationships and promote progress toward goals.

Intervention The third phase of the planned change process during which intervention plans are implemented, monitored, and modified as needed.

Knowledge Understanding of professional terminology, facts, principles, concepts, perspectives, and theories to be used in social work practice.

Learning edge The need for professionals to lean into innovation and emerging practice in order to pioneer new approaches and move beyond existing competency levels.

Learning organizations Organizations that seek to maintain relevance, work toward best practices, continuously evaluate their services, anticipate needed improvements, and base their growth on sound information and a commitment to their mission.

Learning plan A written document that identifies learning goals, objectives, tasks, timeliness, and evaluation criteria for a practicum student, completed in collaboration with the practicum agency and university social work program.

Least harmful The principle in social work ethical decision making that encourages social workers to choose an intervention alternative that is likely to have the least negative impact on clients.

Lifelong professional learning Engagement in ongoing professional learning that keeps professionals abreast of new and evidence-based practices and that is required for those with professional licenses.

Malfeasance Commission of an unlawful or wrongful act in practice.

Malpractice The provision of professional services that is considered by the profession to be of lower quality than the minimum expected, and that causes harm as a result.

Mandated reporters An individual, usually a professional, who is required by law because of their position and involvement with clients, to report suspected abuse or threats of violence to appropriate authorities.

Membership agency An agency that derives some or all of its budget from membership fees and in which members are involved in setting agency policy and developing agency programs.

Misfeasance Commission of a proper act in practice in a way that is injurious or wrongful.

Negligence A failure on the part of a professional to provide services with the level of care required of a prudent practitioner and that causes harm to a client.

Nonfeasance Failure to act in accordance with one's professional responsibility.

Offensive approach to social justice The proactive, positive, and affirmative practices that promote social justice and build on and capitalize on existing forces for change, resources, and values.

Office culture The general ways an agency operate based on agency history, values, theoretical underpinnings, policies and procedures, and staff interactions.

Office politics The undercurrent of power dynamics created by factors such as conflict between various factions within an organization, uneven distribution of power between those in various levels, personal ambition, individuals or groups jockeying for greater power, lowered staff morale, and efforts to lobby on behalf of a certain opinion.

Official lines of authority The chain of command within an organization that describes authority in decision making, agency policy, supervision, and responsibilities of all agency staff.

Organizational climate　The "tone" of an agency that includes relationships, level of teamwork, morale, communication, and the level of mutual support among employees.

Organizational communication　The oral and written forms of communication used within organizations to facilitate communication among employees, supervisors, and administrators about services, policies, and activities.

Organizational culture　The values of the agency that impact its programs and are the underpinnings of the services provided.

Orienting/explanatory theory　Specific types of conceptual frameworks that explain how and why people and families develop, what aspects of the social environment impact social functioning, what explains social problems, and how the social issues they address can be explained.

Outcome evaluation　The measurement of the results of the intervention process in terms of level of success, achievement of goals and objectives, and changes over time.

Planned change process　The central activity of social work practice at all levels of practice, consisting of the phases of engagement, assessment, intervention, and evaluation, all of which are done in collaboration with the client or client system.

Policies of prevention　Social policies that attempt to prevent certain social and health problems from developing or increasing.

Policies of protection　Social policies that seek to protect people from harm and exploitation, especially those who are most vulnerable.

Policies of rehabilitation and remediation　Social policies intended to correct or minimize the impact of certain conditions.

Positivist view of knowledge building　The belief that professional knowledge is acquired through empirical, scientific means.

Postmodern view of knowledge　The belief that values the contributions of alternative theories and qualitative research to professional knowledge, and that encourages the deconstruction of assumptions that form the basis of knowledge.

Power　The ability to make change happen in some way.

Practice hypotheses　Expected outcomes at all levels of practice, including short- and long-term results, which are based on an understanding of client or client systems' needs and utilized in combination with practice models that are likely to result in positive results.

Practice theory/model　Theories and models that provide specific guidance regarding interventions and strategies to be used in specific situations, are based on an understanding of clients and client systems, are well matched to clients' needs, and are supported by evidence of efficacy.

Practice wisdom　The collective professional experiences and observations of practitioners that supplement empirical knowledge.

Precursor　A preexisting condition or factor that influences the development of a social problem.

Primary role　The responsibility of a practicum student to learn, integrate academic knowledge into practice, and gain competencies of a professional social worker.

Private nonprofit agency　An agency established by private individuals or organizations to meet an identified social need or address a social problem and that does not make a profit.

Privatization　The transfer of public responsibilities and power from public control to private entities, which has the potential to greatly change the ways in which services are provided, as well as what is offered.

Privileged communication　The principle that clients can expect that their social worker will not or cannot share information without their consent because information shared with a profession social worker is protected by law.

Process of evaluation　The measurement of the intervention process in terms of fidelity, the stages of planned change, monitoring and adapting of objectives, and completion of intervention effort.

Professional boundary　Clearly defined separation between a professional's personal and professional life that protects clients from potential misuse of professional power and that helps professionals retain energy, enthusiasm, and optimism while also preventing discouragement and burnout.

Professional communication　Communication in all forms that is in accordance with professional and agency standards, that is constructive and collegial in its tone, and that facilitates both client and agency goals.

Professional education　The teaching and learning of knowledge, theory, and broad principles that can be applied in many practice settings; acquired through academic means such as reading, discussion, critical thinking, and testing; is related to the mission of the social work; and is measured in terms of learning outcomes.

Professional identity　A clear understanding of the purpose of the profession, your roles and responsibilities as a social worker, the profession's core values and ethical guidelines, and the skills and knowledge needed to perform social work tasks and activities.

Professional liability/malpractice insurance　Insurance that provides for the costs of legal representation when social workers are accused of causing harm to clients through negligence and/or malpractice.

Professional licensing and certifications　The written sanction to practice social work in a particular state, based on that state's requirements for level of education for specific levels of practice, scope of practice, supervision requirements, licensing examination passage, and a prescribed number of continuing education hours per year.

Professional perspective　A professional view or lens intentionally used to focus on and examine a particular realm of social functioning in order to complete a thorough assessment for intervention (i.e., strengths perspective, diversity perspective, generalist perspective, ecosystems perspective, feminist perspective, and person-in-environment perspective).

Professional supervision　Supervision of a professional or student in a particular discipline or profession in order to provide orientation, training, support, and encouragement for professional growth and development.

Professional training　Training provided by agencies in regard to agency-specific, established, standard, or typical approaches to social work; is related to the mission of the agency; and is measured in terms of work outcomes.

Protective factor   Conditions and characteristics that buffer, inoculate against, and mitigate social problems.

Proximate cause   An act or omission that is considered to be the cause of harm or injury, and without such act or omission the harm or injury would not have occurred.

Public agency   An agency created by a legislative body at the federal, state, county, tribal, or community level and that is mandated, funded, or empowered to provide services in regard to needs identified within its jurisdiction.

Qualitative evaluation   The measurement of intervention outcomes using a non-numeric approach that allows for the description of outcomes in subjective, individual, narrative, and nonquantifiable ways.

Quantitative evaluation   The measurement of intervention outcomes in a numeric manner that allows for quantification of results, analysis of success, and demonstrated level of change.

Reciprocity   An agreement between states that an individual licensed in one state will be accepted for licensure in another state, at times with additional requirements specific to a particular state.

Risk factor   Conditions and characteristics that increase the likelihood that individuals, families, groups, and communities will experience social problems.

Rollback or reversal of social policies   A change or reversal in existing social policy based on dissatisfaction with the results or philosophy of existing social policies.

Scope of practice   The defined areas in which social workers are trained and licensed to practice based on their education and possession of a license and that those without a social work license are not allowed to practice.

Secondary role   The responsibility of a practicum student to provide services to agency clients and to meet the expectations of the practicum agency.

Secondary/vicarious traumatic stress   The negative impact on social workers of bearing witness to the pain and suffering of others and taking on the pain and trauma themselves.

Self-awareness   An accurate view of oneself as it pertains to the use of self in professional practice, including how one is perceived by clients and colleagues.

Skill-building continuum   The structured process and timeline by which a practicum student or social worker gains skills through practice, supervision, reflection, and refinement.

Skills   The behaviors of practice that include the techniques and procedures used by social workers to bring about desired change and enhancement of the social functioning of clients or in social systems with which clients interact.

Social asset   Strength in social functioning that put individuals, families, groups, and communities in a better position to insulate themselves from the negative impacts of the social problems they face and even to extricate themselves from challenging situations.

Social asset cluster   A set of strengths in social functioning that create and/or enhance each other, providing positive attributes and circumstances that can provide a buffer between the individual, family, group, or community and the social problems they face.

Social change strategy   An agency strategy to expand the number and types of life-enhancing opportunities available to people, take actions that will improve the environment in which people must function, and reduce or eliminate negative and destructive forces in their social environment.

Social condition   A factual reality that can be observed and measured. It can be positive or negative, and may or may not rise to the level of a social problem.

Social construction   The belief that knowledge of a social phenomenon is shaped and limited by the context in which it was studied by our individual assumptions and values, by our position in relation to the problem, and by the language used to describe it.

Social control strategy   An agency strategy to monitor and restrict the activities of those who exhibit self-destructive or dangerous behavior.

Social functioning   The ability to fulfill desired and required social roles, meet one's own basic needs, make adequate contributions to family and community life, and to achieve autonomy and satisfaction in the pursuit of one's life goals.

Social indicator   A measure of social conditions and social problems, including how those conditions and problems change over time and compare with similar communities.

Social integration strategy   An agency strategy to encourage and help people interact more effectively with other individuals and with the social systems or resources they need in order to function effectively and cope with problems.

Social justice   The basic fairness and moral rightness of the social arrangements and institutional structures that impact the people of a community or society.

Social policy   A decision made by public or governmental authorities regarding the assignment and allocation of resources, rights, and responsibilities and expressed in laws and governmental regulations.

Social policy analysis model   A conceptual framework to guide an examination and analysis of the social policies that impact the operation of an agency and either support or undermine the social functioning of the clients and groups of people.

Social policy practice   The level of social work practice that works for broad social change and social policy formation that is instrumental in helping large numbers of people and in promoting social justice.

Social problem   A social condition that negatively impacts the social functioning of individuals or communities, and as a situation in which the welfare, values, and well-being of at least a portion of society may be compromised.

Social problem analysis model   A structured format for identifying and assessing a social problem, including its definition, scope, scale, causes, impact, and interaction with other social problems, all of which can lead to an understanding of how to research, prevent, and intervene with the identified social problem.

Social role An individual or family expectation that supports its social functioning or that of others (e.g., parent, partner, citizen, employee, neighbor).

Social stressor An event, series of events, or crisis experienced by a vulnerable individual, family, group, or community that moves the social condition to the status of a social problem.

Social welfare policy A social policy that focuses primarily on the distribution of economic, educational, and health benefits to those in need.

Socialization strategy An agency strategy to assist and encourage people to understand, learn, and abide by the norms of society for their own benefit and that of the family, community, or society.

Stakeholders A person or social system with a specific personal, financial, civic, or policy-making perspectives on the need for, design of, and goals for state and federal social welfare policies.

Standard of care The type, level, and specific type of treatment or intervention that is indicated and appropriate for a specific client with a particular condition.

Standards of practice The minimum quality of professional practice expected by the members of a particular profession.

Strategic planning Engagement of agencies in a process of reexamination of their program effectiveness; review of their mission and goals; and adjustment of their objectives based on changing political climate, community need, or financial resources.

Subpoena A formal notice that one's appearance is required in court in a specific proceeding.

Supervision The process of educating, training, supporting, teaching, monitoring, and evaluating professional staff members and students with the ultimate goal of providing the highest quality of services possible, and with the additional goal of preparing students for professional practice.

Supportive function of supervision The facet of supervision that sustains staff morale, cultivates a sense of teamwork, builds commitment to agency goals and mission, encourages staff, deals with work-related problems among staff, encourages self-awareness among staff, and creates a positive work environment.

Tort A private or civil wrong or injury that results from actions other than the breach of a formal legal contract and the commission of a crime.

Transformational leader A leader who understands and embodies the interpersonal and moral aspects of leadership, inspire others and are motivated by the welfare of everyone involved in a common effort.

Unintentional discrimination Behavior rooted in denial of one's own racism or stereotypical thinking and that can have a negative impact even though such a consequence was not intentional.

Value A strong personal or professional preference rooted in one's deepest beliefs and commitments; affect one's personal or professional choices, decisions, and actions.

Vicarious liability The legal principle that describes the liability a supervisor assumes for the potentially ineffective or unethical actions of those he or she supervises.

Written communication All forms of written documents within agency settings that guide, describe, document, and record organizational processes, both internal and external, and that must meet professional standards of quality, timeliness, privacy, and accuracy.

Index